Cricket's Big Day Out

THE

BENSON and HEDGES CUP

1972 TO 1998

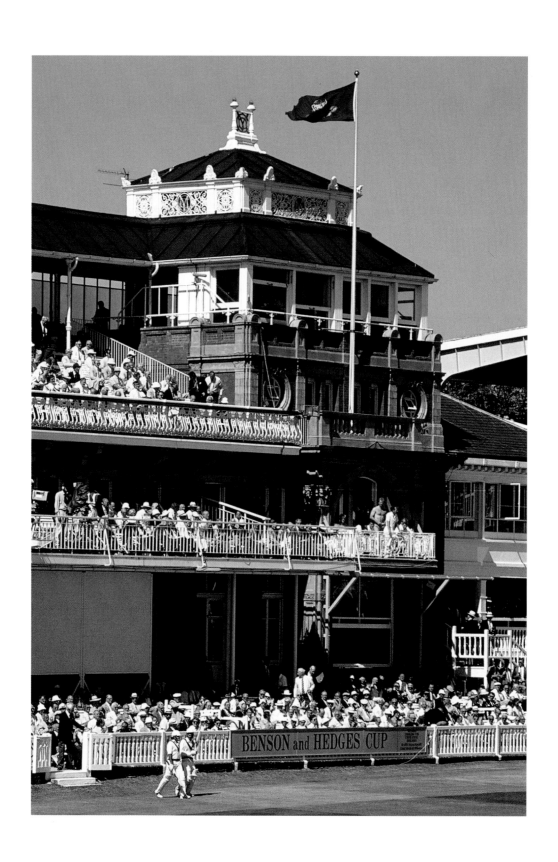

Cricket's Big Day Out

THE BENSON and HEDGES CUP

1972 TO 1998

ANDRE
DEUTSCH

Edited by
PETER BAXTER AND PHIL McNEILL

Statistics by
WENDY WIMBUSH

Designed by
ROBERT KELLAND AND ADRIAN WADDINGTON

With thanks to
Louise Dixon, Tim Forrester,
Eve Cossins, Dave Crowe, Joe Crowe, Catherine McNeill,
Mark Peacock and Audrey Todd

First published in Great Britain in 1998 by André Deutsch Ltd
76 Dean Street, London W1V 5HA
www.vci.co.uk

André Deutsch is a subsidiary of VCI plc

Text copyright © Generation Publications 1998

A catalogue record for this title is available from the British Library

ISBN 0 233 99445 9

Printed and bound in Great Britain
by Jarrold Book Printing, Thetford

– Contents –

– Our golden memories –

This book marks a bittersweet time for everyone at Benson and Hedges. Naturally we are sad that our 27-year involvement in the Benson and Hedges Cup is at an end. But we can look back with great fondness and pride at a competition that brightened up the early part of the cricket season and gave it its mid-summer Big Day Out.

Benson and Hedges were the longest standing supporter of cricket in this country. The Benson and Hedges Cup was launched when one-day cricket was in its infancy, and we are proud to have been associated with a competition that helped to develop an exciting part of the game. We have thoroughly enjoyed these 27 years. Not only have we developed wonderful friendships since the Benson and Hedges Cup was launched in 1972, but we were able to make a significant financial contribution to the sport.

Now all we have left is the memories – but what memories! In this book, we tilt the cup and the golden moments come spilling out. There is Ray Illingworth recalling how he masterminded Leicestershire's victory in the very first Benson and Hedges Cup final. And at the other end of the timescale there is Paul Prichard of Essex, the last captain to savour that thrilling moment on the Lord's balcony when he raises the gold cup triumphantly above his head. Perhaps there would have been a nice symmetry if Leicestershire had managed this year to regain the trophy they first won 27 years earlier – though I dare say Essex supporters would probably disagree!

Talking of Essex brings to mind Graham Gooch's many stirring deeds in the Benson and Hedges Cup; in particular his unforgettable 120 in the 1979 Final. But let's not forget his county colleague John Lever, whose record haul of 149 Benson and Hedges Cup wickets will now never be beaten.

Often, of course, the most memorable moments occurred in the earlier rounds as the Benson and Hedges Cup helped our cricketers to shake off the lethargy of winter and produce their first heroics of the season. Remember Brian Davison's 158 not out for Leicestershire against Warwickshire – the first Benson and Hedges century, scored in the very first season. If we had any doubts about the competition's value, that superlative innings instantly put them to rest.

Remember Mike Procter's four-wickets-in-five-balls for Hampshire versus Gloucesterhire in 1977 – a feat that would be overtaken in 1996 when his fellow South African Shaun Pollock took four wickets in *four* balls on his Warwickshire debut. And remember the young Somerset player who batted on gamely against Hampshire in 1974 after having his teeth knocked out by Andy Roberts – what was his name again? Oh yes, Ian Botham. So many golden memories, and you'll find them all here in Cricket's Big Day Out.

A one-day cricket match is not the easiest sporting event to organise, because it is so vulnerable to the vagaries of weather and the light. Each year for 27 years we have marvelled at the skill of the MCC and the groundstaff as they have prepared Thomas Lord's lovely old cricket ground for its big day. In these pages, John Jameson describes the anticipation of matchday morning – a mixture of anxiety and excitement that we at Benson and Hedges know only too well. It has been a joy and a privilege to work with everyone at Lord's and the ECB for the past 27 years, and we thank them for their unstinting help and support.

We must also thank the supporters who made every Benson and Hedges Cup Final an electrifying occasion … and, of course, everyone who came along to the zonal matches, the quarter-finals and the semi-finals. But above all we must thank all the teams (not forgetting the Universities, the Minor Counties, Scotland and Ireland). It was their efforts – and the many scintillating individual performances – that made the Benson and Hedges Cup a highlight of the cricket season.

Our thanks to all the contributors to Cricket's Big Day Out – Jonathan Agnew, Michael Atherton, Ian Botham, Chris Cowdrey, Mike Denness, Aravinda de Silva, Graeme Fowler, Raymond Illingworth, John Jameson, Andy Lloyd, Vic Marks, Paul Prichard and Alec Stewart – and to the editors, Peter Baxter and Phil McNeill, designers Rob Kelland and Adrian Waddington, and the publishers, André Deutsch.

We trust that this book will give you, the reader, as much pleasure as it gives us at Benson and Hedges. Thank you for being with us for the past 27 years. We enjoyed every minute and we hope you did too.

Jim Elkins

JIM ELKINS
Special Events Director • Benson and Hedges

— The B&H Cup Story —

*For 27 years it gave us cricket's big day out. On an unforgettable midsummer's day,
Lord's became the focal point of the best-loved one-day competition in the English game.
PETER BAXTER recalls the highs and lows of the Benson and Hedges Cup*

W hen we think of the Benson and Hedges Cup, naturally we think of the Finals – Lord's in all its finery, strawberries and champagne, audacious deeds and heady celebrations. But the B&H also stood for the county ground in early spring – seam bowlers running in on a misty morning, three-sweatered fielders squinting as an attempted six comes steepling down in the fading light… What a marvellous competition it was.

For many, the B&H was the first 'real' cricket of the year, adding a much-needed rush of adrenalin to the early part of a season which seems to start so sheepishly in the shadow of almighty football. It will be sorely missed.

The Benson and Hedges Cup – the only county competition linked to one sponsor throughout its lifetime – was the last of the four major competitions to arrive on the scene … and, sadly, the first to depart.

County one-day cricket started in 1963 with the Gillette Cup. Wisden, for one, did not give it a terribly warm welcome, referring to the scenes at Lord's as "resembling an Association Football Cup Final more than the game of cricket".

In the late Sixties, Sunday afternoon television

*The first Benson and Hedges winners, Leicestershire, show off the Cup in 1972.
The B&H may well be remembered as the last one-day competition played in white*

used to carry a complete game featuring a star-studded International Cavaliers side, usually against county opposition. The success of that enterprise convinced the game's authorities that cricket's dwindling popularity would benefit from a county Sunday league, which was born in 1969.

On January 5th 1971 what is generally held to be the first one-day international was staged in Melbourne, to compensate for a rained-off Test – though, like the first ever Test, its status took some time to be acknowledged. It was portrayed in Wisden as 'Australians v MCC' and given three

lines. Nevertheless, this new format soon caught on enough for 1975 to see the first World Cup.

Indeed, as the Seventies dawned there was an evident appetite for one-day cricket. In 1971 the Test and County Cricket Board decided that, instead of six Tests the following year against Australia, they would have five Tests and three one-day internationals. And to beef up the early part of the county season, a new one-day tournament should be started, with the mouth-watering prospect of a mid-season Lord's final. It would have a league element, to give all counties a decent run. The Benson and Hedges Cup was born.

Its original format was to find quarter-finalists from four regional groups of five, with Minor Counties North and South and Cambridge Universities making the numbers up. Over the years the regional theory was dropped in the interests of fairness. Since its first days in 1972 it has been popular with crowds and players, while attracting the attentions of those who felt that changes were needed in the domestic game. For two years in the Nineties, for instance, it became a straight knock-out. Its 55-over format was changed to 50, in order to give our game one competition played to standard ICC regulations, and the same fielding restrictions were imposed. In future years, though, we may come to remember with affection that this was the last limited-over competition played throughout in whites.

But now the Benson and Hedges Cup is gone. The axe that had threatened its place in the changing structure of the domestic game has fallen. This book is a series of snapshots of its history, framed by some of those who took part in the years between Ray Illingworth lifting the fine old gold cup for Leicestershire in 1972 and Paul Prichard raising the same cup for Essex in 1998.

Both their stories encapsulate the romance and heartbreak of the Cup. Illingworth had come to Leicester from Yorkshire, only to find himself opposed to his old county in the first Final. But if it was a question of who had the most Yorkshire grit, Illingworth had more than enough to leave his former supporters in tears. Prichard, 26 years later, had had to fight back from appalling injury to play in the last Final. He was dismissed just eight runs short of a century and you can tell from his contribution that he is already starting to regret it.

Though in the first year there was no success for a Cambridge University side including Majid Khan and Phil Edmonds, when Oxford took their place in 1973 they did achieve the first of 10 victories for university sides in the competition's history. That Oxford side, which beat Northamptonshire, contained Imran Khan and the future chief executive of the ECB, Tim Lamb.

Kent played the first of a record eight finals in 1973 and won it with an all-round performance from a great Lord's favourite, Asif Iqbal. But it was Leicestershire who returned in the next two years. They lost to Surrey in 1974 despite a hat-trick from Ken Higgs, but Norman McVicker's four wickets put paid to Middlesex the following year.

Kent returned to Lord's in 1976 and their captain, Mike Denness, tells in this book how a wounded Basil d'Oliveira almost undid them.

We also read Chris Cowdrey's account of the quarter-final heroics which brought Kent to the 1977 Final. Cowdrey scored a century in his very

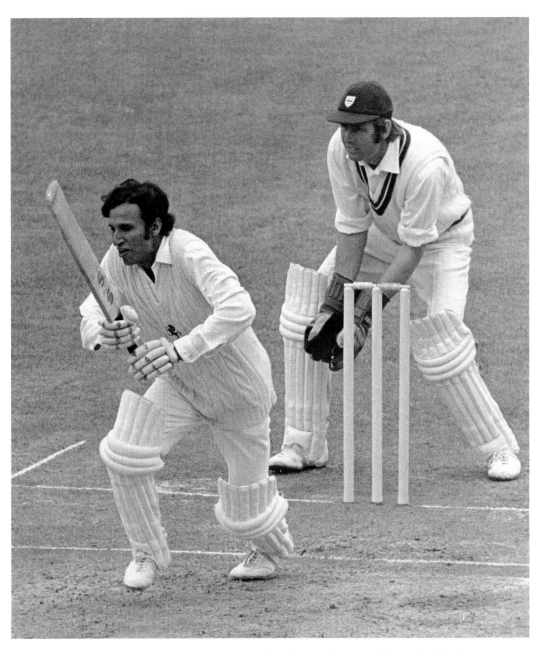

A perennial Lord's favourite, Asif Iqbal makes his mark on the second Benson and Hedges Cup Final, where he scored 59 runs and took four wickets to receive the Gold Award from Sir Leonard Hutton

first B&H innings – but that feat was outshone in the semi-final by Mike Procter's four-wickets-in-three-balls against Hampshire. And it was Procter's team which prevailed in the Final.

Kent returned for a third successive Final in

1978 in which the bowling of their West Indian, John Shepherd, kept Derbyshire to a low total. Bob Woolmer took them to victory, but only after being dropped twice in as many balls off Mike Hendrick.

The 'scandal' of the astonishing declaration at

Worcester in 1979 is recounted in this book by the Somerset captain responsible, Brian Rose. But, fortunately, there were happier things to remember that year.

Essex were always seen as a 'fun' side who enjoyed their cricket. But, as the Seventies came to an end, they had never won a major trophy. They put that right in 1979 and did it in fine style. Graham Gooch made 120 in what was to remain the highest total in a Final – 290 for six – against Surrey. It also won him one of his record 22 Gold Awards: twice as many as anyone else.

Gooch made 60 in the first Final of the Eighties, but this time it was in defeat in the first Final to be played on a Monday after a deluge on the Saturday. And the man who dismissed Gooch? That same Tim Lamb of Northamptonshire who had once helped Oxford University beat the county

The 1997 B&H Final was won for Surrey by what Wisden described as "an innings of innocent near-genius" from Ben Holioake

he now played for. Gooch also holds the record for the highest score in the Benson and Hedges Cup. In a group match at Hove in 1982 he made 198 not out – and then took three Sussex wickets.

But 1982 was Somerset's year; their second in a row. In this book Vic Marks reflects on the joy of the cider county.

There was a sour note behind Middlesex's triumph in 1983. Their rained-off quarter-final with Gloucestershire was decided by the toss of a coin, prompting calls for a new system. This was to lead to the 'bowl-out', applied twice in later years. In fact the Final, which featured Essex for the third time in five years, was a thriller, with a late burst of bowling by Norman Cowans winning it for Middlesex by four runs.

Peter May raised some eyebrows in 1984 when

he presented the Gold Award in the Final to a man who had made nought and had not bowled. Graeme Fowler explains the decision in this book. And Jonathan Agnew tells of a peculiarly one-sided semi-final in which he played in 1985, the year Leicestershire won the Cup for the third time with Gower getting the better of Gooch.

Scotland achieved their first win in 1986, beating Lancashire by three runs at Perth. The final was tighter still, with Graham Dilley needing to hit the last ball from Middlesex's Simon Hughes for six to give Kent victory. It was too much to ask.

Tighter even than that two-run margin was the 1987 Final which Yorkshire won with the scores level by virtue of having lost fewer wickets. Jim Love was the batsman who kept his head and blocked the last ball from Northamptonshire's Winston Davis, knowing that protecting his wicket was all that was required.

B y 1988 only one county had never experienced the big day out of a Lord's final. But now Hampshire put it right, meeting Derbyshire. The outcome was decided in the first hour by a spell from Hampshire's South African swing bowler Steve Jefferies, taking four for one in eight balls. Hampshire won with 23 overs to spare.

Mike Atherton's Combined Universities team came within a hair's breadth of a place in the 1989 semi-finals. They had reached the quarter-finals by beating Surrey and Worcestershire and at Taunton, with Durham University's Nasser Hussain making 118, it really looked as if further history was to be made. They fell three runs short.

Essex contested their fifth Final that year and it produced a gripping finish, with Nottinghamshire's last batsman Eddie Hemmings needing to hit the last ball of the last over from John Lever

for four to win. Against all predictions, he did it.

The Finals of 1990 and 1991 both featured Lancashire and Worcestershire. And they each won one. Lancashire took the first as the first part of that year's Double, with a bowling spell from Wasim Akram proving decisive. In the second match, Graeme Hick made the runs he had been

Lord's looks splendid as the scoreboard celebrates the silver anniversary of the gold Cup.
Opposite: Surrey's Ben Hollioake on his way to a sensational 98 off 113 balls in 1997

denied the year before to seal the Worcester win. Malcolm Marshall had missed two Lord's finals with Hampshire, and so July 11th 1992 was a very big day for him. In fact, the match with Kent was just about evenly split between Saturday and Sunday, so it was on the 12th that Marshall took three for 33 and saw Mark Nicholas hold the Cup for the second time.

The Cup winners in both 1993 and 1994 had

come through by winning a bowl-out. After a rained-off match in each case, five bowlers had had to bowl at a set of undefended stumps. On a rain-soaked ground at Taunton in 1993, Derbyshire's bowlers hit the stumps six times out of 10 to Somerset's three, and in the Final Dominic Cork blazed 92 not out to defeat Lancashire.

Warwickshire's bowl-out triumph over Kent in the Edgbaston indoor school the next year was more controversial, because Kent were unhappy about the pre-match covering. Both Lord's finals that year were Warwickshire v Worcestershire and both were won by Warwickshire, as was the County Championship. The year of the Bear.

Lancashire won for the third time in 1995, but the scene was stolen by a small Sri Lankan genius – Aravinda de Silva. His account of his great day at Lord's is in this book. By the time Lancashire also took the trophy in 1996, they had won 15 consecutive completed Benson and Hedges Cup matches. Ian Austin's four for 21 was decisive in the defeat of Northamptonshire.

A little-known leprechaun called Hansie Cronje jumped up to take Middlesex by surprise in the 1997 competition. Making 92 and taking three wickets, he helped Ireland to their first win over a first-class county. The Final was won for Surrey by what Wisden described as "an innings of innocent near-genius from Ben Hollioake". Alec Stewart, who batted with him, tells his tale here.

And so to the final rites. Benson and Hedges always knew how to throw a good party, and the dinner and dancing under the ancient eyes of the dinosaurs in the Natural History Museum on the eve of the last Final showed that they were determined to go out in style. What a pity they could not control the weather the next day.

1972

– Leicestershire lift the first trophy –

The first Benson and Hedges Cup Final pitted Ray Illingworth against his former county, Yorkshire guaranteed a fiery Final

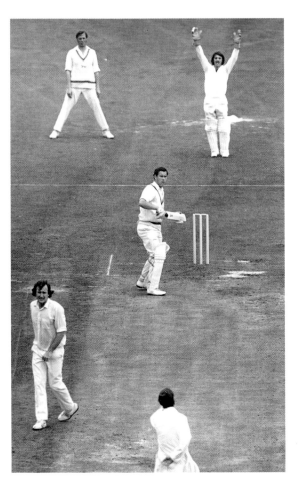

Graham McKenzie traps John Hampshire lbw, during his excellent bowling spell of 11-2-22-3

There was an obvious line for the headline-writers to latch on to in the approach to the first Benson and Hedges Final. Ray Illingworth – Yorkshire to his bootstraps – was now leading Leicestershire against players who had been his teammates. In 18 seasons with Yorkshire (1951-1968), he had been a member of seven Championship-winning sides and in first-class matches for the county he had the fine all-round record of 1,390 wickets and 14,829 runs.

Yorkshire were now captained by Geoffrey Boycott, who had infused a fresh spirit of competitiveness into the side. In 1971 he had hit 13 hundreds in his 2,503 runs, to become the only English batsman ever to average 100 in a season (100.12). But the great man was injured and would be on the sidelines today.

Illingworth had led Leicestershire through to the Final with crushing victories in every match they had played, including seven-wicket wins in both quarter-final and semi-final over Lancashire and Warwickshire respectively – both of them in front of packed Grace Road crowds.

Their Rhodesian batsman Brian Davison had also set a B&H record with a stunning innings against Warwickshire in a zonal match. Davison's

> *Yorkshire captain Geoffrey Boycott had given his team a spirit of competitiveness but he would be on the sidelines today*

158 not out had come in just 92 minutes off 30.5 overs, with 11 sixes and 10 fours. In other words, Leicestershire were hot.

Yorkshire had lived more dangerously. They had come through the group stage thanks to a rule then in force that awarded an extra point to a team who had bowled the opposition out. That extra point had pulled Yorkshire and Lancashire through the Northern Group over Nottinghamshire.

In the Cup Final programme, Illingworth wrote: "Over the last three years we have been doing fairly well in the one-day game, improving all the time. If there was anything we lacked it was in the seam bowling department and the arrival of Ken Higgs has helped us a great deal there. We are also a very good fielding side. The

"One day we'll be able to come to Lord's dressed in gorilla suits…" Young fans watch Leicestershire build their innings

GOLD AWARD WINNER 1972

Chris Balderstone

golden memories

balderstone's aggressive 41* ensured Leicestershire's victory in a low-scoring match. A sound right-handed batsman and slow left-arm bowler, he had played for Yorkshire from 1961 to 1969 without keeping a regular place in the side and was better known as a professional footballer (he played for Huddersfield, Carlisle, Doncaster and Queen of the South). He followed Ray Illingworth to Leicestershire in 1971, but only made his way into the side permanently at the end of this 1972 season, playing just three first-class matches that year. Between 1973 and 1985 he made over 1,000 first-class runs in 11 seasons and had a marvellous B&H career record with 2,059 runs at 45.75. He played two Tests for England against the West Indies in 1976 at the age of 35. On September 15, 1975 he played cricket for Leicestershire against Derbyshire at Chesterfield, before an evening soccer match for Doncaster Rovers against Brentford.

Gold Awards have been pretty well shared around. We're the only team that has not lost a game and we've bowled out every other side. Probably we lack a star batsman but on the credit side is the fact that we all can make runs."

Boycott also praised his team's spirit. "I am delighted that after a lean spell in limited over cricket Yorkshire are now back at the top. We have put in a lot of hard work and now we are seeing the success of our efforts. This stems from last season when we started to put our mind to the game, think about it more and work hard at it from every aspect.

"We have shown that we are a very good fielding side and I think today's Final will be a good one. We will be approaching it with the same attitude we have had through the competition and that is to get one run more than the opposition."

Heavy rain in London early in the morning did threaten the first Final but, thankfully, a crowd of 18,000 saw the game begin on time, with Yorkshire batting, having won the toss. In Ken Higgs and Australian Graham McKenzie, Leicestershire had the ideal bowlers to exploit the conditions, and the going was not easy.

A blow on the wrist for Barry Leadbeater had him off the field for a period, too. He returned later and was top scorer with 32, but a 55-over total of 136 for nine was surely not enough, even though Yorkshire had achieved – just – the

The Benson and Hedges Cup Final 1972.

Lord's Cricket Ground, Saturday, 22nd July.

Balderstone's 41 not out earned the Gold Award

RAY ILLINGWORTH
THE FIRST FINAL: LEICESTERSHIRE V YORKSHIRE, 22ND JULY 1972

RAY ILLINGWORTH WAS THE FIRST CAPTAIN TO RAISE THE GOLD
BENSON AND HEDGES CUP AND THERE WAS A SPLENDID IRONY IN THE
FACT THAT HE HAD WON THE FINAL WITH LEICESTERSHIRE AGAINST HIS
OLD COUNTY, YORKSHIRE.

have always said that I was more nervous in that match than any other match in my life. I had come to Leicestershire three years before from a Yorkshire side that had just won the Championship. When I arrived – as captain – I said that it would take three years to develop any sort of side. So I felt that if we could win this match, we would go forward, but if we lost it, it might take another two or three years to pick up again.

The fact that it was a final against my old county was not a big problem for me. I got on well with all the lads there, and had done even when I was leaving. But it was certainly a big day for me.

That year we had bowled out every side we had played in all the stages of the competition. We had a good, balanced attack. We had spinners, we had seamers, we had quicker bowlers and of course in those days you could put your fielders where you wanted them, which was very important. No side got away and made 200 against us. So we always felt that, provided we bowled first, our batsmen could play a normal sort of game and didn't have to go mad.

That first final day was really overcast and the ball swung around, so the bare scores don't really tell the whole story, but Yorkshire became the first side we hadn't bowled out. Still, we had them nine wickets down at the end and they'd only made 136. Graham McKenzie took three for 22 in 11 overs, Ken Higgs got a couple of wickets and so did I.

We lost our top four batsmen getting to 84 and when I was out for five it was 97 for five and it felt a bit tight at that stage. But the sun just came through and the conditions got a bit easier and Chris Balderstone and Paul Haywood put on 43 together and took us home. There were eight overs in hand, but it was not as easy a win as it may look by any means. Still, the fact that we won it meant that Leicestershire could go from strength to strength over the next few years.

The thing that has changed most since those early days of one-day cricket is the restrictions on field placings. You can see that the scores were lower then, because captains could put ten men on the boundary in the last few overs if they wanted to. Batsmen have probably also become better at improvising, too.

I am not sure that it is a better game for the fielding regulations. I have always felt that a captain should be allowed to put his fielders where he wants to and maybe in another few years we'll have eleven spots on the field where

Raymond Illingworth's moment of triumph: the first captain to hold the B&H Cup

they've all got to stand. I've always had a soft spot for the Benson and Hedges Cup. Obviously from our point of view, with three finals in the first four years, it was a great competition and we got wonderful crowds at Leicestershire. I shall miss the Benson and Hedges.

Above: The Leicestershire fans enjoy their big day out.
Left: Howard Cooper claims one of his two victims –
Roger Tolchard, caught by a young David Bairstow

1972 IN CRICKET

England, under **Ray Illingworth**, retain the Ashes, by drawing the series two-all. At Lord's, Bob Massie takes 16 wickets for Australia for 137, but at Headingley **Derek Underwood** takes 10 wickets with the aid of a fungus called Fusarium in the pitch.... **Dennis Amiss** scores the first ever one-day international century as England beat Australia 2-1 to take the first Prudential Trophy... With Illingworth taking the winter tour off, **Tony Lewis** leads the MCC tour and wins his first Test match in Delhi on Christmas Day.

1972 IN SPORT

Alex Higgins wins the snooker world title... **Gordon Banks** retires after injuring his eye in a car crash... Palestinian terrorists shoot 11 Israeli athletes at the Munich Olympics. US swimmer **Mark Spitz** breaks seven world records.

distinction of being the only side not to have been bowled out by Leicestershire in the B&H competition. McKenzie had taken three for 22 in his 11 overs and Higgs two for 33.

Against Chris Old and Tony Nicholson, Leicestershire started no more surely, but the opener Mick Norman steadied the innings, fifth out for 38.

Even then, with 40 still wanted there was anxiety in the Leicestershire ranks, until Chris Balderstone took the bull by the horns and forced them home, making 41 not out and winning himself the Gold Award from Peter May for the top score in such a low scoring match.

County Champions: Warwickshire
John Player League Champions: Kent
Gillette Cup Winners: Lancashire

FINAL SCOREBOARD 1972

LORD'S • 22ND JULY

– Yorkshire –

won the toss

*P J Sharpe, c Tolchard, b Higgs	14
R G Lumb, b McKenzie	7
B Leadbeater, run out	32
J H Hampshire, lbw b McKenzie	14
R A Hutton, c Spencer, b Steele	8
J D Woodford, c Spencer, b Illingworth	1
C Johnson, b Higgs	20
C M Old, lbw, b Illingworth	6
†D L Bairstow, c Tolchard, b McKenzie	13
H P Cooper, not out	7
A G Nicholson, not out	4
Extras (lb 9, nb 1)	10
Total (55 Overs, for 9 wkts)	**136**

Fall of wickets: 1-17, 2-21, 3-60, 4-65, 5-77, 6-83, 7-113, 8-122, 9-124.

Bowling: McKenzie 11-2-22-3, Higgs 11-1-33-2, Spencer 7-2-11-0, Davison 11-2-22-0, Illingworth 10-3-21-2, Steele 5-1-17-1.

– Leicestershire –

B Dudleston, c Bairstow, b Nicholson	6
M E J C Norman, c Sharpe, b Woodford	38
† R W Tolchard, c Bairstow, b Cooper	3
B F Davison, b Cooper	17
J C Balderstone, not out	41
*R Illingworth, c Bairstow, b Hutton	5
P R Haywood, not out	21
Extras (b 2, lb 2, w 4, nb1)	9
Total (46.5 overs, for 5 wkts)	**140**

Did not bat: J F Steele, G D McKenzie, K Higgs, CT Spencer

Bowling: Old 9.5-1-35-0, Nicholson 9-2-17-1, Hutton 11-1-24-1, Cooper 9-0-27-2, Woodford 8-1-28-1.

Fall of wickets: 1-16, 2-24, 3-58, 4-84, 5-97.

Gold Award Winner: J C Balderstone
(Adjudicator: P B H May)

Umpires: D J Constant & T W Spencer

– Leicestershire won by five wickets –

1973

– Asif hadn't read the script –

In the year of the underdog, Norman Gifford was praying for Worcestershire to "do a Sunderland". But Kent's dynamic all-rounder Asif Iqbal had other ideas

By the time the second Benson and Hedges Cup Final was staged at Lord's on July 21 before a crowd of 23,000 people, it was firmly established as a highlight of the cricket calendar. In the 93 B&H matches played to date, we had already seen two of the highest individual innings to be scored in the competition's entire 27-year history, courtesy of two overseas stars – Gordon Greenidge of Hampshire and the West

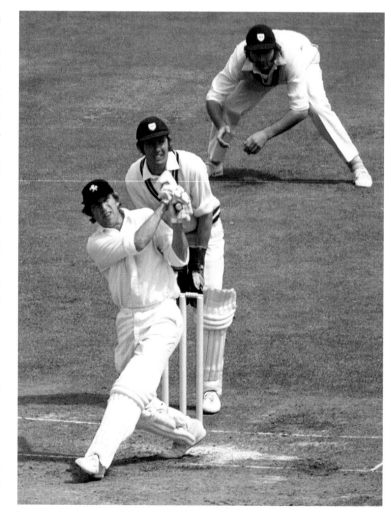

Indies, and Brian Davison of Leicestershire and Rhodesia. Davison's unbeaten 158 against Warwickshire in 1972 had already been overtaken, earlier in the 1973 season, by Greenidge's thunderous 173 not out against the Minor Counties (South) at Amersham. (Perhaps Greenidge could be accused of cashing in on lesser opponents here; but it is interesting to note that the rest of the all-time top 10 B&H scores were played against first-class opposition.) That Greenidge innings also included what we now know was the highest partnership in 27 years of the B&H Cup – an unbroken second-wicket stand

> *'This could be the year for the sporting underdogs. Just remember what Sunderland achieved in the FA Cup Final. If they did it, why not us?'*
> — NORMAN GIFFORD

Above: Where's it gone? Mike Denness and Norman Gifford looking for the coin after the toss. Left: Brian Luckhurst hits a six off Basil d'Oliveira during his superb innings of 79

Rodney Cass can only watch helplessly as Asif Iqbal starts to turn the Final Kent's way with a quickfire knock of 59

of 285 with David Turner. The 1973 B&H competition also brought the first major upset, when Oxford University beat Northamptonshire in a zonal match.

What's more, that year's semi-finals had seen arguably the closest match ever to be played in the Benson and Hedges Cup. Lancashire and Worcestershire both scored 159 but Worcestershire won because they had lost fewer wickets – nine as opposed to 10! To make matters worse for Lancs, they had lost their last wicket with the final ball of their 55 overs. Had the same fate befallen Worcestershire, Lancashire would have won. But the final ball of Worcestershire's innings brought not the 10th wicket, but the 159th run.

Worcestershire had already ridden their luck in the fifth of their five zonal games. Playing Warwickshire in what amounted to a knockout fix-

A Cup quartet: Iqbal, Denness, Shepherd and Underwood

ture, they had overhauled their neighbours' 211-4 with one ball to spare. Worcestershire owed their victory to middle order batsman Ted Hemsley, who was better known as a footballer for Sheffield United. His innings of 73 earned him the first of three Gold Awards – the second footballer to win

Asif Iqbal

g o l d e n   m e m o r i e s

asif Iqbal's Gold Award was his third of the summer. With 59 he helped Brian Luckhurst put on 116 runs for Kent's third wicket, and opening the bowling he took 4-43, including three crucial middle-order wickets. Asif was a brilliant batsman, fast of foot with wristy drives and cuts. He made his first-class debut for Hyderabad in India before emigrating to Pakistan in 1961, and his Test debut as a medium-fast bowler, taking 18 wickets in three Tests in New Zealand in 1965. He concentrated on his batting from 1967 when he scored the first of 11 Test centuries, against England at The Oval, batting at No 9 and putting on a Test record 190 for the ninth wicket with Intikhab Alam in 170 minutes. In Tests he scored 3575 runs at 38.85, and took 53 wickets at 28.33. He played for Kent from 1968 to 1982, and was a highly regarded captain in 1977 and 1981-2.

The man of the moment: Asif Iqbal

Kent captain Mike Denness shows the Benson and Hedges Cup to the county's supporters, as his teammates applaud

Asif Iqbal took four wickets to destroy Worcestershire

1973 IN CRICKET

Bomb scare stops play. The players huddle in the centre of the pitch as Lord's is evacuated during a Test. The West Indies win by an innings and 226 runs, with centuries by **Rohan Kanhai**, **Gary Sobers** and **Bernard Julien**, to take the series 2-0. Their other victory came at The Oval, where **Keith Boyce** hit 72 batting at No 9 and took 11 wickets… **Bev Congdon** scores 176 and **Vic Pollard** 116 as New Zealand make the second-highest last innings total ever — 440 — but still lose to England by 38 at Trent Bridge.

1973 IN SPORT

Both **Charlton** brothers retire from football… **Gareth Edwards** finishes off rugby's greatest try, for the Barbarians vs the All Blacks… **Red Rum** overhauls Crisp to win the Grand National in record time… An FA Cup Final fairytale: Second Division Sunderland beat Leeds 1-0… **David Bedford** slashes 8 seconds off **Lasse Viren**'s 10,000m record… **Jackie Stewart** wins the Formula One world title despite quitting before the end of the season when Tyrrell colleague **Francois Cevert** dies in practice.

---

one, but not the last (was there anything Ian Botham didn't do?).

By a strange coincidence, Worcestershire had another soccer player in their ranks – Aston Villa goalkeeper Jim Cumbes – while middle-order batter Jim Yardley had played reserve-team football for West Bromwich Albion. But the presence of three footballers at Lord's was not the only gem for trivia fans in the 1973 Final. Worcestershire's opening batsman was Ron Headley, whose son Dean would also appear in a Benson and Hedges Final … for Kent. Dean actually went one better than his dad, playing in the Finals of 1995 and '97; sadly, neither father nor son was ever a Benson and Hedges Cup-winner.

Kent went into the '73 Final with a galaxy of

> *Brian Luckhurst and Asif Iqbal lit up Lord's with a dashing partnership of 116 in 29 overs*

stars. The experienced Mike Denness had replaced Colin Cowdrey as captain the previous year, but Cowdrey was still there, batting way down at No 7 in an extremely strong team that included Brian Luckhurst, Asif Iqbal, Alan Knott, Bob Woolmer and Derek Underwood.

Worcestershire captain Norman Gifford made no bones about the fact that his team were the underdogs, and noted hopefully: "That suits us fine! This could be the year for the sporting underdogs. Just remember what Sunderland achieved in the FA Cup Final. If they did it, why not us?"

But Worcestershire did have the season's most in-form county batsman – Glenn Turner, who had scored 1,018 runs at an average of 78 by

Ealham leaves the field to the B&H girls. Note the Lord's groundstaff member on the right: believe it or not, it's Ian Botham

● FINAL SCOREBOARD 1973 ●

LORD'S • 21ST JULY

– Kent –
won the toss

B W Luckhurst, run out	79
G W Johnson, run out	9
*M H Denness, c d'Oliveira, b Cumbes	0
Asif Iqbal, b Gifford	59
A G E Ealham, c Headley, b Johnson	15
J N Shepherd, c Gifford, b Brain	12
M C Cowdrey, not out	29
†A P E Knott, run out	12
Extras (b 4, lb 5, nb 1	10
Total (55 overs, for 7 wkts)	**225**

Did not bat: R A Woolmer, D L Underwood, J N Graham

Fall of wickets: 1-23, 2-23, 3-139, 4-165, 5-172, 6-198, 7-225.

Bowling: Brain 11-2-26-1, Cumbes 11-1-37-1, Gifford 11-2-46-1, d'Oliveira 11-2-45-0, Hemsley 2-0-17-0, Johnson 9-0-44-1.

– Worcestershire –

R G A Headley, c Knott, b Graham	13
G M Turner, b Woolmer	25
E J O Hemsley, run out	23
†G R Cass, c Denness b Underwood	19
J A Ormrod, c & b Asif Iqbal	12
*N Gifford, b Asif Iqbal	33
B L d'Oliveira, c Underwood, b Asif Iqbal	47
T J Yardley, not out	3
I N Johnson, b Shepherd	2
B M Brain, b Asif Iqbal	0
J Cumbes, run out	1
Extras (lb 8)	8
Total (51.4 overs)	**186**

Fall of wickets: 1-26, 2-57, 3-69, 4-85, 5-98, 6-168, 7-181, 8-184, 9-185, 10-186.

Bowling: Graham 9-0-38-1, Asif Iqbal 11-1-43-4, Shepherd 11-0-41-1, Woolmer 11-0-36-1, Underwood 9.4-1-20-1.

Umpires: C S Elliott & A E G Rhodes

Gold Award Winner: Asif Iqbal
(Adjudicator: Sir Leonard Hutton)

– Kent won by 39 runs –

the end of May, and would hit 2,416 in the season for Worcs and New Zealand.

They also had the man with the most amusing name in cricket, Brian Brain. And it was Brain who raised Worcestershire's hopes as Denness chose to bat under gloomy skies. He and Jim Cumbes opened the bowling with such a niggardly spell that after 20 overs Kent had only reached 34 for two, with Graham Johnson run out and Denness sent back to the pavilion for a duck.

But Brian Luckhurst and Asif Iqbal lit up Lord's with a dashing partnership of 116 in 29 overs, including a fine six by Luckhurst, who was run out for 79 by a brilliant long throw by Basil d'Oliveira. Asif went for 59, yorked by Gifford, but Cowdrey marshalled the late order to such good effect that Kent put on 53 in the final eight overs to reach 225-7.

Kent's opening bowlers, Norman Graham and

Asif Iqbal, were just as economical as Worcestershire's had been, and Headley and Turner were well tied down. The biggest blow came when Woolmer bowled Turner in the last over before tea. Worcestershire's last hope lay with their two England veterans, 33-year-old Gifford and 41-year-old d'Oliveira. They put on 70 in 12 overs in a sixth-wicket stand until d'Oliveira tried to hit Asif Iqbal for the second six in an over and was caught by Underwood at midwicket.

Worcestershire slumped to an ignominious 186 all out. Asif Iqbal finished with four for 43, including the wickets of Gifford and d'Oliveira. After his rollicking innings, it was a formality for Sir Leonard Hutton to hand Asif the Gold Award.

County Champions: Hampshire
John Player League Champions: Kent
Gillette Cup Winners: Gloucestershire

1974

— When the going gets tough —

*Ray Illingworth's Leicestershire were back at Lord's once more,
determined to regain the Cup they considered their property.
But they ran into Surrey's John Edrich at his most obdurate*

The first break-up of the regional aspect of the Benson and Hedges Cup group rounds came about after Middlesex pointed out that their South zone was the only one that consisted entirely of first-class counties. It did them little good. They were swapped with Cambridge University and found themselves making the Midlands an all first-class zone. Middlesex lost all four games.

It was Leicestershire and Worcestershire who qualified from that group by virtue of a better strike rate of balls bowled for each wicket taken over Warwickshire. Leicestershire then had a close quarter-final win over Kent and an overwhelming semi-final victory over Somerset, who had, in the quarter-final, discovered the remark-

able all-round talents of Ian Botham. So Ray Illingworth brought Leicestershire back to Lord's only two years after they had won the first B&H Cup Final – and he was determined to repeat what he described as "the greatest day in Leicestershire's history".

Illingworth's message to Leicestershire's opponents was: "Congratulations to Surrey on making the day with us. And a final word of warning to my old friend John Edrich – Hands off our Cup!"

Surrey had never won a one-day competition since their inception. They had had a close

*Right: The Surrey team
celebrate victory at Lord's*

Warm-up: The Band of 1st Battalion, The Green Howards

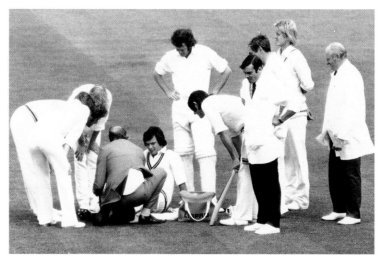

Robin Jackman requires the physio's attention but umpire Dickie Bird is not impressed

*Above: Ken Higgs bowled
brilliantly (7-2-10-4) but
could not stop Surrey
from winning the Cup*

John Edrich

golden memories

i n his second year as Surrey captain, Edrich batted cautiously for his 40 in the final, but this proved important in a low-scoring game, and his shrewd handling of his bowlers gave him his third Gold Award of the season. (He had also won Awards in the opening zonal match against Sussex and in the semi-final against Lancashire.) This was the one trophy that Surrey won during Edrich's spell as captain 1973-7. Edrich holds the Surrey record with nine B&H Gold Awards in all. Born into a notable cricketing family on 21 Jun 1937, John joined Surrey from Norfolk in 1956 and followed his older cousin Bill into the England team. A stalwart, left-handed opening batsman he scored 5138 runs in Tests for England at an average of 43.54, with 12 centuries, between 1963 and 1976, and just short of 40,000 runs in his first-class career.

Edrich: 40 vital runs in the low-scoring Final

encounter with Geoff Boycott's Yorkshire in the quarter-final and a bigger margin of victory over David Lloyd's Lancashire in the semi.

John Edrich was in his second year as captain, and he was in fine form: his average at that point of the season stood at 73.72. He had been recalled to the England team and had scored 100 not out against India at Old Trafford and 96 at Lord's – passing 4,000 Test runs in his 61st Test.

Edrich's contribution to the B&H Final, after he won the toss on July 20th, was crucial. His painstaking 40 took Surrey to 99 before they lost

Little did we realise that this new idea would become established so quickly

their third wicket. Although Edrich scored just 18 runs in the first 24 overs, his stubborn resistance took Surrey past the hundred before he gave a low return catch to slow left-armer John Steele with Surrey's total on the dreaded 111.

Younis Ahmed played some aggressive shots in making 43, but Ken Higgs made sure that the later batsmen did not get away with a challenging target. Higgs took a hat-trick to dismiss Alan Butcher, Pat Pocock and Arnold Long – the only hat-trick ever taken in a B&H Cup Final. He finished with four for 10 in his seven overs and Surrey were all out in the last

IAN BOTHAM
QUARTER-FINAL: SOMERSET V HAMPSHIRE, 1974

IN 1971 A LARGE 15-YEAR-OLD CALLED IAN BOTHAM PLAYED FOR THE FIRST TIME FOR SOMERSET 2ND XI. A SPELL ON THE LORD'S GROUNDSTAFF FOLLOWED AND A COUPLE OF MATCHES FOR THE COUNTY IN THE SUNDAY LEAGUE IN 1973. BUT IT WAS IN 1974 THAT THE NAME BOTHAM FIRST HIT THE HEADLINES. THE STAGE WAS TAUNTON AND A BENSON AND HEDGES CUP QUARTER-FINAL.

At that time I could not be certain of a place in the side and it wasn't till I arrived at the ground in the morning that Brian Close told me I was playing. It was, I suppose, one of the biggest games in the club's history, because we hadn't won anything at that stage and here we were in the Bensons quarter-final. Nowadays people talk about pressure, but I'd been fighting to get in the side and I just went out there to enjoy myself, as I think any 18-year-old would.

Still, Richards and Greenidge were not the worst pair of opening batsmen to be bowling against and they were to take plenty of runs off me in my career. But on this day I bowled Richards for 13, Graham Burgess got the wickets of Greenidge and Gilliat and with Turner run out for nought, they went from 22 for no wicket to 22 for four.

Ian Botham gets an Andy Roberts special delivery full in the face. He lost four teeth but refused to go off, and carried on batting with Hallam Moseley to take Somerset to victory

from the last 15 overs with not a lot left in the hutch. Early on I took a ball in the mouth from Andy Roberts, who was a bit quicker than anything I'd come across in the second XI cricket I'd been playing. It was quite a shock. I don't know what sort of shot I was trying to play, but I was very late on it and I paid for it with four of my teeth. I think it probably woke me up.

Hallam Moseley played out of his skin. He fancied himself as the new Seymour Nurse, so we nicknamed him Seymour and he played some of the most exquisite cover drives.

And as the runs came – 63 of them in 13 overs for the ninth wicket – the excitement got too much for two young members of the Somerset staff on scoreboard duty, who got into something of a tangle

Trevor Jesty and Peter Sainsbury pulled them back into it with a stand of 95, but I had Sainsbury caught by Viv Richards for 40. I ended with two for 33 and Hallam Moseley finished them off to take three for 28. They were all out for 182.

Today you would think a target like that was a bit of a doddle, but I think there's a bit more science in the game now than there was then and we made hard work of it. We never really got on top of it, even though Derek Taylor made 33 and Brian Close 28. We collapsed to Trevor Jesty's bowling.

I came in at 113 for seven, which was soon 113 for eight. We still needed 70

with the numbers and were roundly jeered by the spectators for their efforts. Their names: Peter Roebuck and Vic Marks.

Hallam Moseley played really well, but when he got out for 24, we still needed seven to win off the last two overs as our last man, Bob Clapp came in. Now, Bob's batting record was hardly going to scare the opposition.

I can remember us scrambling for a three to make sure I kept the bowling and as we crossed he seemed to take off in a long dive, with his bat outstretched to make his ground. Whether he would have been called in by a third umpire with a replay, we'll never know. It must have been a very tight call, but he was in.

I had got the strike. I played and missed a couple of times, but then I got

Botham is applauded off the field, looking for a dentist

one through the off side to pick up the boundary to win the game. Next morning I woke up to the newspaper headlines – and rather a sore head, which, of course I put down to the four teeth getting knocked out and having to rush off to the dentist. The evening of the game, if you'd given me open heart surgery I wouldn't have felt it as we celebrated the way we'd come back from the dead in that match. It was a great night, believe me.

Hampshire 182 *(53.3 overs) (T E Jesty 79;*
P J Sainsbury 40; H R Moseley 3-28; I T Botham 2-33)
Somerset 184-9 *(54 overs) (I T Botham 45 n.o.;*
T E Jesty 4-28)
In the semi-final, Somerset were heavily defeated by Leicestershire, who themselves lost to Surrey in the final.

1974 IN CRICKET

England, under **Mike Denness**, enjoy three big wins over India in the first series of the summer. Denness makes two centuries and **David Lloyd** an unbeaten 214 at Edgbaston. But the weather and the dead Oval pitch make a closer series against Pakistan a stalemate... **John Jameson** and **Rohan Kanhai** set a world record unbroken second wicket stand of 465 for Warwickshire (Jameson 240, Kanhai 213)... England set off for Australia to defend the Ashes, but run into a revitalised **Dennis Lillee** and his sensational new partner **Jeff Thomson**. Old trouper **Colin Cowdrey** finds himself whisked out to face them as he approaches his 42nd birthday.

1974 IN SPORT

Gary Player wins the US Masters and the Open after being written off as too old... **Don Revie** wins the League with Leeds then becomes England manager... **Denis Law**, in his last League match, scores a late goal for Manchester City and sends his old club Manchester United into the Second Division... South Africa lose their first ever rugby union home series to **Willie-John McBride**'s Lions... **Chris Evert** is engaged to **Jimmy Connors**. Both win Wimbledon... **Franz Beckenbauer**'s West Germany win the World Cup, beating the 'Total Football' of Johan Cruyff's Netherlands in the final... Rumble in the Jungle – **Muhammad Ali** beats **George Foreman** in Zaire.

over for 170. So Illingworth's captaincy skills in the field had done it again – or so it seemed. A target of 171 looked like an easy task.

But Geoff Arnold saw to it that they had the worst possible start, by bowling Barry Dudleston with the first ball of their innings. Arnold and Jackman took a stranglehold on the batsmen, though it was medium-pacer Graham Roope who made the next inroads.

Alan Butcher and Pat Pocock, too, proved impossible to score off and the last man out was Illingworth himself in the penultimate over, bowled by Arnold with 28 runs still needed. Arnold finished with three for 20 while Pocock's off-breaks took three for 26.

For his gritty innings and his handling of his side in the field, Freddie Brown gave the Gold Award to Surrey skipper John Edrich.

County Champions: Worcestershire
John Player League Champions: Leicestershire
Gillette Cup Winners: Kent

❖ FINAL SCOREBOARD 1974 ❖

LORD'S • 20TH JULY

– Surrey –
won the toss

*J H Edrich, c & b Steele	40
L E Skinner, lbw, b Higgs	0
G P Howarth, c Tolchard, b Booth	22
Younis Ahmed, c Dudleston, b Booth	43
G R J Roope, b McKenzie	13
S J Storey, lbw, b Illingworth	2
R D Jackman, c Tolchard, b McKenzie	36
A R Butcher, c Tolchard, b Higgs	7
P I Pocock, b Higgs	0
†A Long, c Tolchard, b Higgs	0
G G Arnold, not out	0
Extras (lb 5, nb 2)	7

Total *(54.1 overs)* 170

Fall of wickets: 1-4, 2-36, 3-99, 4-111, 5-118, 6-137, 7-168, 8-168, 9-168, 10-170.

Bowling: McKenzie 10.1-0-31-2, Higgs 7-2-10-4, Booth 8-1-30-1, McVicker 8-1-25-0, Illingworth 11-0-36-2, Steele 10-0-31-1.

– Leicestershire –

B Dudleston, lbw, b Arnold	0
J F Steele, run out	18
M E J C Norman, lbw, b Roope	24
B F Davison, c Howarth, b Arnold	13
†R W Tolchard, lbw, b Roope	0
J C Balderstone, b Pocock	32
*R Illingworth, b Arnold	23
N M McVicker, c Edrich, b Pocock	10
G D McKenzie, st Long, b Pocock	0
P Booth, c Arnold, b Jackman	5
K Higgs, not out	8
Extras (b 1, lb 5, nb 4)	10

Total *(54 overs)* 143

Fall of wickets: 1-0, 2-46, 3-46, 4-50, 5-65, 6-113, 7-129, 8-129, 9-131, 10-143.

Bowling: Arnold 10-4-20-3, Jackman 11-1-34-1, Roope 11-2-30-2, Butcher 11-1-23-0, Pocock 11-1-26-3.

Umpires: W E Alley & H D Bird

Gold Award Winner: J H Edrich
(Adjudicator. F R Brown)

– Surrey won by 27 runs –

1975

– Brearley outfoxed by Illingworth –

Leicestershire were becoming a fixture in the B&H Final. This time their opponents were Middlesex. Mike Brearley's team were about to embark on a remarkable era of success … but not just yet

Leicestershire were in their third Benson and Hedges Final in four years, but both finalists had finished second in their groups. The Midlands one, from which Leicestershire had emerged, now featured a combined Oxford and Cambridge Universities side, which included Imran Khan and scored victories over both Worcestershire and Northamptonshire.

Middlesex had been restored to the South, while Surrey swapped places with Minor Counties (South) and moved to the West zone.

Leicestershire's relative luck with the draws continued with home ties in the quarter-final, in which they had a narrow squeak with Lancashire, and in the semi, where Gordon Greenidge's hundred for Hampshire was matched by one from

The jubilant Leicestershire team celebrate their decisive win over Middlesex

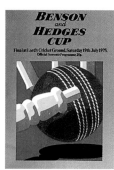

A fine diving catch by Leicestershire's dynamic wicketkeeper Roger Tolchard finally ends Mike Smith's long vigil

John Steele hits out during an innings of 49 which formed the cornerstone of Leicestershire's march to victory

Norman McVicker

golden memories

McVicker came on as first change for Leicestershire in the final and took the wicket of Phil Edmonds with his first ball. He proceeded to bowl his 11 overs without a break to record 4-20, taking the first four Middlesex wickets to fall. A right-arm fast-medium bowler, McVicker played Minor Counties cricket for Lincolnshire (1963-8) and only joined a first-class county at the age of 28, playing for Warwickshire in 1969-73 and Leicestershire in 1974-6. He met with considerable success as is seen by his career first-class figures of 413 wickets at an average of 25.47 and B&H career figures of 38 wickets at 20.23 (conceding a miserly 3.16 runs per over). Perhaps surprisingly this was the one B&H Gold Award of his career. In 1975 he also played a major role in helping Leicestershire to their first ever County Championship, with 482 runs at 34.42 and 46 wickets at 25.82 in that competition.

Chris Balderstone in a five-wicket win. Middlesex had had a semi-final century from Clive Radley to enable them to beat Warwickshire.

The final zonal matches had produced two controversies which did not involve the finalists. At Chelmsford, in the last over of the Essex innings against Sussex, Brian Edmeades was 'caught' on the long-on boundary by Marshall. Edmeades was on his way to the pavilion when a commotion on the boundary caused the umpire, Donald Oslear, to go and investigate. There the majority view, corroborated by Marshall himself, was that in making the catch he may have put one foot on the boundary rope. Had the catch stood, it would have given Sussex the extra wicket they needed to go into the quarter-finals instead of Middlesex.

At The Oval, Surrey's match with Gloucester had ended with the scores level on 218, but the West Country team were named winners because they had lost only five wickets to Surrey's nine. John Edrich was less than pleased when he discovered that the umpire had called a wide in the 52nd over, but not added an extra ball. A run off that ball would have given Surrey victory. Equally, another wicket would have confirmed Gloucester's win.

The Final pitted that wily old fox Ray Illingworth, then aged 43, against a man 10 years his junior – Mike Brearley. At the time, it seemed that Brearley had long ago blown his chances of ever becoming an England player.

He had been captain of Middlesex for five years without winning a trophy and this was the county's first one-day final. Although they were fated to lose the B&H Final that day, it was a foot in the door, and it heralded a period of great success for Middlesex under Brearley and then Mike Gatting.

> '*The popularity of one-day cricket owes a great deal to the B&H Cup. It provides a good competitive start to the season and helps focus attention on the summer game.*'
>
> PRINCE PHILIP,
> PRESIDENT OF THE CRICKET COUNCIL,
> IN THE 1974 CUP FINAL PROGRAMME

Great bowling: McVicker's 11-3-20-4

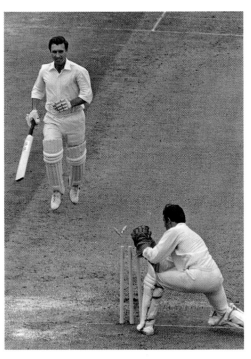

The Leicestershire fans rejoice after winning the Benson and Hedges Cup twice in its first four years

Fred Titmus smiles ruefully as he is run out for a duck

1975 IN CRICKET

Battered England reel away from Australia after losing the Ashes to **Lillee** and **Thomson** by 4-1. They only win the last Test in the absence of Thomson… New Zealand batsman **Ewen Chatfield** 'dies' when struck on the temple by England's **Peter Lever**. His heart actually stopped beating, but he was revived by England physio **Bernard Thomas**… The first World Cup is staged in England. The West Indies beat Australia by 17 runs in a final graced by a superlative 102 in 85 balls from **Clive Lloyd**… A four-Test series with Australia sees captain **Mike Denness** replaced by **Tony Greig**. **David Steele** – 'the bank clerk going to war' – takes on **Lillee** and **Thomson** but

can't regain the Ashes… **Graham Gooch** bags a pair in his first Test… A day of Championship cricket is abandoned in June in Buxton – because of snow.

1975 IN SPORT

Barry Sheene nearly dies in a crash at Daytona but bounces back to win the 500cc world title in 1976 and '77… **Jack Nicklaus** beats **Johnny Miller** and **Tom Weiskopf** on the 18th hole in 'the best ever Masters'… Czech **Martina Navratilova**, 19, defects to the USA… Southern League Wimbledon beat First Division Burnley in the FA Cup, then draw at Leeds… The Thriller in Manila – **Muhammad Ali** beats **Joe Frazier** in an epic battle.

Brearley was well aware of its significance. "For Middlesex this is a new lease of life," he wrote in the Cup Final programme, "and I'm sure our increased support in London will prove that. If anyone thinks we are the underdogs – well and good. We've been branded that all season and look where we are today!"

But Illingworth saw this as a day of destiny. "This is our third Benson and Hedges Final at Lord's and we aim to make it the best yet," he wrote. "We won the Cup in 1972 against Yorkshire, a sweet triumph. Last year we slipped up against Surrey. Today, it is Middlesex on their home territory. But if Mike Brearley thinks that's an advantage, he had better think again. We congratulate Middlesex on their success but the whole Leicester side – no, the whole county – aims to see the B&H trophy on the Grace Road mantelpiece again. That is its proper home."

> *In an early example of what would later be known as pinch-hitting, Phil Edmonds opened the innings and hooked Graham McKenzie's first ball for six*

In the Final, there was an early example of what would later be known as 'pinch-hitting', when Phil Edmonds opened the Middlesex innings – Mike Brearley having pushed himself down to four in the order – and hooked his first ball from Graham McKenzie for six. But Norman McVicker inflicted early damage on the Middlesex batting, reducing them to 87 for four including the wicket of Brearley, brilliantly caught in the slips by Brian Davison.

Mike Smith, later to serve Middlesex as scorer, played the sheet-anchor role, making 87, but they could not break the shackles. Opening bowler Ken Higgs put on another fine show: his 10 overs cost only 18 runs and he took the crucial wicket of Larry Gomes. Middlesex were all out in the 53rd over for 146.

Leicestershire took no risks in getting the runs, though there were two run-outs and a pair

Raymond Illingworth carries the Benson and Hedges Cup back to Leicestershire, saying: "That is its proper home"

Ken Higgs bowled a tidy spell of 10 overs for just 18 runs

of wickets for the veteran off-spinner Fred Titmus along the way.

There was a slight wobble when Leicestershire lost two wickets on 67, including Brian Davison for a duck to the deceptively innocuous bowling of Larry Gomes. But the doughty John Steele and bustling Roger Tolchard eased them to a comfortable win by five wickets, with three and a half overs to spare.

Norman McVicker won the Gold Award for his bowling and the Leicester fox was still running well ahead of the pack. They still had another title to win that year, while Middlesex still had another Lord's final to play … and lose.

County Champions: Leicestershire
John Player League Champions: Hampshire
Gillette Cup Winners: Lancashire

◗ FINAL SCOREBOARD 1975 ◗

LORD'S • 19TH JULY

– Middlesex –
won the toss

M J Smith, c Tolchard, b Booth	83
P H Edmonds, c Illingworth, b McVicker	11
C T Radley, c Higgs, b McVicker	7
*J M Brearley, c Davison, b McVicker	2
N G Featherstone, c Tolchard, b McVicker	11
H A Gomes, b Higgs	3
G D Barlow, b Illingworth	7
†J T Murray, c Cross, b Steele	1
F J Titmus, run out	0
M W W Selvey, c Tolchard, b Booth	6
J S E Price, not out	2
Extras (lb 10, nb 3)	13
Total (52.4 overs)	**146**

Fall of wickets: 1-26, 2-37, 3-43, 4-87, 5-99, 6-110, 7-117, 8-119, 9-141, 10-146.

Bowling: McKenzie 7-2-20-0, Higgs 10-3-18-1, McVicker 11-3-20-4, Booth 8.4-1-25-2, Cross 2-0-9-0, Illingworth 9-1-31-1, Steele 5-0-10-1.

– Leicestershire –

B Dudleston, run out	17
J F Steele, c Selvey, b Titmus	49
J C Balderstone, run out	12
B F Davison, c Murray, b Gomes	0
†R W Tolchard, not out	47
G F Cross, lbw, b Titmus	0
*R Illingworth, not out	13
Extras (b 3, lb 9)	12
Total (51.2 overs, for 5 wkts)	**150**

Did not bat: N M McVicker, P Booth, G D McKenzie, K Higgs

Fall of wickets: 1-32, 2-67, 3-67, 4-118, 5-121.

Bowling: Price 9-3-26-0, Selvey 9.2-2-33-0, Titmus 11-2-30-2, Gomes 11-4-22-1, Edmonds 11-2-27-0.

Umpires: W L Budd & A E Fagg

Gold Award Winner: N M McVicker
(Adjudicator: E R Dexter)

– Leicestershire won by five wickets –

1976
– D'Oliveira goes down fighting –

Graham Johnson of Kent won the Gold Award, but the highlight of the Final was an innings by the injured Basil d'Oliveira that nearly pulled off a impossible win for Worcestershire

If the Gold Award goes to the player who makes the match, maybe in this instance it should have gone to someone on the losing side, who made a one-sided game into a contest.

It was Basil d'Oliveira who provided the heroics in this match. The veteran Worcestershire all-rounder's stubborn resistance against the odds and when carrying an injury would have brought a smile to the face of another old trouper. Colin Cowdrey knew all about gallantry in a losing cause, having less than two years before been flown out to face Dennis Lillee and Jeff Thomson in Australia. Cowdrey was now retired, but the former Kent captain took the opportunity in the Cup Final programme to give his thoughts on the passing of an era when there was no one-day cricket, and selected a squad "from those I have played with but who have never had the opportunity to play in one-day cricket". He went for a bowling line-up selected from Brian Statham, Alec Bedser, Derek Shackleton, Bob Appleyard, Jim Laker and Johnny Wardle; Trevor Bailey ("the best all-rounder of my time"); Godfrey Evans ("tailor-made for one-day cricket, a great wicketkeeper and dangerous attacking batsman); and batsmen selected from Hutton, Washbrook, Compton, Edrich, May and Graveney. Quite a handy side…

In the earlier rounds of the B&H Cup, the

> *'This will be our fourth one-day cup final and I have been lucky enough to have been involved in all four. Unfortunately we have lost each one!'*
>
> — NORMAN GIFFORD

Alan Knott watches as Basil d'Oliveira, batting with a hamstring injury, tries to win the match by hitting boundaries

There is no finer sight in cricket than a full house at Lord's. This is the start of the Worcestershire reply

Graham Johnson

golden memories

With Bob Woolmer (61), Johnson set Kent well on course to victory during an opening stand of 110, the first ever century opening partnership in a Lord's one-day final. Johnson went on to score 78 and, fielding on the boundary, caught out four of Worcestershire's first five batsmen. A right-handed batsman and off-break bowler, Johnson gave stalwart service to Kent in a 20-year career with the county from his debut at the age of 18 in 1965 to 1985. In his first-class career he scored 12,922 runs at 24.51 and took 567 wickets at 31.04 as well as 316 catches. He scored over 1,000 runs in a first-class season each year 1973-5 and, as his bowling became more important, took over 50 wickets three times, 1978, 1981 and 1983. In all he won three B&H Gold Awards.

Asif Iqbal enjoying another B&H final at Lord's

regional arrangement of the zonal groups had now all but totally been abandoned. Thus Yorkshire, for instance, found themselves in the same group as Sussex – but, more interestingly, as Oxford and Cambridge Universities. They met at Barnsley, the Universities captained by one Vic Marks and including unknown undergraduates Peter Roebuck, Chris Tavaré, Paul Parker and Andrew Wingfield-Digby. Yorkshire were beaten by seven wickets with seven overs to spare. It cost Yorkshire a place in the quarter-finals.

The semi-finals were splendid matches, a Mike Denness century being the difference in Kent's favour at The Oval, and 143 from Glenn Turner doing the job for Worcestershire at Edgbaston.

Worcestershire skipper Norman Gifford was appearing in his fourth one-day cup final. But he had a big hurdle to overcome. "This will be our fourth Cup Final since 1963," he observed, "and I have been lucky enough to have been involved in all four. Unfortunately, we have lost each one!"

At Lord's Gifford won the toss and put Kent in. He may well have regretted it as Graham

Johnson during his crucial innings of 78

MIKE DENNESS

THE FINAL: KENT v WORCESTERSHIRE, 17TH JULY 1976

MIKE DENNESS CAPTAINED KENT FROM 1972 TO 1976 AND IN THAT TIME THEY
BECAME A FINE ONE-DAY SIDE, WINNING THE GILLETTE CUP, THE SUNDAY LEAGUE
THREE TIMES AND THE BENSON AND HEDGES CUP TWICE. ON THIS DAY, HOWEVER,
THEY LOOKED AS IF THEY MIGHT HAVE THEIR THUNDER STOLEN BY A REMARKABLE
PERFORMANCE.

At the start of this successful period for Kent, we had not won anything since 1913 and so it was important to show people what we could do by getting to Lord's finals. In the Benson and Hedges Cup we had enjoyment – and disappointment as well.

On this occasion we were given a good start by Graham Johnson and Bob Woolmer, who put on 110 for the first wicket. That's the sort of thing you try and plan for, and it gave Asif Iqbal the chance to play as only he could. The problem of batting with him was that he was so quick between the wickets that as he passed you he would say maybe "two" or "three" or even "four" and unless you were quick enough, he could be lapping you.

During our innings Basil d'Oliveira pulled a hamstring in the field and had to go off after bowling only four overs. That was a big handicap for them, because be bowled in these games at a slow pace that meant that you had to put the impetus on the ball. Seeing him go off we were also rather hoping that it would handicap him when they batted, too.

By today's standards, you might think that after a start like that we should have got more than our 236 for seven, but these were the days of no limitations on field placings. We had a side full of useful all-rounders, like Woolmer, John Shepherd and Asif. I can't remember many times when any individual bowler was really taken apart by the opposition batting. And then of course we had Underwood.

The great thing about Derek was that you could rely on him to bowl to a certain field. He would get into his line and length very quickly. He was just natural in his rhythm and he always made it very difficult for the batsman to score runs and the rest of the players took confidence from that and that helped to give us our great team spirit.

At 90 for four, thanks to three good boundary catches by Johnson, we felt we had Worcestershire in trouble, with the new batsman – the injured Basil d'Oliveira – batting with Glenn Turner as his runner. We thought, "well, he can't move his feet, so he's not going to be able to strike the ball". But he just stood there and belted it.

We talked to the bowlers about trying to get him to move his feet with change of length and direction, because if you bowled a consistent off-stump line on a good length, all Basil did was pick you up over midwicket or smash you

Happy days! Johnson, Denness and Woolmer share their moment of victory

through the covers and that proved hard for the bowlers, because they were in a rhythm.

We got into the situation where Basil was winning the game for Worcester. I was standing in the middle with Alan Knott and the bowler Kevin Jarvis, talking about how we were going to deal with this, when Basil walked past us and I said to him: "Which bowler would you like now?"

And he said to me: "Mike, I'm getting very tired. Just put anybody on."

He didn't last too much longer. He was bowled by Kevin for 50, which he'd made out of 75 scored in the 14 overs he was in for. He'd made it a close-run thing for us.

That was a swansong for me. I finished with Kent at the end of that season and went off to have an enjoyable few seasons with Essex.

1976 IN CRICKET

The West Indies arrive in England smarting from a 5-1 defeat in Australia, just in time to hear the England captain, **Tony Greig**, say that when they are on top they are great, but when they're down 'they grovel'. "We aim," he says, "to make them grovel." If the tourists need any incentive, that will do. They take the series in a heatwave summer by 3-0, ending with a remarkable bowling performance by **Michael Holding**, taking 14 wickets on an unhelpful pitch. **Tony Greig** 'grovels' on the parched Oval outfield when his side has been set their final target of 435… Women play at Lord's for the first time, when England meet Australia for the St Ivel Cream Jug.

1976 IN SPORT

John Curry wins the Winter Olympics figure skating gold… Liverpool, with strikers **Kevin Keegan** and **John Toshack**, do the Double of League and Uefa Cup… **Bobby Stokes'** goal wins the FA Cup Final against Manchester United for Second Division Southampton… **Severiano Ballesteros**, 19, is six ahead going into last round of The Open. He fades to finish behind **Johnny Miller**… **Nadia Comaneci**, 14, scores the first ever perfect score in Olympic gymnastics… **James Hunt**, in his first Formula One season, wins the title from **Niki Lauda** by one point. after Lauda makes a miraculous return to racing six weeks after a fire at Nurburgring in which he is scarred for life.

The turning point as d'Oliveira is bowled by Jarvis

Johnson and Bob Woolmer put on the first century opening stand in any Lord's final. Johnson made 78 and Woolmer 61 and during their partnership there was a significant injury as Basil d'Oliveira pulled up in the field clutching a hamstring. Quite apart from the loss of his bowling (though his four overs so far had gone for 21 runs), Worcestershire needed his batting.

Asif Iqbal's usual improvisations and sharp running, making 48 not out, took the Kent score to 236 for seven. Ormrod and Turner made a fair start, until the first bowling change brought on John Shepherd, who removed Turner and Neale. Derek Underwood came on and shackled Alan Ormrod at last. He, Imran Khan and Hemsley were all caught on the boundary by Johnson. (This was to be Imran's only cup final with Worcestershire. He left at the end of the season, saying he found life in the county too boring!)

Now Worcestershire were in trouble at 126 for five. D'Oliveira had just arrived at the crease –

with Turner as his runner. A strong man, he swung from a static position and for a time the Kent bowlers seemed unable to find any way to bowl at him. Suddenly the possibility of a remarkable Worcestershire win was stirring the crowd as they cheered d'Oliveira's heroics.

The task was still demanding – 75 were needed for the last ten overs. But as long as d'Oliveira was still there, Worcestershire were in the hunt. Kent were mightily relieved when he was bowled by Kevin Jarvis for 50 and limped off to a standing ovation. Worcestershire succumbed to be all out for 193.

Basil d'Oliveira had made it a match after all. But Graham Johnson, who had been the top scorer and had taken no fewer than four catches, deserved his Gold Award.

County Champions: Middlesex
John Player League Champions: Kent
Gillette Cup Winners: Northamptonshire

◆ FINAL SCOREBOARD 1976 ◆

LORD'S • 17TH JULY

– Kent –

G W Johnson, b Boyns	78
R A Woolmer, c Inchmore, b Gifford	61
*M H Denness, c Wilcock, b Inchmore	15
Asif Iqbal, not out	48
A G E Ealham, c Ormrod, b Boyns	11
J N Shepherd, c Boyns, b Gifford	8
†A P E Knott, b Imran Khan	1
C J C Rowe, run out	0
Extras (b 2, lb 10, nb 2)	14
Total (55 overs, for 7 wkts)	**236**

Did not bat: R W Hills, D L Underwood, K B S Jarvis

Fall of wickets: 1-110, 2-155, 3-171, 4-194, 5-215, 6-220, 7-236.

Bowling: Imran Khan 9-1-26-1, Inchmore 11-0-57-1, Pridgeon 9-1-35-0, d'Oliveira 4-1-21-0, Gifford 11-3-38-2, Boyns 11-0-45-2.

– Worcestershire –

won the toss

J A Ormrod, c Johnson, b Underwood	37
G M Turner, c Knott, b Shepherd	14
P A Neale, c Johnson, b Shepherd	5
Imran Khan, c Johnson, b Underwood	12
E J O Hemsley, c Johnson, b Underwood	15
B L d'Oliveira, b Jarvis	50
C N Boyns, c Knott, b Jarvis	15
†H G Wilcock, not out	19
*N Gifford, c Knott, b Jarvis	0
J D Inchmore, c Underwood, b Asif Iqbal	2
A P Pridgeon, b Jarvis	8
Extras (b 1, lb 12, w 1, nb 2)	16
Total (52.4 overs)	**193**

Fall of wickets: 1-40, 2-52, 3-70, 4-90, 5-126, 6-161, 7-166, 8-172, 9-175, 10-193.

Bowling: Jarvis 10.4-2-34-4, Asif Iqbal 9-0-35-1, Shepherd 7-0-17-2, Woolmer 11-3-27-0, Underwood 9-2-31-3, Hills 6-0-33-0.

Umpires: D J Constant & T W Spencer

Gold Award Winner: G W Johnson
(Adjudicator: Sir Garfield Sobers)

– Kent won by 43 runs –

1977

– The Cup goes to Proctershire –

Mike Procter yearned for a big stage on which to display his talents. His Gloucestershire colleagues made sure that it was their day – and Kent went home empty-handed for the first time

Gloucestershire and Kent both had new captains for 1977, and both were popular, dynamic figures. Gloucestershire's skipper was their remarkable South African all-rounder Mike Procter. Kent's was also an international all-rounder – and a former Benson Hedges Final Gold Award winner, to boot – Asif Iqbal of Pakistan. Writing in the Cup Final programme, he said: "In one-day cricket there is no room for errors and for both Mike Procter and myself, today will be a great challenge as we are both new captains.

"We know that Gloucestershire are hard opponents to beat. On the other hand Kent thrive

Right: One of the greatest B&H performances – Mike Procter during the spell against Hampshire in which he took four wickets in five balls

on hard-fought matches. If experience counts for anything, we must be favourites to make this our third Benson and Hedges Cup Final victory."

Procter obviously had other ideas. Denied the stage of Test cricket during these isolation years for his country, for him a Lord's final was a great day. And not for nothing were his county now being popularly called 'Proctershire'.

A devastating fast bowler who famously bowled 'off the wrong foot', his three for 15 had helped Gloucestershire beat Middlesex in the

Zaheer Abbas played a majestic innings of 70 for Gloucestershire, ensuring a sizeable total for their bowlers to defend

Andy Stovold

g o l d e n m e m o r i e s

In his fifth year with Gloucestershire, Stovold had a splendid season, scoring 1,223 runs at 34.94 in first-class cricket and taking 63 dismissals as their wicket-keeper. He had a superb match in the B&H Final, top-scoring with 71 and taking three catches behind the stumps. Stovold relinquished the wicket-keeping duties to Andy Brassington the following year, and thenceforth concentrated on his hard-hitting batting, playing for the county until 1990, with a best season of 1,671 first-class runs at 42.84 in 1983. His value in limited-overs cricket is shown by the fact that his career averages for the B&H of 37.34 (2,134 runs) and NatWest of 37.93 (1,138 runs) are well above that for first-class cricket, where he scored a total of 17,601 runs at 29.78. He set Gloucestershire records with nine B&H Gold Awards (including three in 1977) and 69 appearances.

Andy Stovold top scored with 71

quarter-final. Then, in the semi-final at Southampton, he really set the supporters alight with a hat-trick which started with the great Barry Richards. His six-wicket haul in that match included four wickets in five balls – and cost him just 13 runs. It was also the best bowling performance recorded in the B&H Cup to date.

Procter also had the third best batting score thus far in the B&H – 154 not out against Somerset in 1972. He had won four Gold Awards in the B&H competition, two of them in 1977. No wonder many people regarded him as the outstanding all-rounder in the world.

But Kent were B&H holders – and favourites. Chris Cowdrey's hundred had beaten Sussex in the quarter-final and Bob Woolmer's all-round performance saw them through at Northampton.

On July 16th, Procter won the toss and launched a commanding performance from the Gloucestershire batsmen. Andy Stovold's brilliant 71 contained ten fours and his mantle was taken on by the bespectacled Zaheer Abbas with a

CHRIS COWDREY
QUARTER-FINAL: KENT V SUSSEX, CANTERBURY, 8TH JUNE 1977

CHRIS COWDREY FIRST PLAYED FOR KENT IN 1976 AND THE NEXT YEAR MADE HIS FIRST-CLASS DEBUT AT THE AGE OF 19. HE CARRIED THE ADDITIONAL BURDEN OF BEING THE SON OF THE GREAT COLIN AND ON THIS, THE OCCASION OF HIS BENSON AND HEDGES DEBUT, THE ANXIOUS FATHER COULD BE SEEN STALKING ROUND THE CANTERBURY BOUNDARY.

It is a thrill for any 19-year-old to be included in a Kent squad for a Benson and Hedges quarter-final. With local rivals Sussex the visitors and a guaranteed full house at Canterbury, the match takes on even great significance.

I was under no illusions. I had been included as a specialist substitute fielder or perhaps a standby for a last-minute injury. Yet it was an injury to me as my knee collapsed in practice two days before the match which seriously threatened my chances of any contribution at all.

Written off by a knife-happy orthopaedic surgeon, I was ushered off to a faith healer as a desperate measure. As I hobbled away she gave me a clean bill of health. I was unconvinced and consequently enjoyed a rather more social evening than usual on the eve of a big match.

It came as a major surprise when my captain Asif Iqbal approached me on arrival in the dressing room with "You're in, Cow, good luck." I was so amazed I couldn't bring myself to admit to any fitness doubt. The healer had told me not to worry and miraculously I strode out with the Kent team at 11.00am, secretly pleased that we had lost the toss. I had been told I was to open the batting with Bob Woolmer and I felt rather apprehensive about facing my boyhood hero, John Snow.

For the next few hours, though, we were smashed to all parts of the ground by Kepler Wessels, Roger Knight and Javed Miandad as Sussex amassed a total of 264, which in those days was considered an almost unattainable target. However there were several factors in our favour, such as a magnificent pitch for batting, fervent Kent support and a team who expected to win. Oh… and we had a plan.

During the qualifying rounds Kent had lost to Sussex largely due to the new-ball bowling of Mike Buss. He bowled his 11 overs for nothing with his gentle, swinging, left arm seamers and someone had to take him on this time to ensure there was no repeat. Cometh the hour…

I was a very strong legside player or, as some preferred to say, 'strokeless on the off side' and I had been given a free licence to slog Mike Buss out of the

Chris Cowdrey matched his father by scoring a century in his first B&H game

attack. Well, Plan A worked as I farmed Buss over square leg a few times and we got off to a flier, but when Asif Iqbal was out at 111-3 we needed something special to get anywhere near the Sussex total. Although I was still playing my strokes running purely on adrenalin, Alan Ealham gave the innings the real injection it needed. We put on 146 and he scored a spectacular 94 not out.

There was no happier man in the ground than Ealham when I reached my hundred. He hugged me around the neck so tight I could hardly breathe, but he knew then that our partnership had won the game. I was out soon afterwards for 114 and the reception I received from the capacity crowd is still the greatest memory of my career.

Alan Ealham deserved the Gold Award, but it was my day and on the advice of Derek Underwood I celebrated in style. In jest he said, as he always did after a teammate's hundred, "Celebrate on the night, son, you'll never get another one." Actually, I never did get another hundred in the Benson and Hedges and a week later I was lbw Buss 0 at Maidstone.

At least the occasion provided the happy family statistic that my father and I had both scored centuries in our first innings in the Benson and Hedges Cup. My score was higher than his, though!

Sussex 264 for 5 *(55 overs) (R D V Knight 91; K C Wessels 64; Javed Miandad 56 n.o.)*
Kent 268 for 4 *(52.1 overs) (C S Cowdrey 114; A G E Ealham 94 n.o.)*
Kent won by 6 wickets.

Above: Zaheer Abbas catches Alan Knott as Gloucestershire close in on victory.
Left: Over-excited Gloucestershire fans battled with police. MCC secretary Jack Bailey
said: "It was disgraceful, but it will be a sad day if we ever have to cage supporters in"

FINAL SCOREBOARD 1977

LORD'S • 16TH JULY

– Gloucestershire –
won the toss

Sadiq Mohammad, c Hills, b Woolmer	24
†A W Stovold, c Underwood, b Shepherd	71
Zaheer Abbas, c Underwood, b Jarvis	70
*M J Procter, c Knott, b Julien	25
J C Foat, not out	21
D R Shepherd, b Jarvis	9
D A Graveney, c Underwood, b Julien	1
M J Vernon, not out	3
Extras (lb 7, w 2, nb 4)	13
Total (55 overs, for 6 wkts)	**237**

Did not bat: M D Partridge, J H Shackleton, B M Brain

Fall of wickets: 1-79, 2-144, 3-191, 4-204, 5-220, 6-223.

Bowling: Jarvis 11-2-52-2, Julien 11-0-51-2, Shepherd 11-0-47-1, Woolmer 11-0-42-1, Underwood 11-1-32-0.

– Kent –

R A Woolmer, c Shackleton, b Graveney	64
G S Clinton, b Brain	0
C J C Rowe, c Stovold, b Procter	0
*Asif Iqbal, c Stovold, b Vernon	5
A G E Ealham, c Stovold, b Vernon	11
B D Julien, b Graveney	1
J N Shepherd, c Procter, b Brain	55
†A P E Knott, c Zaheer Abbas, b Partridge	14
R W Hills, c Procter b Shackleton	6
D L Underwood, b Brain	8
K B S Jarvis, not out	0
Extras (lb 7, nb 2)	9
Total (47.3 overs)	**173**

Fall of wickets: 1-4, 2-5, 3-24, 4-64, 5-65, 6-100, 7-122, 8-150, 9-166, 10-173.

Bowling: Procter 7-1-15-1, Brain 7.3-5-9-3, Vernon 11-1-52-2, Shackleton 10-0-40-1, Graveney 9-2-26-2, Partridge 3-0-22-1.

Umpires: H D Bird & W L Budd

Gold Award Winner: A W Stovold
(Adjudicator: F S Trueman)

– Gloucestershire won by 64 runs –

1977 IN CRICKET
An earth-shattering year. After winning a Test series in India, **Tony Greig** takes his side to Melbourne for the Centenary Test. It ends in the same margin of victory for Australia as the original in 1877 – 45 runs. **Derek Randall**'s defiant 174 is the star attraction... But behind the scenes Australian TV magnate **Kerry Packer** is setting up his own circus of cricketers to break the Australian Broadcasting Corperation's monopoly of TV rights. The plot is uncovered and Greig, as one of the recruiters, is sacked as England captain... His replacement is **Mike Brearley**, who regains the Ashes at Headingley in the match where **Geoff Boycott** scores his 100th hundred... **Ian Botham** makes his Test debut, modestly taking five for 74.

1977 IN SPORT
Red Rum wins his third Grand National (as well as two seconds) and retires... **Bjorn Borg** beats **Jimmy Connors** to win his first Wimbledon title in an epic final. **John McEnroe**, 18, is the first qualifier to reach the semi-finals... **Virginia Wade** wins during the Queen's Jubilee... Liverpool do the League and European Cup double but are beaten by **Tommy Docherty**'s Manchester United in the FA Cup final... Docherty is sacked by United for leaving his wife to live with the club physio... **Jack Nicklaus** and **Tom Watson** smash the Open record as Watson wins by one stroke with 268 at Turnberry.

---

magnificent innings of 70, including a huge six off John Shepherd.

Kent's target was 238 – and normally they would expect to get there. But it quickly looked a tall order, when Procter and Brian Brain had them reeling at five for two. Martin Vernon added the crucial wickets of Asif Iqbal and the captain, Alan Ealham, cheaply and when David Graveney – later to become chairman of selectors – had bowled Bernard Julien, it was 65 for five.

Bob Woolmer, who had opened and been watching the mayhem at the other end, was now joined by John Shepherd and they took the score up to 100 before Graveney had Woolmer caught at deep midwicket for 64. Now the writing was on the wall, even after a defiant six from Alan Knott and Shepherd going on to make 55.

Kent were all out in the 48th over for 173 and Gloucestershire had won the title against all the predictions by the substantial margin of 64 runs.

Schweppes County Champions: Kent & Middlesex
John Player League Champions: Leicestershire
Gillette Cup Winners: Middlesex

1978

— Kent get back in the winning habit—

The previous year, a great South African all-rounder had spoilt Kent's big day out. Now, in place of Mike Procter, they were facing Derbyshire's Eddie Barlow. Surely lightning couldn't strike twice?

Kent were back again, for their third Final in a row. The previous year had been an intense disappointment to them, and they were looking to make a better job of it under their third captain in three years – Alan Ealham.

"Lord's on a Benson and Hedges Final day is like a second home to us," Ealham said. "If experience counts for anything, we must be favourites to win the Cup in our third consecutive Final. But that is how we felt about last year's Final! We had won in 1973 and 1976 and thought we knew more than most about the game. But in one-day cricket there is no room for complacency.

"Our record in one-day competition speaks for itself. Hardly a season has passed in the Seventies without us winning one of them. Our players love the pressures of this type of cricket and I think this is reflected in our results.

"For me, of course, this year provides a different, very special challenge. This is my first season as captain of Kent and reaching this Final has made a marvellous start for me. I hope I can cap it by winning a record third victory in the Benson and Hedges Cup."

If Kent were Lord's veterans, Derbyshire were new boys. Their captain, Eddie Barlow, was a very experienced all-rounder, having played for South Africa way back in 1961. Even during South Africa's exclusion from Tests, he had played for the Rest of the World against England – and took four wickets in five balls. Earlier in the 1978 season he won a Benson and Hedges Gold Award for taking six for 33 against Gloucestershire.

He observed: "This will be Derbyshire's first visit to Lord's as B&H Cup Finalists. Indeed, this is the first year that we have survived the zonal rounds! But then a lot of things are happening to Derbyshire that have not happened to us for a long time. Three players in an England Test 12 for one thing (Bob Taylor, Geoff Miller and Mike Hendrick).

"Nobody has ever rated us as one-day cricket specialists but it won't be bothering us to be the underdogs. We have a young team at Derbyshire and it will be a new experience to savour."

Barlow won the toss and decided to bat, which gave Lord's another new experience. When Derbyshire opener Alan Hill emerged from the Pavilion, he became the first batsman to wear a helmet in a Benson and Hedges Final.

It didn't help him too much. He outstayed his opening partner, Tony Borrington, but when Hill and Barlow fell in quick succession to John Shepherd and Derek Underwood, Derbyshire had made a dreadful start and were 33 for three. The other Derbyshire South African, Peter Kirsten, helped Geoff Miller put on 55 for the fourth wicket, but the going was painfully slow and only 60 runs came in the first 30 overs.

Kirsten eventually fell to Asif Iqbal for 41. Shepherd returned to bowl Miller for 38 and

Cowdrey, Downton and Underwood: We won the Cup!

Above: No doubt about that one, mate! Kent's Chris Tavaré is bowled by Phil Russell without troubling the scorers

Super Kent! But little did they realise that their third Benson and Hedges trophy would also be their last…

◊ GOLD AWARD WINNER 1978 ◊

Bob Woolmer

g o l d e n   m e m o r i e s

In his third successive B&H Final, Woolmer followed scores of 61 in 1976 and 64 in 1977 with a match-winning innings of 79, made out of 117 while he was at the wicket. Woolmer made his debut for Kent in 1968 and for several years was a useful medium-fast bowler and middle-order batsman. He made a late breakthrough as a top-class batsman, accelerated when he started opening in 1976. He made his Test debut for England in 1975 and had a very successful series against Australia in 1977, when he played most fluently for 394 runs at an average of 56.28, including two centuries. He then decided to join Kerry Packer's World Series cricket and was unable to regain a regular place but he played four Tests on his return in 1980-1. He became a highly successful coach with Kent and Warwickshire, before taking on the same job for South Africa in 1994.

Bob Woolmer scored over half of the winning total

Above: Chris Tavaré takes a spectacular diving catch to dismiss Alan Hill – the first B&H Cup finalist to wear a helmet. Below left: John Shepherd calmly saw Kent to victory

1978 IN CRICKET

Kent win the first sponsored County Championship… In a summer split between Pakistan and New Zealand, England win five Tests out of six, the Headingley match with Pakistan falling foul of the weather. Bizarrely, England have just returned from tours of both countries on which **Mike Brearley** broke his arm, giving **Geoff Boycott** the captaincy. At the end of the year Brearley is taking England to Australia for the defence of the Ashes… **David Gower** debuts with four off his first ball against Liaquat Ali of Pakistan, then scores a century against New Zealand… Australia, needing 382 to beat Pakistan at Melbourne, pass 300 with only three wickets down – but then lose their last seven wickets for just five runs to the bowling of **Sarfraz Nawaz**… Two great England players of the past leave us – **Herbert Sutcliffe** and **Frank Woolley**.

1978 IN SPORT

Wales do the Grand Slam and **Gareth Edwards** retires… **Ray Reardon** wins his sixth and last world snooker title… **Brian Clough** and **Peter Taylor**'s newly-promoted Nottingham Forest win the League by seven points… **Ingemar Stennmark** of Sweden wins his third successive skiing World Cup… **Martina Navratilova** wins her first Wimbledon title… Scot **Archie Gemmill** scores an all-time great World Cup goal against Holland. **Mario Kempes** scores twice in the final as Argentina beat Holland… **Bernard Hinault** wins the first of a record five Tours de France… Liverpool retain the European Cup… **Ardiles** and **Villa** sign for Spurs… **Muhammad Ali**, 36, beats **Leon Spinks** to become the only man to win the world heavyweight title three times… Racing driver Ronnie Peterson dies at Monza.

Above: The Kent team celebrate on the Lord's Pavilion balcony after winning their third Benson and Hedges Cup.
Below: Peter Kirsten played with dogged resistance for 41 but Derbyshire failed to set Kent a difficult target

quickly added the wickets of Ashley Harvey-Walker and Taylor to take his haul to four for 25. Derbyshire were all out in the last over for 147.

It should not have been a stiff target and it wasn't. Bob Woolmer led the way with 79, which brought him the Gold Award, though he did have the good fortune to be put down twice off successive balls from Hendrick, uncharacteristically in both cases – by Barlow at slip and by Taylor, the wicketkeeper, diving right.

When Woolmer was gone, Shepherd and captain Alan Ealham saw Kent home with six wickets and over 13 overs to spare.

Schweppes County Champions: Kent
John Player League Champions: Hampshire
Gillette Cup Winners: Sussex

FINAL SCOREBOARD 1978

LORD'S • 22ND JULY

– Derbyshire –
won the toss

A Hill, c Tavaré, b Jarvis	17
A J Borrington, c Downton, b Shepherd	0
P N Kirsten, c Shepherd, b Asif Iqbal	41
*E J Barlow, b Underwood	1
G Miller, b Shepherd	38
H Cartwright, c Ealham, b Woolmer	12
A J Harvey-Walker, b Shepherd	6
†R W Taylor, c Downton b Shepherd	0
P E Russell, c Downton, b Jarvis	4
R C Wincer, not out	6
M Hendrick, run out	7
Extras (lb 10, w 4, nb 1)	15
Total (54.4 overs)	**147**

Fall of wickets: 1-11, 2-32, 3-33, 4-88, 5-121, 6-127, 7-127, 8-132, 9-134, 10-147.

Bowling: Jarvis 9.4-3-19-2, Shepherd 11-2-25-4, Underwood 11-3-21-1, Woolmer 10-2-15-1, Asif Iqbal 8-1-26-1, Johnson 5-0-25-0.

– Kent –

R A Woolmer, c Hendrick, b Barlow	79
G W Johnson, c Barlow, b Russell	16
C J Tavaré, b Russell	0
Asif Iqbal, c Taylor, b Russell	9
*A G E Ealham, not out	23
J N Shepherd, not out	19
Extras (lb 3, w 1, nb 1)	5
Total (41.4 overs, for 4 wkts)	**151**

Did not bat: C J C Rowe, C S Cowdrey, D L Underwood, †P R Downton, K B S Jarvis

Fall of wickets: 1-32, 2-34, 3-70, 4-117.

Bowling: Hendrick 11-2-23-0, Wincer 7-0-29-0, Russell 11-2-28-3, Barlow 8.4-0-44-1, Miller 2-0-8-0, Kirsten 2-0-14-0.

Umpires: D J Constant & J G Langridge

Gold Award Winner: R A Woolmer
(Adjudicator: A V Bedser)

– Kent won by six wickets –

1979

– Gooch's golden moment –

*Essex supporters knew all about Graham Gooch already.
In the 1979 Final he unveiled all his shots and began to lay
down the blueprint for the record-breaking career to come*

For years Essex had attracted a great deal of affection as an endearing and amusing side. They were a good and improving side, too, but they had never won a major trophy in their 103-year history.

This is how captain Keith Fletcher saw it in the Cup Final programme: "This is Essex's first B&H Cup Final and we are now poised to win the first title in the club's history. It may have taken us sometime to get to a final, but now we are here we really mean business.

"Our record this season shows we are one of the strongest sides in the country and, as we proved in the semi-final against Yorkshire, we have strength in depth – an important asset in one-day games. What's more, we have a small matter to rectify with Surrey. They defeated us by a mere seven runs in this year's zonal rounds. Today we will try to ensure that the score is reversed and by a bigger margin!"

Fletcher's acumen as one of the shrewdest captains in the game had undoubtedly been a large factor in Essex's challenges in the various competitions in recent years. In the Final he was up against another highly seasoned professional. Although Roger Knight did not have Fletcher's international experience, he was one of a very few players to have won caps for three counties – and he had even won Benson and Hedges Gold Awards for each of them: two for Gloucestershire,

Gooch in full cry. Opposite: Jack Richards smiles ruefully after failing to dismiss Essex's centurion

one for Sussex and one for Surrey. And, of course, his team had won the Cup before. Many of his teammates had been present for that triumph, even if Knight had not.

He said: "In 1974 Surrey found out what winning the Benson and Hedges Cup was all about. It was a tremendous experience which we aim to repeat today. Our opponents that day were

Leicestershire and we knew it would be a tough match. Today's game, I suspect, will be even tougher. Essex are in form, but we have the advantage of knowing we can beat them, as we did earlier in the competition this year."

Surrey's old boy, Younis Ahmed, had made a hundred against them for Worcestershire in the quarter-final, but it had been a lone effort and

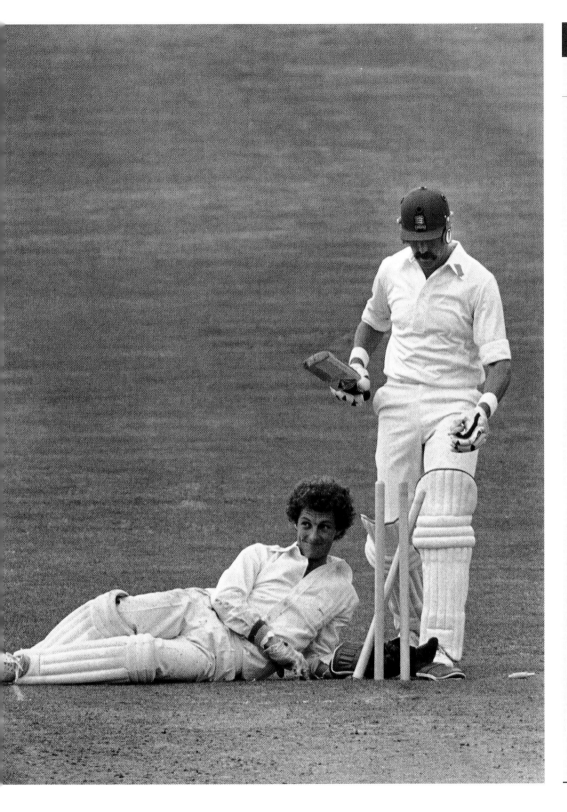

GOLD AWARD WINNER 1979

Graham Gooch

g o l d e n   m e m o r i e s

Gooch's match-winning innings of 120 won him his fourth Gold Award. It was by no means his last. By the time he retired, he had amassed a whole cupboard full – 22 Gold Awards, twice that of his closest rival. His record in every aspect of the B&H Cup is incomparable. His aggregate of 5,176 runs is more than 2,000 ahead of the next highest (Mike Gatting) in the history of the competition. Gooch also holds the record for the highest score (198 not out), the most centuries (15), the most catches by a fielder (68), the most runs in a season (591 in 1979), and even the most matches played (115). In adddition to his batting and fielding feats, Gooch took 69 wickets (at an average of 31.81) in B&H matches. Gooch went on to many triumphs, but Essex supporters will always treasure his innings at Lord's on July 21, 1979 as perhaps his finest moment.

The Gold Award winner among Gold Award winners

BRIAN ROSE
GROUP MATCH: WORCESTERSHIRE V SOMERSET, MAY 23RD/24TH 1979

A GAME THAT SHOCKED THE CRICKETING WORLD AND LED TO A CHANGE IN THE RULES GOVERNING ONE-DAY CRICKET. WISDEN RECORDS: "THE SOMERSET CAPTAIN, ROSE, SACRIFICED ALL KNOWN CRICKETING PRINCIPLES BY DELIBERATELY LOSING THE GAME." THIS IS HIS STORY.

This was our final match in our group. In those days it was three points for a win and one for no result. We already had nine points from winning all our previous three games. Worcestershire and Glamorgan had each won two and had six points. Although we were top, we could be levelled on points and then the formula to decide the top team was bowlers' strike rate – balls bowled divided by wickets taken.

Our strike rate was the best in the group, but not by a lot and Glamorgan were due to play the Minor Counties (South) at the same time, so they were likely to win and to improve their strike rate.

The weather was awful and the first day was washed out. I think the idea came to us in the dressing room as we sat watching the rain come down. It built up in that sort of atmosphere. Everyone got involved in the discussions, even the chairman of the cricket committee. If we declared after one over, we could not make our strike-rate any worse.

When the possibility had been discussed, I visited the Worcestershire secretary's office to ring the TCCB at Lord's, to confirm the position with the Board Secretary, Donald Carr.

We did start on the second day, with probably no more than 100 paying spectators in the ground. I think the Worcestershire team did have an inkling that something was up, but they didn't know what until it happened.

I opened with Peter Denning. Vanburn Holder bowled the opening over, which had one no-ball in it, and then I declared. It was one for no wicket declared. I think their players were astonished. The press certainly were, along with the few spectators who were there. Glenn Turner took 10 balls to score the two singles to win the match.

I think we knew that people weren't going to like us very much, but the storm of controversy did take us rather by surprise. I think you have to put it into the context of Somerset's recent cricket history. The previous year we had lost the Sunday League only on run-rate and we had lost the Gillette Cup Final as well. So we had geared ourselves up to be hard and firm in the following season. This was going to be our year and perhaps we had decided to be a bit mean and aggressive. Not really the traditional Somerset image, but that was what we were trying to overcome. We'd played 100 years without winning a competition and we knew we had the class in the side.

Rose captained Somerset to their first trophies in 1979 but also to B&H disqualification

As it turned out, the rain washed out Glamorgan's match at Watford, so we didn't need to have done it, anyway. We had qualified on points. The trouble with the bad weather was that there was no other cricket news to talk about for a week and the publicity was intense. At the end of that week, the TCCB met at Lord's and disqualified us for bringing the game into disrepute.

I regret it if we hurt the spirit of the game. We always wondered about that. Personally I regretted it because it was a difficult time for me, but the irony is that it made us even more determined to win something and we did. We won the Gillette and Sunday League and I think that situation of being booted out of the Benson and Hedges made us a more intense and internally together team.

Somerset 1 for 0 dec. *(1 over)*
Worcestershire 2 for 0 *(1.4 overs)*
Worcestershire won by 10 wickets.

1979 IN CRICKET

Mike Brearley's England retain the Ashes with a 5-1 series win in Australia against a side shorn of Packer players… In the final of the second World Cup, England are overwhelmed by the West Indies, for whom **Viv Richards** makes an undefeated hundred and **Joel Garner** sweeps away a hamstrung England… **Ian Botham**, after a thrilling hundred against India at Headingley, achieves the double of 1,000 Test runs and 100 wickets at The Oval, in only his 21st Test – a record distance… The Packer split is being healed and England agree to join the West Indies in a unifying tour of Australia… Less unifying is **Dennis Lillee**'s decision to bat at Perth with an aluminium bat, which is soon outlawed.

1979 IN SPORT

Trevor Francis becomes first £1m player in a transfer from Birmingham to Nottingham Forest… **Jim Watt** becomes the lightweight world champion. **Maurice Hope** wins the light middleweight title… **Sevvy Ballesteros** wins the Open at 22, the youngest this century… **Billie Jean King** wins her 20th Wimbledon title – the doubles with **Martina Navratilova**… **Troy** wins the 200th Derby by seven lengths… Arsenal beat Manchester United 3-2 in the FA Cup Final after being 2-0 up with five minutes to go… **Sugar Ray Leonard** wins the world light welterweight title… 15 die in a storm during the Fastnet yacht race off Plymouth.

Surrey had won by seven wickets. Their low-scoring semi-final at Derby had been a tighter affair. Knight joked: "It is said that a tough semi-final sharpens a team for the final. If that is so, our match with Derbyshire will stand us in good stead!"

Essex had the good fortune to be drawn at home for both quarter-final and semi-final. Graham Gooch hammered 138 off Warwickshire and then 49 off Yorkshire who, with a century opening partnership, had looked likely to post a more challenging total than 173. That three-wicket win saw Essex into their first Lord's final.

Essex captain Keith Fletcher and Graham Gooch hoist the prize

Knight put Essex in, despite the fact that he was missing Sylvester Clarke from his attack. After Mike Denness had gone for 24, the aggressive South African Ken McEwan joined Gooch in a stand of 124. McEwan hit ten boundaries in making 72 and was followed by the Essex captain, Keith Fletcher with a typically stylish 34. But all the while Surrey had no answer to Gooch in imperious form, hitting three sixes as he recorded the first hundred in a B&H Final. When he eventually became Hugh Wilson's fourth wicket for 120, Essex, at 273 for five were already heading for a large total. It was, in the end, 290 for six.

Surrey did not appear to baulk at their target. While Howarth, with growing fluency, and Knight, who started the momentum, were adding 91 for the third wicket, anything seemed possible. Keith Pont accounted for both of them – Knight for 52 and Howarth for 74. Though Graham Roope tried to keep up the challenge with 39 not out, the bolt was shot and when John Lever bowled Wilson in the gathering gloom, Essex at last had a trophy – not, it turned out their last of the summer.

It was appropriate that an Essex man, Trevor Bailey, should be the one to hand Graham Gooch the Gold Award.

Schweppes County Champions: Essex
John Player League Champions: Somerset
Gillette Cup Winners: Somerset

● FINAL SCOREBOARD 1979 ●

LORD'S • 21ST JULY

– Essex –

M H Denness, c Smith, b Wilson	24
G A Gooch, b Wilson	120
K S McEwan, c Richards, b Wilson	72
*K W R Fletcher, b Knight	34
B R Mardie, c Intikhab Alam, b Wilson	4
K R Pont, not out	19
N Phillip, c Howarth, b Jackman	2
S Turner, not out	1
Extras (b 3, lb 8, w 1, nb 2)	14
Total *(55 overs, for 6 wkts)*	**290**

Did not bat: †N Smith, R E East, J K Lever

Fall of wickets: 1-48, 2-172, 3-239, 4-261, 5-273, 6-276.

Bowling: Jackman 11-0-69-1, Wilson 11-1-56-4, Knight 11-1-40-1, Intikhab Alam 11-0-38-0, Pocock 11-0-73-0.

– Surrey –

won the toss

A R Butcher, c Smith, b Lever	13
M A Lynch, c McEwan, b East	17
G P Howarth, c Fletcher, b Pont	74
*R D V Knight, c Smith, b Pont	52
D M Smith, b Phillip	24
G R J Roope, not out	39
Intikhab Alam, c Pont, b Phillip	1
R D Jackman, b East	1
†C J Richards, b Turner	1
P I Pocock, b Phillip	7
P H L Wilson, b Lever	0
Extras (b 4, lb 16, w 1, nb 5)	26
Total *(51.4 overs)*	**255**

Fall of wickets: 1-21, 2-45, 3-136, 4-187, 5-205, 6-219, 7-220, 8-226, 9-250, 10-255.

Bowling: Lever 9.4-2-33-2, Phillip 10-2-42-3, East 11-1-40-2, Turner 11-1-47-1, Pont 10-0-67-2.

Umpires: H D Bird & B J Meyer

Gold Award Winner: G A Gooch
(Adjudicator: T E Bailey)

– Essex won by 35 runs –

1980

– Essex fail to see the funny side –

Keith Fletcher's Benson and Hedges Cup-holders were known to enjoy a joke. But they sometimes batted like a bunch of comedians… and it was Northants who enjoyed the last laugh

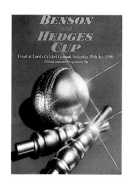

Northamptonshire won their first trophy in an exciting finish when 1979 B&H Cup-winners Essex failed to make the 12 runs they needed off the last over bowled by Sarfraz Nawaz.

It was not the climax that seemed probable when Graham Gooch and the stylish South African Ken McEwan had taken Essex past the 100 mark in the 31st over on a good pitch. This was the same partnership which had taken Essex to victory over Surrey the previous year at Lord's,

and it looked like history was repeating itself. But then came the dramatic turning point, which Allan Lamb recalls in his autobiography: "At 112 for one, Goochie was 60 and with Kenny McEwan starting to motor, we looked like losing. Then Tim Lamb came on, and the scorebook reads: 'Gooch c A Lamb b T Lamb'. He middled one like a tracer to me at mid-on and it might not have gone in cleanly, but it stayed and we were on our way…"

Ten minutes later, off-spinner Peter Willey got rid of McEwan, bowling him with his quicker ball for 38. When Brian Hardie went for a duck, playing on to Jim Watts, Essex suddenly began to look precarious. 112 for one had become 129-5. Keith Fletcher was struggling to gain momentum and his side had fallen behind the clock. Watts turned the screw with the off-spin of Richard Williams, who bagged the wicket of Pont.

By the time Sarfraz returned for his final bowling stint, Essex wanted 50 off six overs. Sarfraz, who had taken five for 21 in the semi-final against Middlesex, bowled tightly to finish with figures of 3-23 off his 11 overs. But at the other end it was a different ball game thanks to Essex's hard-hitting West Indian Nobby Phillip, whose assault on Jim Griffiths' medium pace produced 30 off two overs.

But Phillip was stranded at the non-striking end when Sarfraz began the last over. Essex, on 197-8, needed 12 runs for a tie which would have

John Lever salutes Ken McEwan's run-out of Jim Watts

given them victory because they had lost fewer wickets. Their No 9 batsman Neil Smith had watched Phillip's smash-and-grab act from 22 yards away, and if he had been thinking straight he would have tried to poach a single off Sarfraz and give his partner the strike. Instead he lashed out at the Pakistani paceman's second ball, aiming for the boundary, and was bowled.

Brian Hardie is bowled by Jim Watts

Joy and despair: George Sharp does a jig as Ken McEwan sees his bails dislodged by a ball from Peter Willey

Allan Lamb

g o l d e n   m e m o r i e s

batting at No 4, Lamb played a beautiful innings of 72 to ensure that Northamptonshire achieved a decent total of 209 in a final played on the Monday, following a Saturday washed-out by rain. Lamb was born in South Africa of British parents, and after making his first-class debut for Western Province in 1972/3, came to England to play for Northants in 1978. He met with immediate success, and averaged over 60 in first-class cricket three years in a row (1980-2). He duly made his Test debut for England as soon as he was eligible in 1982 and over the ensuing decade made 4,656 Test runs at 36.09, being even more successful in one-day internationals (4010 runs at 39.31). In first-class cricket he scored 32,502 runs at 48.94 and his effectiveness in one-day cricket is exemplified by his B&H career record of 2,636 runs at a highly impressive average of 47.07, with a total of nine Gold Awards.

Essex supporters' nerves would not have been calmed by the sight of Ray East walking to the wicket, as his motto at the crease sometimes seemed to be taken from Dad's Army's Corporal Jones – "Don't panic!" – with a method of running between the wickets to match. But Essex's resident comedian got a single off the third ball, putting Nobby on strike at last.

Now Essex needed 10 from three – and Phillip kept his team in the hunt by getting two of them off the fourth. So eight runs were required off the last two balls. The game was up when Phillip failed to connect with Sarfraz's fifth delivery, and although he and

Northants urgently needed some inspiration, and it came from the brilliantly unorthodox bat of Allan Lamb

East were able to take two off the last ball of the match, it was not enough.

The ninth Benson and Hedges final was played on a Monday, in front of a crowd of 23,263, after heavy rain washed out any play on the Saturday. It made a fitting climax to the career of Northants skipper Jim Watts, who scored a valuable 22 in a match-winning partnership of 59 with Allan Lamb before being run out by McEwan. When Essex batted, Watts contributed eight useful overs for just 30 runs, and directed the team's affairs with a shrewd touch as Northants reined Essex in. Immediately after the match, with the trophy in his hand, he announced his retirement from cricket.

John Lever began the day for Essex by bowling his first six overs for seven runs but it was medium pacer Keith Pont who took the first three wickets as Northants were pinned down by keen outcricket. Two more wickets fell to medium pace

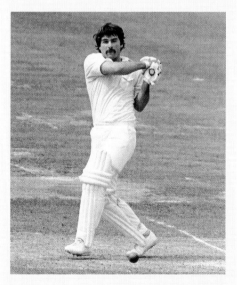

Lamb's fine knock of 72 secures the Gold Award

ANDY LLOYD

YORKSHIRE v WARWICKSHIRE AT HEADINGLEY, 10TH MAY 1980

THE BENSON AND HEDGES CUP ENDED EACH YEAR WITH THE BIG DAY OUT AT LORD'S IN JULY, BUT EVEN THE EARLIEST MATCHES OF THE SEASON COULD BE THRILLERS. FORMER WARWICKSHIRE CAPTAIN ANDY LLOYD REMEMBERS WARWICKSHIRE'S FIRST GROUP MATCH OF 1980.

It was Bob Willis's first season as captain of Warwickshire. He had won the toss and put Yorkshire in. Before we went out onto the field he said, "I'm going to get Boycott on the back foot early on and if it hits him on the pads, lads, give it all you've got."

I was at second slip as Bob came in up the hill from the rugby stand end to bowl the first ball to Geoffrey. Sure enough, it nipped back at him and hit him on the pad, plumb in front of middle. Up we went – the biggest shout you've ever heard. Dickie Bird was the umpire. "Not out." Boycott went on to get 40 and got Yorkshire off to a good start. They eventually made 268 for four.

That was quite a good score for what wasn't a very easy pitch. We got off to a pretty good start, though, before our opening stand was broken by Amiss being bowled by Boycott. He was bowling in his cap, round the wicket, those little in-duckers. They could be useful, too, but Amiss's wicket was a prize that truly delighted him, because Dennis was the only man who had run him out more times in Tests than he'd run out his partners. Dennis was furious.

I was out to Alan Ramage, who had a reasonable bit of pace. He didn't always get it in the right place, but he did on this day and I was lbw for 11, one of three wickets for him, though this wasn't the end of his part in this game.

We were muddling along, but we were always a little bit behind the clock. When our last two batsmen came together we needed 23 and that, we thought, was a few too many. When it came to the last over, with Chris Maynard and our Indian left-arm spinner Dilip Doshi at the wicket, we still needed 10 to win. Now Dilip was an excellent bowler, but his batting was not the strongest part of his game and his running between the wickets wasn't great. So, with Chris Old

Bob Willis orchestrated his team's appeal against Geoffrey Boycott, but Dickie Bird said: "Not out"

bowling the last over for Yorkshire and Dilip to face, we didn't think we'd got much chance.

The field was spread out as in came Old to bowl to Doshi, who had one shot, which was a kind of smear to mid-off. And, sure enough, he connected with the first one and it went to deep mid-off, where Alan Ramage came in to pick up. Chris Maynard, who was very quick between the wickets, had set off from the non-striker's end and was up and back in a flash to complete the second run as Ramage threw the ball to Old at the bowler's stumps while Dilip was still waddling towards the striker's end.

The next ball the same thing happened. He smeared it off to mid-off and in came Ramage, but this time Dilip got under it and it was a skier out to Ramage at deep mid-off. But he dropped it and in that time thay ran a comfortable two.

Now the crowd were going berserk and giving Yorkshire a really hard time. The next two balls each went straight to Alan Ramage and somehow they scrambled two each time. We had won by one wicket with one ball to spare. I think it was the most amazing last over I've ever seen.

Dilip came back to the dressing room, peering through his heavy-rimmed glasses and said: "Now I know God is not a Tyke."

Yorkshire 268 for 4 *(55 overs) (J H Hampshire 85 n.o.; K Sharp 45; G Boycott 40)*
Warwickshire 269 for 9 *(54.5 overs) (K D Smith 65; J A Claughton 52; A Ramage 3-63)*
Warwickshire won by one wicket.

Sharp looks sharp and Phillip gets a flier as they flee the pitch invasion at the end of an excitingly close-run match

FINAL SCOREBOARD 1980

LORD'S • 19TH (NO PLAY) 21ST JULY

— Northamptonshire —
won the toss

G Cook, c Gooch, b Pont	29
W Larkins, c Denness, b Pont	18
R G Williams, c McEwan, b Pont	15
A J Lamb, c Hardie, b Phillip	72
P Willey, c McEwan, b Turner	15
T J Yardley, c Smith, b Gooch	0
†G Sharp, c Fletcher, b Pont	8
*P J Watts, run out	22
Sarfraz Nawaz, not out	10
T M Lamb, lbw, b Turner	4
B J Griffiths, b Turner	0
Extras (b 1, lb 8, w 4, nb 3)	
Total (54.5 overs)	**209**

Fall of wickets: 1-36, 2-61, 3-78, 4-110, 5-110, 6-131, 7-190, 8-193, 9-209, 10-209.

Bowling: Lever 11-3-38-0, Phillip 11-1-38-1, Turner 10.5-2-33-3, Pont 11-1-60-4, Gooch 11-0-24-1.

— Essex —

M H Denness, b Willey	14
G A Gooch, c A J Lamb, b T M Lamb	60
K S McEwan, b Willey	38
*K W R Fletcher, b Sarfraz Nawaz	29
B R Hardie, b Watts	0
K R Pont, b Williams	2
S Turner, c Watts, b Sarfraz Nawaz	16
N Phillip, not out	32
†N Smith, b Sarfraz Nawaz	2
R E East, not out	1
Extras (b 1, lb 5, w 3)	9
Total (55 overs, for 8 wkts)	**203**

Did not bat: J K Lever

Fall of wickets: 1-52, 2-112, 3-118, 4-121, 5-129, 6-160, 7-180, 8-198.

Bowling: Sarfraz Nawaz 11-3-23-3, Griffiths 7-0-46-0, Watts 8-1-30-1, T M Lamb 11-0-42-1, Willey 11-1-34-2, Williams 7-0-19-1.

Umpires: D J Constant & B J Meyer

Gold Award Winner: A J Lamb
(Adjudicator: K F Barrington)

— Northamptonshire won by 6 runs —

1980 IN CRICKET

Ian Botham becomes the first player to score a century and take 10 wickets in a match as England beat India in Bombay ... Tourists West Indies beat England 1-0. **Joel Garner**'s 26 wickets earn him Man of the Series ... The 100th anniversary of Test cricket in England is celebrated in the Centenary Test against Australia at Lord's. **Kim Hughes**, **Graeme Wood** and **Geoffrey Boycott** score centuries in a drawn match as ten hours are lost to rain ... **John Arlott** receives an ovation from the players as he finishes his final commentary during the Centenary Test with the words: "28 Boycott, 15 Gower, 69 for two. And after a few words from Trevor Bailey it'll be Christopher Martin-Jenkins."

1980 IN SPORT

Bjorn Borg wins his fifth Wimbledon singles title, beating **John McEnroe** in possibly the greatest final ever ... Britain's **Steve Ovett** wins the Moscow Olympics 800 metres but **Sebastian Coe** gets dramatic revenge in the 1500m ... **Severiano Ballesteros** becomes the youngest ever winner of the US Masters.

either side of lunch as Peter Willey fell to a rash shot off the bowling of Stuart Turner, and Gooch dismissed Jim Yardley.

Northants urgently needed some inspiration, and it came from the brilliantly unorthodox bat of Allan Lamb. Just as he had done in the Gillette Cup Final the previous year – which Northants lost to Somerset despite his dashing 78 – Lamb held things together with an innings of true class.

His 72 included an audacious six over midwicket off Lever, and was to win him the Gold Award from Ken Barrington. But Lamb fell to a terrific diving catch at long-on by Brian Hardie, and the match swung back towards Essex ... until Lamb's own juggling act to dismiss Gooch, which set up that dramatic last over by Sarfraz.

Schweppes County Champions: Middlesex
John Player League Champions: Warwickshire
Gillette Cup Winners: Middlesex

1981

– King Viv's royal tournament–

When Garner and Botham were in their pomp, there
was only one man who could outshine them.
Unfortunately for Surrey, he played for Somerset too…

A full house of 21,000 spectators were treated to a fantastic display of batting from Richards and Botham

With the world's best batsman, the world's best bowler and the world's best all-rounder in their team, many would say it was about time Somerset put their stamp on the Benson and Hedges Cup. The Final was played out before 21,130 specators who were treated to two of the greatest performances ever seen at Lord's as Somerset became the seventh winner in the 10 years of the B&H competition.

Neither team had had an easy route to the Final, as both had come through tough qualifying groups. Somerset had conspired with their semi-final opponents Surrey to keep holders Essex out of the quarter-finals, while the runners-up in Somerset's group had included Hampshire and Middlesex.

Surrey captain Roger Knight pointed out in the Benson and Hedges programme that his team had been the losers in both the B&H Final of 1979 and the NatWest Final of 1980, and they were anxious not to make it three in a row. Sadly for him, their wish was not granted.

Surrey and Somerset were both very strong teams on paper, but on the day one team was obviously more 'up for it' – and in the early Eighties, when Somerset were in the mood there was no stopping them. Viv Richards, with yet another sumptuous one-day hundred, and Joel Garner with his masterly bowling, played the starring roles as Somerset strode confidently to their first success in this event. By the time Ian Botham had helped Richards to finish the business in style, with an unbroken partnership of 87, the West Countrymen had strolled home with seven wickets and more than 10 overs to spare.

Surrey, having been put in to bat by Brian Rose, made a sticky beginning. At the end of 17 overs they had prodded their way to just 15 for one as 'Big Bird' Garner turned in his usual immaculate performance, with Botham operating from the other end. But Knight gave his team its backbone with an invaluable 92 and there were brief flurries from Monte Lynch, Sylvester Clarke and Graham Roope as the men from The Oval counter-attacked late in the innings.

> *On the day one team was obviously more 'up for it' – and in the early Eighties, when Somerset were in the mood there was no stopping them*

Fetch that! Beefy on the attack

No... it's my bat!

Vivian Richards

golden memories

t he batting of Vivian Richards was so often seen to best effect on the great occasion. He had scored 138* in the World Cup Final of 1979 and here, two years later, there was another such Lord's occasion as his brilliant 132* ensured that Somerset passed Surrey's 194 with over ten overs to spare. Born in St John's, Antigua, on 7 March 1952, nobody could touch Richards at his imperious best as a commanding batsman and his average of just over 50 for his 8,540 runs in Tests for the West Indies (1974-91) was backed by one of 47.00 for 6,721 runs in limited-overs internationals. Although he ended his English career with Glamorgan, he gave great service to Somerset from 1974 to 1986, often in the company of his great friend and similarly barn-storming cricketer, Ian Botham. Each won six B&H Gold Awards while playing for Somerset.

But no one could hit Garner. He finished with the remarkable figures of five for 14, while off-spinner Vic Marks took two wickets for 24 in his 11 overs.

At the end of their 55 overs, Surrey must have known that a total of 194 for eight was not enough to daunt Somerset's bat-ting power. They needed at least another 30 runs to exert greater pressure on their opponents.

However, their bowlers began well enough by dismissing the two Somerset openers for only five runs. Although West

Viv Richards always put on a show at Lord's

VIC MARKS
TWO CONSECUTIVE FINALS:
SOMERSET V SURREY 1981, SOMERSET V NOTTINGHAMSHIRE 1982

THE SOMERSET SIDE THAT WAS JUST COMING INTO ITS OWN WHEN THE YOUNG IAN BOTHAM PLAYED HIS MEMORABLE QUARTER-FINAL IN 1974 FIRST WON THE CUP IN 1981 AND REPEATED THE FEAT IN THE FOLLOWING YEAR. IN EACH MATCH THEIR OFF-SPINNING ALL-ROUNDER VIC MARKS TOOK TWO FOR 24 FROM HIS ELEVEN OVERS, WINNING THE GOLD AWARD IN THE '82 FINAL FOR THE CRUCIAL WICKETS OF DEREK RANDALL AND CLIVE RICE.

In 1981 and 1982 cricket's big days out at the Benson and Hedges Final did not last too long. Somerset won both matches comprehensively. We were delighted by the manner of the victories; so were our supporters, but those neutrals who pottered through the Grace Gates were probably disappointed that they were denied a breathtaking finish.

There were some breathtaking moments however. In 1981 against Surrey the crowd were treated to one of those rare occasions when Viv Richards and Ian Botham combined with devastating effect. To polish off the match this pair added 87 in thirteen overs so that the victors had 10.3 overs and seven wickets to spare. Richards hit a blistering 132 not out and inevitably won the Gold Award. This was his stage and the Surrey bowlers unwittingly fed him his lines.

In truth the damage had been done earlier in the day. Joel Garner tormented the Surrey batsmen, who needed 13 overs to reach double figures. The great telegraph pole finished with figures of five for 14 from his 11 overs; only Roger Knight with a defiant 92 could offer any resistance, shepherding his side to a modest total of 194. Spare a thought for Garner. In five victories in Lord's finals (one for the West Indies and four for Somerset) his figures were 5-38, 6-29, 5-14, 3-13 (the following year against Nottinghamshire) and 2-15 yet he never won the man of the match award – usually because Viv Richards had blasted a stunning century.

The game against Nottinghamshire in 1982 was even more one-sided. By then Somerset were a relaxed team when Lord's finals came along. The night

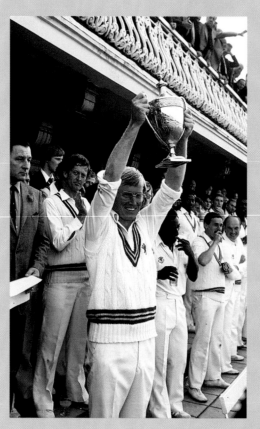

1981: Brian Rose holds Somerset's first B&H Cup aloft

before the game we would have a rare team dinner and, once the port had been passed, an equally rare team meeting, which seldom bore any relation to what happened the following day. We would discuss all the opposition batsmen before reaching the inescapable conclusion that "he might struggle against Joel", conveniently forgetting that the big man could only bowl eleven overs.

In 1982 we were concerned about Richard Hadlee. Peter Roebuck, who had never faced him, was informed that he was quicker than Joel but moved the ball both ways – just to ensure a peaceful night's sleep for Somerset's opener. Ian Botham advised us to keep the ball up to Hadlee when he batted and the next day greeted him with a succession of bouncers. We inevitably spent twenty minutes discussing Mike Hendrick's batting and Derek Randall's bowling. Brian Rose, our captain, after some sage opening remarks would sit back in his chair with a cigar and patiently wait for us all to shut up so that he could go to bed. Not the most scientific of systems, but it seemed to work.

Nottinghamshire appeared to be paralysed by the occasion. They mustered just 130 so that Richards only had time to crack a half century. So did Roebuck despite his nightmares about Hadlee. This time the target was reached with 22 overs and nine wickets to spare. Tom Graveney, that most perspicacious of adjudicators, had a tricky dilemma regarding the Gold Award. It might have been Garner (again) or Richards or Roebuck, but in the end wise old Tom decided to give it to me for the removal of Randall and Rice.

The Somerset team: From left, back, Jeremy Lloyds, Dennis Breakwell, Peter Roebuck, Joel Garner, Colin Dredge, Nigel Popplewell, Vic Marks, Peter Denning; front, Derek Taylor, Ian Botham, Brian Rose, Viv Richards, Hallam Moseley

Indies quickie Clarke was bowling with a bad back, he shot out Peter Denning for a duck, while England's Robin Jackman bowled Rose for five.

These setbacks obliged Richards to apply himself with some care in the early stages of his innings, but this was simply the calm before the storm. Soon he was bestriding the Lord's stage at his imperious best while Peter Roebuck kept him staunch company, scoring 22 in a partnership of 105. There was never a doubt that Jim Laker would nominate King Viv for the Gold Award – though, as Vic Marks points out opposite, Joel Garner had good reason to feel hard done by.

Richards' 132 not out was the highest individual innings in any Benson and Hedges Cup Final, while his West Indian teammate Joel Garner's

five for 14 was the second best bowling return in a B&H Final. Later in the summer of 1981, Somerset finished third in the County Championship, equalling their best position ever, and second in the John Player League.

Schweppes County Champions: Nottinghamshire
John Player League Champions: Essex
NatWest Bank Trophy Winners: Derbyshire

1981 IN CRICKET

1981 and all that: **Ian Botham** and **Bob Willis** bring England back from the dead at Headingley to beat Australia after following on. With England 135-7 in the second innings, still 92 behind, Botham scores 149 off 148 balls then Willis takes eight for 43 as Australia lose by 18 runs. Captained by **Mike Brearley**, England recover from 1-0 down to take the series 3-1.

Botham, sacked as captain after the first two Tests, is Man of the Match in all three victories… Earlier in the year, England's Test in Guyana is cancelled after **Robin Jackman** is deported for playing in South Africa, and assistant manager **Ken Barrington** dies of a heart attack in Barbados, as **Clive Lloyd**, **Michael Holding** and **Viv Richards** condemn England to a 2-0 series defeat.

1981 IN SPORT

Steve Davis wins his first snooker world title… **Bob Champion** and **Aldaniti** win the Grand National after Champion had beaten cancer… **Shergar** wins the Derby by the biggest margin ever… **Ricky Villa** scores the greatest goal in an FA Cup Final as Spurs beat Manchester City 3-2… **John McEnroe** wins Wimbledon, beating **Bjorn Borg** in the final.

LORD'S • 25TH JULY

– Surrey –

G S Clinton, c Roebuck, b Marks	6
†C J Richards, b Garner	1
*R D V Knight, c Taylor, b Garner	92
G P Howarth, c Roebuck, b Marks	16
M A Lynch, c Garner, b Popplewell	22
D M Smith, b Garner	7
S T Clarke, c Popplewell, b Garner	15
G R J Roope, not out	14
D J Thomas, b Garner	0
R D Jackman, not out	2
Extras (b 2, lb 14, w 2, nb 1)	19
Total (55 overs, for 8 wkts)	**194**

Did not bat: P I Pocock

Fall of wickets: 1-4, 2-16, 3-63, 4-98, 5-132, 6-166, 7-182, 8-183.

Bowling: Garner 11-5-14-5, Botham 11-2-44-0, Dredge 11-0-48-0, Marks 11-5-24-2, Popplewell 11-0-45-1.

– Somerset –

won the toss

*B C Rose, b Jackman	5
P W Denning, b Clarke	0
I V A Richards, not out	132
P M Roebuck, c Smith, b Knight	22
I T Botham, not out	37
Extras (nb 1)	1
Total (44.3 overs, for 3 wkts)	**197**

Did not bat: N F M Popplewell, V J Marks, D Breakwell, J Garner, †D J S Taylor, C H Dredge

Fall of wickets: 1-5, 2-5, 3-110.

Bowling: Clarke 8-1-24-1, Jackman 11-1-53-1, Thomas 5.3-0-32-0, Pocock 11-1-46-0, Knight 9-0-41-1.

Umpires: H D Bird & B J Meyer

Gold Award Winner: I V A Richards
(Adjudicator: J C Laker)

— Somerset won by seven wickets —

1982

– Somerset stroll to two in a row –

No one had won the Benson and Hedges Cup twice in a row.
And Somerset would have to overcome a strong Nottinghamshire
side to achieve it. Could they do it? No problem…

Joel Garner, the best bowler never to win a Benson and Hedges Cup Final Gold Award, in action against Notts

Somerset became the first county to retain the Benson and Hedges Cup by winning a damp squib of a contest in which the losers failed to do themselves justice on their first appearance in a one-day final.

This was particularly disappointing for Nottinghamshire, as they had been expected to put up a good show. They were the reigning County Champions, having won the title for the first time since 1929, and although they had never even reached the B&H semi-finals before, they seemed to have an ideal one-day team.

Their strong batting lineup included future England opener Tim Robinson, the peripatetic Derek Randall (the Jonty Rhodes of his day) and two of the world's most exciting all-rounders in South African Clive Rice and New Zealander Richard Hadlee. And on top of that they had a street-wise bowling squad in which Hadlee was supported by England stalwart Mike Hendrick and off-spinner Eddie Hemmings, who many rated the best in the country.

> *"Then I will tell them to make sure, above everything else, that they must enjoy themselves."*

Rice was clearly inspired by the prospect of his team's first big day out. In the Cup Final programme he wrote: "Perhaps the final words I will

Vic Marks, Viv Richards, Brian Rose, Ian Botham and Peter Denning enjoy the view from the players' balcony

GOLD AWARD WINNER 1982

Vic Marks

g o l d e n   m e m o r i e s

Somerset retained the B&H trophy, winning this match easily, with Viv Richards again to the fore with a delightful innings of 51*. Somerset achieved their target of 131 with 22 overs to spare, and a major factor in that easy victory was the good work of their bowlers. Marks was outstanding as his intelligent display of off-spinning brought him figures of two for 24 in 11 overs. His two wickets were vital ones – Derek Randall and Clive Rice. Marks, captain of Oxford University in 1976 and 1977, played for Somerset from 1975 to 1989 before becoming cricket correspondent of The Observer and a member of the Test Match Special team on BBC Radio. He played six Test matches for England, but had more success in one-day internationals, capturing 44 wickets at 25.79 in his 34 matches. In his best season in first-class cricket, 1984, he scored 1,262 runs at 52.58 and took 86 wickets at 25.96.

An all-rounder who plays, writes and talks cricket

say to the side this morning will best sum up what playing in our first Cup Final at Lord's means to us all. I will tell them exactly what I expect of them cricket wise, insisting on performances which will do justice to themselves as professionals playing for a side being groomed to dominate the rest of the 1980s. Then I will tell them to make sure, above everything else, that they must enjoy themselves.

"It is an occasion many cricketers will never taste in their careers, an experience I doubted I would ever share. When I retire, it will obviously be a day I will look back upon as one of the highlights of my playing career. That is why it is essential we should enjoy it."

Rice was right about the success that lay ahead for Notts. Winning the Championship in 1981 signalled the start of a decade in which they would finally pick up a one-day trophy – the NatWest – in 1987, in their third Lord's final in six seasons, and then go on to win the Sunday League in 1991.

But whether Rice will look back on July 24,

Viv Richards during his undefeated innings of 51

Yippee... the first wicket. Viv Richards celebrates as Joel Garner bowls Paul Todd for two and Somerset are on their way

1982 IN CRICKET

England captain **Keith Fletcher** apologises for hitting his stumps in anger after being given out in India... **Geoffrey Boycott** scores 105 in Delhi to become the world's top Test scorer. During the next Test, before a world record 394,000 in Calcutta, Boycott is too ill to field – but not too ill to play golf. He then leaves the goes home 'by mutual agreement'... Australia's **Dennis Lillee** and Pakistan's **Javed Miandad** nearly come to blows when Lillee kicks Miandad after a collision. Lillee is suspended for two one-day matches... Rain stops play at Lord's with **Mohsin Khan** on 199. When he reaches his 200 four hours later, he kisses the ground in relief... **Ian Botham** hits what is believed to be the fastest 200 in Test history, against India at The Oval. One crashing shot breaks close fielder **Sunil Gavaskar**'s fibula... **Boycott**, **Gooch** & Co go to South Africa and are banned for three years.

1982 IN SPORT

Steve Davis makes snooker's first televised maximum break... Racing driver **Gilles Villeneuve** is killed in practice at the Belgian Grand Prix... **Jimmy Connors** beats **John McEnroe** in a thunderous Wimbledon final... Wolves avoid bankruptcy by three minutes; saved by **Derek Dougan**... **Ron Greenwood**'s England go out of the World Cup unbeaten. **Paolo Rossi**'s six goals win the trophy for Italy... **Bobby Robson** becomes England football manager.

1982, as one of the highlights of his career is another question. It just wasn't Nottinghamshire's day.

Rice's opposite number Brian Rose approached the Final in far more relaxed vein. He knew that in Botham, Richards and Garner he had match-winners who were the envy of the world, and of course he had last year's success behind him.

"A summer for us would not be a summer without a visit to a Cup Final at Lord's," he wrote in the Cup Final programme. "Here we are on our second successive visit. But

Left: Nottinghamshire's Basharat Hassan plays a cut during his innings of 26.
Right: And a good time was had by all

there is no question of us thinking we only have to turn up to claim it. We are well aware that Kent and Surrey both lost when they went back to Lord's as holders. Every player's contributions will be vital if we are to be the first county to retain the trophy."

Nottinghamshire, asked to bat first by Rose (as Surrey had been a year before), struggled against a keen and accurate attack, and never looked like building the sort of score that would put their opponents' batting under any pressure. By lunch their innings was already in rubble at 89 for four.

Inevitably it was Joel Garner who started the slide, shooting out Paul Todd in his second over with that famous yorker that rocketed down at the batsman's feet from a very great height. The third wicket, shortly after Robinson fell to Dredge, was equally crucial: Randall rashly gave himself room to cut Vic Marks's second ball and was bowled.

Marks it was, too, who put paid to the ever-dangerous Rice, who had previously hit him for six. Rice's 27 turned out to be Nottinghamshire's top score, and they were bowled out in just over 50 overs for the lowest total so far recorded in the last round of this competition.

When Somerset replied, chasing an easy target of 131 to win, they lost Peter Denning, caught off Hendrick at 27, but that was Notts' last hurrah. Peter Roebuck and Viv Richards completed the job without difficulty.

Richards struck three resounding fours in one over from Hadlee, who was shackled by injury, and he and his partner managed to time it so that they both reached 50 just before Richards nonchalantly flicked away a legside delivery from Kevin Cooper to put Notts out of their misery. It was all over before half past five, with nearly 22 overs to spare.

Vic Marks won the Gold Award for 11 overs of shrewd and tidy off-spin.

Schweppes County Champions: Middlesex
John Player League Champions: Sussex
NatWest Bank Trophy Winners: Surrey

Peter Roebuck and Viv Richards both get half-centuries

Brian Rose lifts the Cup for the second time in two years

◊ FINAL SCOREBOARD 1982 ◊
LORD'S • 24TH JULY

– Nottinghamshire –

P A Todd, b Garner	2
R T Robinson, c Richards, b Dredge	13
D W Randall, b Marks	19
S B Hassan, c Taylor, b Dredge	26
*C E B Rice, b Marks	27
J D Birch, b Moseley	7
R J Hadlee, b Garner	11
†B N French, c Taylor, b Botham	8
E E Hemmings, b Botham	1
K E Cooper, b Garner	3
M Hendrick, not out	0
Extras (lb 5, w 7, nb 1)	13
Total (50.1 overs)	**130**

Fall of wickets: 1-3, 2-40, 3-40, 4-86, 5-102, 6-106, 7-122, 8-123, 9-130, 10-130.

Bowling: Garner 8.1-1-13-3, Botham 9-3-19-2, Dredge 11-2-35-2, Moseley 11-2-26-1, Marks 11-4-24-2.

– Somerset –
won the toss

P M Roebuck, not out	53
P W Denning, c French, b Hendrick	22
I V A Richards, not out	51
Extras (b 5, w 1)	6
Total (33.1 overs, for 1 wkt)	**132**

Did not bat: *B C Rose, I T Botham, V J Marks, N F M Popplewell, †D J S Taylor, J Garner, C H Dredge, H R Moseley

Fall of wickets: 1-27.

Bowling: Hadlee 9-0-37-0, Hendrick 8-0-26-1, Cooper 5.1-0-41-0, Rice 6-2-11-0, Hemmings 5-0-11-0.

Umpires: D J Constant & D G L Evans

Gold Award Winner: V J Marks
(Adjudicator: T W Graveney)

– Somerset won by nine wickets –

1983

– Essex are all in the dark –

It was nearly nine o'clock when Essex lost the Cup to Middlesex
– and they must have thought they were having a bad dream.
They had as good as won it … but somehow they threw it away

Those who watched the Benson and Hedges Cup Final in July 1983 were left in no doubt at the end of the day that they had witnessed a thrilling cricket match with a most unexpected outcome. The start of the match was delayed for 50 minutes by rain, and perhaps this

Radley enjoys the sunshine before the evening's drama

had a bearing on the bizarre dénouement. Essex, who looked to be cruising to victory for most of the day, inexplicably collapsed as the shadows grew long over Lord's and finally capitulated in the gloom at the start of the final over at 8.49pm.

This was a meeting of two teams who were both familiar with this special day. Essex intended to win the title for a second time and Middlesex were anxious to record their first success, having narrowly lost to Leicestershire in 1975.

Middlesex could count themselves lucky to be in the final at all, having 'beaten' Gloucestershire on the toss of a coin in a rain-ruined quarter-final at Bristol in which only four overs were possible. But both teams had made short shrift of their semi-final opponents. Essex reached the final with a crushing win over Kent at Canterbury, while Middlesex scored an equally resounding victory over Lancashire at Lord's.

Now these two fierce local rivals were ready to put on a show for the capital's big day out. As Keith Fletcher wrote presciently in the Cup Final programme: "I am quite grateful we have avoided Middlesex so far in the competition. I always thought that the two of us would make the best final." How right he was…

Middlesex, sent in to bat by Fletcher, had trouble coming to terms with the movement generated by their home pitch, as the ball swung and seamed in the hands of Essex's medium-pacers.

Clive Radley's 89 not out set up Middlesex's triumph

Graham Gooch, the slowest of the five, bowled his 11 overs for just 21 runs, while Stuart Turner went for 24 and Neil Foster took three for 26.

Things began to look rather a formality for Essex when Middlesex managed only 196 for eight off their 55 overs, despite Radley's 89 not out.

It was four o'clock by the time Essex began their reply, and they immediately started to make up for lost time. With Gooch in majestic form and Hardie making good use of the edge of his bat as usual, they had 79 on the board after just 11 overs. When Gooch was caught behind, Ken McEwan joined Hardie and together they took it on to 127 for one. Just 70 runs needed with nine wickets in hand and 25 overs to go. It should have been a doddle – but that gifted Essex team had a strange

Mike Gatting comtemplates Dickie Bird's decision as he is run out after making 22

Clive Radley

g o l d e n   m e m o r i e s

Radley came in at the fall of the first Middlesex wicket, and batted through to the end of the innings for 89 not out. This was the only 50 in a match won by Middlesex by just four runs and a typical fighting innings by a most determined cricketer. After a season with Norfolk, Radley played for Middlesex for over 20 years, 1964-87, scoring 26,441 runs in his first-class career. An accumulator of runs rather than an entertainer, Radley had just one year of Test cricket, when at the age of 34 in 1978 he scored 481 runs at an average of 48.10 in three series. His 158 in 648 minutes against New Zealand in his second Test was then the slowest-ever 150, but his record showed that he might well have been used more often and he played a major part in Middlesex's five limited-overs trophies won from 1977 to 1986.

Clive Radley was a popular choice as Gold Award winner

knack of making life difficult for themselves.

It was after seven o'clock when things took a dramatic turn. McEwan flashed at Phil Edmonds and gave a hard chance which Norman Cowans snatched up in the covers. It was here that Mike Gatting, in his first season as Middlesex skipper, seized the initiative. Gatting had stepped into Mike Brearley's shoes when the maestro retired, and he knew he had a lot to live up to. It was in this match that he showed he had the nerve and the knowledge to match his distinguished predecessor. Changing his bowlers astutely, marshalling his fields with great skill, he soon had Essex trapped in a spiral of confusion and disarray.

Gatting himself happily admitted that his team was not built to strangle the life out of the opposition, but to take their wickets. "In the eyes of some people we are not ideally equipped for one-day cricket, lacking, as we do, the mean type of

> *'I am glad we have avoided Middlesex so far,' said Fletcher. 'I always thought that the two of us would make the best final.' How right he was...*

bowler content with delivering 11 overs for as few as possible. We even have the nerve to include two spinners. I make no apology. We believe in aggression. The taking of wickets is all-important."

It was a spinner who had made the breakthrough – and now all the Middlesex bowlers were about to start snapping up the Essex wickets. Gatting's opposite number Fletcher fell to a bat-pad catch off Edmonds. Keith Pont hit his wicket after being struck on the head by a bouncer from Neil Williams – later to join Essex – and Hardie edged a delivery from Cowans into the gloves of Paul Downton. Four wickets had fallen for 29 runs in the space of 11 overs to a combination of aggressive pace and cunning spin.

But Essex still had time and wickets on their side. Derek Pringle and Turner put their heads down and took the score up to 185 – just 12 runs short of victory with four overs to get them in and

JOHN JAMESON
BEHIND THE SCENES AT THE FINAL

THE BIG DAY OUT IS A VERY BIG DAY AT THE OFFICE FOR THE MCC STAFF AT LORD'S. IT IS MCC, NOT THE ECB, THAT RUNS MATCHES HERE. FORMER WARWICKSHIRE PLAYER JOHN JAMESON IS MCC ASSISTANT SECRETARY (CRICKET), RESPONSIBLE FOR RUNNING THE MATCH.

For all big matches I will have arrived at Lord's by seven o'clock in the morning, though the head groundsman, Mick Hunt, will have been on the ground since six. We don't have a game at Lord's in the five days leading up to a major match, which gives the groundstaff time to prepare the pitch and to get the ground into pristine condition for the big day. Mick keeps a very strict record of his preparations of the pitch, such as when he waters it and when he rolls it and how long he has rolled it. Periodically he will take cores from it to test whether the moisture content is coming out of it and the pitch is becoming dry, because we like to try to get a dry pitch if we possibly can.

I always have an anxious look at the weather first thing because, if it's overcast at Lord's, the ball does swing around and it can ruin the match early on. So our hearts are all lifted if it's a sunny morning. There's a great rush of adrenalin when the time comes to open the gates, because that is the time when we all come into the spotlight. Has everything been prepared? Have we missed anything? Have we remembered to put the discs for the fielding circles out, for instance? All these things start to come into your mind and I suppose Mick Hunt and I and all his staff do breathe a sigh of relief when 11 o'clock comes and the first ball is bowled and we can just hope that the pitch is going to play its best.

Being a match that fell in the middle of the summer, the Benson and Hedges Cup Final was outside the soccer season and some counties have supporters who have been known to be a bit boisterous. As with all major matches, we do contact the police and keep in touch with them regarding possible trouble areas and with counties in a final we will contact their local constabulary to establish a good rapport with them, so that if there are any troublemakers that they know about, we'll be informed about it. As a result, perhaps, we haven't had any serious incidents. A few years ago at a final a police officer spotted a few characters who were known to him and he just let them know that if there was any trouble in that stand, they would be the first to be arrested. They thought it was a bit unfair, but he told them that that was the rule that would be applied. And there was no trouble in that stand that day – but I heard that that bunch left the ground at about five o'clock and within the hour had been arrested in a pub by Baker Street Station.

We do hate it when a final goes into a second day, because, apart from

Lord's groundsman Mick Hunt. In the run-up to the B&H Final he carefully notes every time he waters or rolls the pitch for the match ... then prays that it won't rain

causing us problems, it does spoil it for the spectators, as it did for the last one in 1998. Then the weather was so bad on the Sunday morning that we had a meeting with the ECB, the team captains and managers, the umpires and the broadcasters about what the procedure would be if it came to a bowl-out. Thankfully, it didn't.

We haven't finished our big day even when the cup has been presented. We've still got to make sure the ground has been cleared and no bottles or nails have been dropped on the outfield. (Damage to mowers can be very expensive.) There have occasionally been problems in the past when we've had to get ambulances in for spectators as well, but happily that is a rarity.

At about nine o'clock – very tired – I can leave the ground.

Left: Keith Fletcher is caught by Clive Radley off the bowling of Phil Edmonds for three.
Below: Clive Radley and Mike Gatting get their hands on the Cup

1983 IN CRICKET

Australia's **Terry Alderman** breaks his collar bone trying to repel a pitch invasion at Perth… There is a major upset in the third World Cup Final at Lord's as odds-on favourites West Indies self-destruct against India. Chasing a moderate total of 184, **Clive Lloyd**, **Viv Richards**, **Gordon Greenidge** & co subside to a 43-run defeat by reckless strokeplay and underestimating the tenacity of their opponents. In the next two years India would go on to win the Asia Cup, the Sharjah Four Nations Trophy and the B&H World Championship.

1983 IN SPORT

Shergar is kidnapped… **Sevvy Ballesteros** wins the US Masters by four shots… **Torvill & Dean** win the world ice dance title with all nine judges giving perfect sixes… **Graham Taylor**'s Watford beat champions Liverpool 2-1 on the last day to finish second in the League, five years after being in Fourth Division. Liverpool boss **Bob Paisley** retires… **Carl Lewis** wins three golds at the first World Championships, at Helsinki. Decathlete **Daley Thompson**, the first man in any event to hold Olympic, European and Commonwealth titles and the world record, adds the world title.

five wickets in hand. But then the roof fell in…

Pringle was lbw to Daniel, and Turner skied a catch to long-on, which was well taken by substitute John Carr. Middlesex skipper Mike Gatting held on to a scorching catch from David East, Ray East went into "Don't panic" mode and was run out by Clive Radley; and Cowans settled the matter by bowling Neil Foster with the first ball of the last over. Essex's last five wickets had fallen for seven runs in 19 balls.

Thus Middlesex received the tumultuous congratulations of the breathless and weary crowd of 22,000 as Gatting received the Benson and Hedges Cup. To complete their day, the Gold Award went to Clive Radley for his unbeaten 89. As for Essex, they took revenge later in the season by overhauling Middlesex to win the County Championship.

Schweppes County Champions: Essex
John Player League Champions: Yorkshire
NatWest Bank Trophy Winners: Somerset

FINAL SCOREBOARD 1983

LORD'S • 23RD JULY

– Middlesex –

G D Barlow, b Foster	14
W N Slack, c Gooch, b Foster	1
C T Radley, not out	89
*M W Gatting, run out	22
K P Tomlins, lbw, b Gooch	0
J E Emburey, c D E East, b Lever	17
†P R Downton, c Fletcher, b Foster	10
P H Edmonds, b Pringle	9
N F Williams, c & b Pringle	13
W W Daniel, not out	2
Extras (b 3, lb 9, w 4, nb 3)	19
Total (55 overs, for 8 wkts)	**196**

Did not bat: N G Cowans

Fall of wickets: 1-10, 2-25, 3-74, 4-74, 5-123, 6-141, 7-171, 8-191.

Bowling: Lever 11-1-52-1, Foster 11-2-26-3, Pringle 11-0-54-2, Turner 11-1-24-0, Gooch 11-2-21-1.

– Essex –
won the toss

G A Gooch, c Downton, b Williams	46
B R Hardie, c Downton, b Cowans	49
K S McEwan, c Cowans, b Edmonds	34
*K W R Fletcher, c Radley, b Edmonds	3
K R Pont, hit wicket, b Williams	7
D R Pringle, lbw, b Daniel	16
S Turner, c sub(J D Carr), b Cowans	9
†D E East, c Gatting, b Cowans	5
R E East, run out	0
N A Foster, b Cowans	0
J K Lever, not out	0
Extras (lb 12, w 3, nb 8)	23
Total (54.1 overs)	**192**

Fall of wickets: 1-79, 2-127, 3-135, 4-151, 5-156, 6-185, 7-187, 8-191, 9-192, 10-192.

Bowling: Daniel 11-2 34-1, Cowans 10.1-0-39-4, Williams 11-0-45-2, Emburey 11-3-17-0, Edmonds 11-3-34-2.

Umpires H D Bird & B J Meyer

Gold Award Winner: C T Radley
(Adjudicator: L E G Ames)

– Middlesex won by 4 runs –

1984

– Lancashire have a field day –

Warwickshire came to Lord's as favourites but their big guns got bogged down. Big Jack Simmons said thank you to Nancy, but the surprise performance came from a non-participant … Peter May

Lancashire won the Benson and Hedges Cup for the first time with an efficient victory, comfortably earned. It was their first appearance in a one-day final since 1976, when they lost the Gillette Cup to Kent, but they had won the Gillette title four times before that under the captaincy of Jack Bond, who was now their manager. They were no strangers to a Lord's day out.

Warwickshire had been there as recently as 1982, when they lost the NatWest Final to Surrey, and they had also taken the Sunday League title in 1980. In Bob Willis, Alvin Kallicharran, Chris Old, Dennis Amiss and 44-year-old Norman Gifford they had a strong core of experience. All of those players knew this could be their last Lord's final, and they were determined not to blow their chance.

So it was Warwickshire who started the final as favourites. But Lancashire were a canny team who were perfectly happy being the underdogs. En route to the final they had knocked out the favourites, Essex, in the quarter-final, then the new favourites, Nottinghamshire, in the semi-final. Now they were facing the favourites again…

> *Peter May gave John Abrahams the Gold Award. It seemed a strange choice, as he had been out for a duck and did not bowl*

But this was a Lancashire team just coming into its own. Later that season they would go on to reach the NatWest semi-finals, and haul themselves up to finish fourth in the John Player League. New captain John Abrahams was determined that the 1970s legacy of 'Bond's boys'

Jack Simmons applauds as Gladstone Small is out for two runs and Warwickshire's ninth wicket falls on 134

Alvin Kallicharran was the only Warwickshire batsman to play a long innings, but his 70 was not enough

GOLD AWARD WINNER 1984

John Abrahams

golden memories

never before or since has the Gold Award gone to a man who scored a duck, did not bowl and took just one catch. So the selection of Abrahams by Peter May was certainly a surprise to the crowd, who had seen a fine team performance from Lancashire. As captain Abrahams had, of course, won the toss and put Warwickshire in to bat, and that may well have been decisive in the conditions. Abrahams had also contributed important innings in the earlier rounds and had taken the one other Gold Award of his career in the quarter-final. A Cape Coloured from South Africa, Abrahams played for Lancashire from 1973 to 1988, with two seasons, 1984-5, as captain, and now manages the England Under-19 team. He was a left-handed batsman and occasional off-break bowler, at his best between 1982 and 1986 when he passed 1,000 first-class runs in four of the five seasons.

Great captaincy earned Abrahams the Gold Award

would soon be matched by a new era of success.

On paper, the two teams were well matched. By coincidence, both had a Wisden Player of the Year: Lancashire slow bowler Jack Simmons and Warwickshire wicketkeeper Geoff Humpage. Both players would perform well in the B&H Final. Humpage took four catches – the only Lancashire wickets to fall – but it was Simmons who

> "We fielded well and kept Warwickshire to a low score, then Bob Willis came steaming in and I can remember some quick balls from Gladstone Small. I recall Bob not being too pleased about the pitch. Our captain John Abrahams was happy, though – it was Lancashire's first win in the competition and he got the Gold Award after making a duck! Harvey (Neil Fairbrother) was also in the side and steered us to victory in a stand with David Hughes. It was a different era and hard to believe that I was involved in it."
>
> – Mike Watkinson

would make the decisive contribution. Warwickshire, put in to bat on a pitch offering early life for the quick bowlers, actually did the hard work before lunch, passing the 100 mark with only two wickets down. Their big guns Kallicharran, seemingly poised for a big score, and Amiss had then made 50 together.

But Warwickshire ran out of momentum against a characteristically tight spell from Simmons (11-3-18-0), and their last eight wickets subsided for only 37 against a keen and accurate attack led by Paul Allott with three wickets for 15 runs. More than four of Warwickshire's overs were unused. Only three batsmen reached double figures, and Kallicharran – who scored a priceless 70 – was the only one to pass 20. Lancashire's victory target was a seemingly easy 140.

Warwickshire captain Willis, making his last appearance for his county, soon accounted for England opener Graeme Fowler but Lancashire made steady, unhurried progress until the fall of two quick wickets reduced them to 71 for four.

GRAEME FOWLER
THE FINAL: LANCASHIRE V WARWICKSHIRE, 21ST JULY 1984

LANCASHIRE WON THE BENSON AND HEDGES CUP MORE OFTEN THAN ANY OTHER TEAM. GRAEME FOWLER WAS PART OF THE TEAM FOR THEIR FIRST FINAL IN THIS COMPETITION, A MATCH REMEMBERED PRINCIPALLY FOR THE CONTROVERSIAL CHOICE OF GOLD AWARD WINNER.

1984 was a strange season. My team, Lancashire, arrived at Lord's as Cup Final underdogs to Warwickshire. We were bottom of the Championship and floundering on Sundays. England, after three Test matches (I opened the innings in all of them), were three-nil down. Every team I was involved with was losing. My season, like Lancs', was all or nothing. A double century against Kent and four other centuries (one against West Indies) heavily mixed with low scores.

Not much do I remember about the Final, but what I do remember happened as if it was yesterday.

Paul Allott and myself (Rodney and Del Boy) had organised sponsored suits from a reputable tailor in Chorlton-cum-Hardy. Shiny petrol blue single-breasted with a white shirt and a Lancashire tie – nice! Jack Bond, the Lancashire manager, provided each player with a red rose – the final touch.

However, the late Cedric Rhoades, then the all-powerful Lancashire chairman, heard a whisper about the suits. He demanded that we wear the Lancashire blazer. But we had heard a whisper that the Chairman had heard a whisper. So we whispered to each other and left our blazers behind. On the team bus to London, the manager told us of the Chairman's demand, to which we all shouted, "Left it at home, manager." The dress code was decided, the Chairman furious, the players smiling and smart.

The unlucky John Stanworth was left out. Years later, as Lancashire coach, Stanworth omitted Steve Elworthy, the overseas player, from a Lord's final. Elworthy left the ground. Stanworth stayed – a true team man.

John Abrahams won the toss and fielded. At lunch Warwickshire were 109 for three. With Alvin Kallicharran and Geoff Humpage at the crease, it was even.

After Nancy's huge lunch, fortified by the calories, Paul Allott and in particular Jack Simmons ("Just a couple more spuds, please, Nancy") dominated the game. It is true to say that our ground fielding was spectacular, but you are reliant on your bowlers bowling to their field. They did. Warwickshire fell like a pack of cards. 139 all out.

Neil Fairbrother (with a full head of hair) saw us home in under 43 overs. Job done.

Most famously, John Abrahams, who had made nought and had not bowled, collected the Gold Award from Peter May. When Abrahams' name was

Abrahams was a most surprising Gold Award winner, but still a popular choice

mentioned, the crowd roared and May's reasoning was never heard. Here is what he said: "I would like to present the Gold Award to John Abrahams (roar) to accept it on behalf of the Lancashire team for their fielding."

Did he deserve it? Yes. Who do you think set the field?

1984 IN CRICKET

England opener **Andy Lloyd** spends eight days in hospital after being hit on the head by a **Malcolm Marshall** bouncer. In the same series, **Winston Davis** breaks **Paul Terry**'s arm... **Greg Chappell**, **Dennis Lillee** and **Rodney Marsh** retire. Chappell was the world's top catcher and Australia's top scorer of all time, Lillee was the world's top wicket-taker, and wicketkeeper Marsh had the world's most dismissals. (Marsh is the only one whose record still stands.) It also spelt the end of Test cricket's most common dismissal: c Marsh b Lillee... **Gordon Greenidge** makes light work of the 342-run target set by **David Gower**, scoring 214 not out as West Indies beat England at Lord's. In the same series, **Malcolm Marshall** takes seven England wickets with his fractured left hand in plaster –

and bats one-handed to help **Larry Gomes** get his century... Essex win the Championship with the penultimate ball of season. Notts need four runs off two balls against Somerset to clinch the title when **Mike Bore** holes out.

1984 IN SPORT

Torvill & Dean's finest hour at Sarajevo: 19 six-pointers for Bolero... **Zola Budd** of South Africa becomes 'British' in record time in order to register before her 18th birthday and avoid serving a five-year qualification. It all ends in tears in the Los Angeles Olympics 3,000 metres when Budd collides with **Mary Decker**... **Dennis Taylor** recovers from 8-0 down in the world snooker final to beat **Steve Davis** 18-17... A fire at Bradford City kills 56... **John Francome** retires as champion jockey after a bad fall, having ridden a record 1,138 winners.

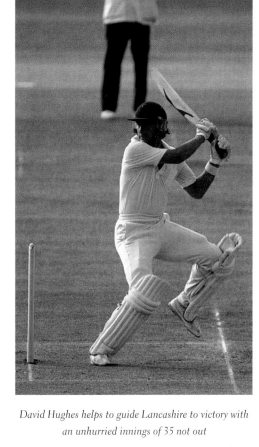

David Hughes helps to guide Lancashire to victory with an unhurried innings of 35 not out

Steve O'Shaughnessy was in the action with bat and ball

Another breakthrough then and Warwickshire might just have been in business. As it was, David Hughes and Neil Fairbrother – described in the Cup Final programme as "a promising left-hander" – took Lancashire home with a dozen overs to spare.

Peter May chose Abrahams for the Gold Award. It seemed a strange choice, since the Lancashire captain was out for a duck at a time when Lancashire were still not entirely sure of victory. But he did take the catch to dismiss Kallicharran, and directed some splendid Lancashire outcricket in a decisive fashion.

Britannic Assurance County Champions: Essex
John Player League Champions: Essex
NatWest Bank Trophy Winners: Middlesex

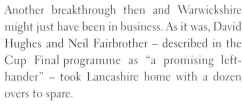

◊ FINAL SCOREBOARD 1984 ◊

LORD'S • 21ST JULY

– Warwickshire –

R I H B Dyer, c Maynard, b Watkinson	11
P A Smith, c Fairbrother, b Allott	0
A I Kallicharran, c Abrahams, b Jefferies	70
D L Amiss, c Maynard, b Watkinson	20
†G W Humpage, c Maynard, b Allott	8
A M Ferreira, c & b O'Shaughnessy	4
C M Old, b O'Shaughnessy	5
Asif Din, c Ormrod, b Jefferies	3
G C Small, lbw, b Jefferies	2
N Gifford, not out	2
*R G D Willis, c Jefferies, b Allott	2
Extras (lb 4, nb 8)	12
Total (50.4 overs)	**139**

Fall of wickets: 1-1, 2-48, 3-102, 4-115, 5-121, 6-127, 7-132, 8-133, 9-134, 10-139.

Bowling: Allott 8.4-0-15-3, Jefferies 11-2-28-3, Watkinson 9-0-23-2, O'Shaughnessy 11-1-43-2, Simmons 11-3-18-0.

– Lancashire –

won the toss

G Fowler, c Humpage, b Willis	7
J A Ormrod, c Humpage, b Ferreira	24
S J O'Shaughnessy, c Humpage, b Ferreira	22
D P Hughes, not out	35
*J Abrahams, c Humpage, b Smith	0
N H Fairbrother, not out	36
Extras (lb 6, w 1, nb 9)	16
Total (42.4 overs, for 4 wkts)	**140**

Did not bat: S T Jefferies, J Simmons, †C Maynard, M Watkinson, P J W Allott

Fall of wickets: 1-23, 2-43, 3-70, 4-71.

Bowling: Willis 9-0-19-1, Small 4-0-30-0, Ferreira 11-2-26-2, Old 10.4-3-23-0, Smith 6-0-20-1, Gifford 2-1-6-0.

Umpires: D J Constant & D G L Evans

Gold Award Winner: J Abrahams
(Adjudicator: P B H May)

– Lancashire won by six wickets –

1985

– Willey plays the decisive hand –

Essex had acquired the winning habit, whereas Leicestershire were starting to look back on their Seventies glory days and wonder where it all went wrong. But on their big day out it all went right

V ictory over the more fancied side by five wickets, with 18 balls in hand, gave Leicestershire something to celebrate in their otherwise disappointing season. To achieve this third success in a competition they had won

in its inaugural year (1972), they needed to make the highest score by a side batting second in the Benson and Hedges Final.

Essex, in the absence of their injured captain Keith Fletcher, were led by Graham Gooch. Even without Fletcher, there was no question who were the favourites: Essex had won both the County Championship and the John Player League less than a year before, and in 1985 they were still a formidable force. (They eventually picked up two trophies again – the NatWest and the Sunday League.) Essex were appearing in their fourth B&H Cup Final in seven seasons.

Leicestershire, on the other hand, had not appeared in a one-day final for 10 years. There were only two players in the current team who had played on that heady day. David Gower had been present in a non-playing capacity, and even he had trouble remembering it.

"My memory is not the most reliable at the best of times," the captain wrote in the Cup Final programme. "I must confess I do not readily recall the details, having been a mere spectator on that occasion, along with Nigel Briers and Paddy Clift, two other youngsters new to the Leicestershire staff. Leicestershire's victory celebrations might have had something to

Peter West interviews the captains before the match

Right: The crowds applaud an excellent match and await the post-match presentation

High-rolling Essex were confident. But Leicestershire's seamers had bowled ominously well in the semi-final

do with my lack of recall but I do, however, remember the sheer joy on the faces of the team, and hoping it would not be long before I could play an active role in one of the finest days of the season. It goes without saying that I did not think I would have to wait another 10 years…"

High-rolling Essex could afford to feel confident. The main omen that Leicestershire might have a little extra up their

Peter Willey
golden memories

Willey was the obvious choice for the Gold Award as, opening the bowling with his off-spin, he pinned down the Essex batsman, taking 1-41 from his 11 overs, and then steered Leicestershire to victory with a fine 86 not out batting at No 4. A tall, very strong man, Willey made his county debut at the age of 16 and played for Northamptonshire from 1966 to 1983 before moving to Leicester, where he stayed until 1991. He is now one of the world's top umpires, calm and resolute. Without quite establishing himself at Test level, he gave good service to England, scoring 1,184 runs, with two centuries, and taking seven wickets in 26 Tests (1976-86). He was at his best against the toughest opposition, against the West Indies in 1980-1 when he scored 510 runs at 42.50. He also played in 26 one-day internationals and in all won seven B&H Gold Awards.

Peter Willey hits a boundary during his 86 not out

sleeves was their stunning victory in the semifinal when, on a day of bright sunshine, their seam bowlers shot out Kent at Grace Road for just 101. Essex had been warned…

Gower, who was captain of England as well as Leicestershire, won the toss and asked Gooch to bat first. On a good pitch lacking pace, Gooch and Brian Hardie laid a prudent and useful foundation, but boundaries were few and far between.

The obvious threat to Leicestershire of a long, accelerating innings by Gooch was cut off when he was bowled by the off-spin of Peter Willey. But

Lever and the injured Fletcher mull over the day ahead

JONATHAN AGNEW
SEMI-FINAL: LEICESTERSHIRE V KENT, 20TH JULY 1985

LEICESTERSHIRE WERE ONE OF THE MOST SUCCESSFUL TEAMS OF THE
BENSON AND HEDGES CUP. THE BBC'S CRICKET CORRESPONDENT PLAYED
HIS PART IN SECURING THEIR EMPHATIC ARRIVAL IN THE 1985 FINAL.

No other match jangles the nerves to anything like the same extent as a major semi-final and that includes a Test match. Absolutely everything is at stake: nobody remembers the losing semi-finalists and, besides, it is every county cricketer's dream to play in a Lord's final.

Kent in the mid-Eighties were a terrific one-day team. Packed with all-rounders, they batted down to No 9 (Graham Johnson – a former opening batsman). Among the bowlers, there was a certain Derek Underwood who rarely conceded more than two runs per over. As it turned out, he did not bowl a single ball in the game!

Meanwhile, at Leicestershire, we were rapidly gaining the reputation of being under-achievers. We had a powerful pace attack and a middle order consisting of David Gower, Peter Willey and James Whitaker but, to the mounting frustration of our followers, had nothing to show for it.

I can remember getting together with the rest of the team on the morning of the match. Everyone was tense until Gower, the captain, breezed into the dressing room at half past nine. As usual, he had been away on Test duty (winning the Ashes as it happened!) and we were always pleased to welcome him back. Besides, his big-match experience would be vital.

There was always a slight concern that, while playing for England, his mind was not totally on events at Grace Road. This was quite understandable but the feeling of unease would result in a borderline player loudly dropping into conversation the fact that he had taken eight for 20 the previous day, for fear of being dropped. Once, we took the field with 12 men; David having forgotten to inform a rather disgruntled Les Taylor that he had been left out!

But this morning was very different. This was a vitally important match and, on the first day of the summer that year, David won the toss and put Kent in to bat. By lunch they were 76 for seven and the match was effectively over. This after the two left-handers Mark Benson and Simon Hinks had put on 24 for the first wicket.

I used to hate bowling to Benson. He had the most aggravating 'leave' in county cricket and no matter how hard you tried to persuade yourself that you had beaten the bat, in fact you knew that he had just pulled it inside the line of the ball. It was maddening!

But I got him: a little edge through to Mike Garnham and he was on his way

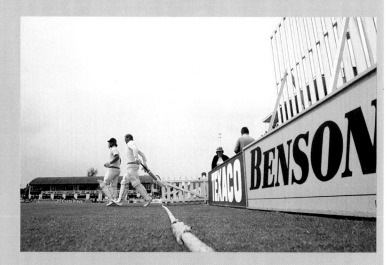
Leicestershire's openers Ian Butcher and Chris Balderstone

for 14. Hinks soon followed him for 11 (Ian Butcher taking a catch at slip) and the most astonishing collapse had begun. As we gathered together at the fall of each wicket our excitement grew. We knew that, for most of us, our first Lord's final was there for the taking.

"Steady on lads, we've still got to get these runs," warned the experienced Chris Balderstone. He was the Gold Award winner in the first Benson and Hedges Cup Final in 1972, and there was tremendous tension in the dressing room as he and Butcher set off in pursuit of 102 to win.

'Baldy' fell early, caught by Alan Knott off Richard Ellison, but Butcher played an excellent, positive knock. He dashed to 55 before Gower and Willey saw us home with more than 33 overs to spare. At twenty past four we were sitting on the players' balcony having already opened our case of Pale Ale (we never had champagne at Grace Road) toasting a truly remarkable day.

Kent 101 all out (45.5 overs) (L B Taylor 3-16; P B Clift 2-20; J P Agnew 2-24)
Leicestershire 102 for 2 (21.5 overs) (I P Butcher 55 n.o.)
Leicestershire won by 8 wickets

Essex, 147 for two at one stage, were going well when Les Taylor's persistent accuracy was rewarded with three good wickets – Paul Prichard, Ken McEwan and Derek Pringle. The Essex innings just couldn't get going after that, and a total of 213 for eight left Essex wishing they had made another 30 runs or so to put their opponents under greater pressure.

With a stand of 83 for the third wicket, Gower and Willey looked to be riding Leicestershire home on a loose rein. But Gower fell to a great catch by Alan Lilley at cover (repeating the feat with which he had dismissed Mike Gatting in the

Captain David Gower and Gold Award winner Peter Willey enjoy their big day out

semi-final). Then Gooch's deceptive swing bowling put paid in quick succession to James Whitaker and Nigel Briers.

Suddenly Leicestershire were wobbling at 135 for five and Essex were firmly back in contention. The favourites were looking good.

But Peter Willey had other ideas. At 35 years old he played one of the most valuable innings seen in a one-day final, and found in wicketkeeper Mike Garnham the flexible partner he needed to finish the job. Eschewing retrenchment, they went on the attack, and romped to victory in a flurry of strokemaking, putting on 80 together in less than a dozen overs.

With the wicket of Gooch as well as his 86 not out, it was an easy task for Denis Compton to select Willey for the Gold Award.

Britannic Assurance County Champions: Middlesex

John Player League Champions: Essex

NatWest Bank Trophy Winners: Essex

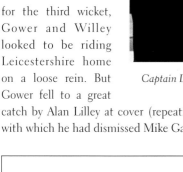

1985 IN CRICKET

At Madras, **Graeme Fowler** scores 201 and **Mike Gatting** 207 – the first time two England batsmen have passed 200 in a Test match – as **David Gower**'s England beat India 2-1…

Graham Gooch, **Peter Willey** and **John Emburey** return after a three-year Test ban for playing in South Africa. Gooch scores two centuries in three one-day games against Australia… England regain the Ashes. **Gower** scores 732 runs in the series at an average of 81.33, including 215 at Edgbaston to clinch the series.

1985 IN SPORT

39 people die when Liverpool fans charge Juventus fans at Heysel, Brussels, during the European Cup Final. **Kenny Dalglish** becomes Liverpool player-manager the next day… **Barry McGuigan** wins the world featherweight title… Unseeded **Boris Becker** is the youngest winner of Wimbledon… Scotland football manager **Jock Stein** dies of a heart attack during a game against Wales… **Sandy Lyle** is the first Briton since **Tony Jacklin** to win the Open. Jacklin's Europe team regain the Ryder Cup after 28 years.

◗ FINAL SCOREBOARD 1985 ◗

LORD'S • 20TH JULY

- Essex -

*G A Gooch, b Willey	57
B R Hardie, c & b Clift	25
P J Prichard, b Taylor	32
K S McEwan, c Garnham, b Taylor	29
D R Pringle, c Agnew, b Taylor	10
C Gladwin, b Clift	14
A W Lilley, b Agnew	12
†D E East, not out	7
S Turner, run out	3
N A Foster, not out	6
Extras (b 1, lb 15, w 1, nb 1)	18
Total *(55 overs, for 8 wkts)*	**213**

Did not bat: J K Lever

Fall of wickets: 1-71, 2-101, 3-147, 4-163, 5-164, 6-191, 7-195, 8-198.

Bowling: Agnew 11-1-51-1, Taylor 11-3-26-3, Parsons 11-0-39-0, Clift 11-1-40-2, Willey 11-0-41-1.

- Leicestershire -

won the toss

J C Balderstone, c Prichard, b Pringle	12
I P Butcher, c Prichard, b Turner	19
*D I Gower, c Lilley, b Foster	43
P Willey, not out	86
J J Whitaker, b Gooch	1
N E Briers, lbw, b Gooch	6
†M A Garnham, not out	34
Extras (b 2, lb 9, w 2, nb 1)	14
Total *(52 overs, for 5 wkts)*	**215**

Did not bat: P B Clift, G J Parsons, J P Agnew, L B Taylor

Fall of wickets: 1-33, 2-37, 3-120, 4-123, 5-135.

Bowling: Lever 11-0-50-0, Foster 11-2-32-1, Pringle 10-0-42-1, Turner 10-1-40-1, Gooch 10-1-40-2.

Umpires: H D Bird & K E Palmer

Gold Award Winner: P Willey
(Adjudicator: D C S Compton)

- Leicestershire won by five wickets -

1986

– Kent so near and yet so far –

Two runs short. How Kent must have been kicking themselves. But after a game of dramatic swings and roundabouts, when the music stopped there could only be one winner – and that was Middlesex

This was the closest and, at its climax, the most exciting of all Benson and Hedges finals. Kent fell a tantalising two runs short of a moderate target. But that constituted a remarkable recovery from the depths of 20 for three and 72 for five – a recovery which all but brought them a record fourth victory in the competition.

Middlesex, the reigning County Champions, were making their seventh appearance in a Lord's

Right: Clive Radley discovers that batting is not always easy on a pitch like this one.
Left: Roland Butcher dejectedly departs, caught Marsh bowled Ellison, for nought

final. They had recently beaten Essex in the 1983 B&H Final – and Kent in the NatWest Bank Trophy Final the year after that. Kent were playing in their 10th one-day final, and had won the Benson and Hedges Cup three times, but not since 1978. Middlesex were the team who had the winning habit.

In the semi-finals, Middlesex had completed a comparatively easy victory over Nottinghamshire at Lord's, with John Emburey pinning the

That winning feeling! Clive Radley, Norman Cowans and Mike Gatting enjoy victory in the close-fought Final

John Emburey

golden memories

this was one of the tightest of finals, as Kent failed to reach Middlesex's total of 199 by just two runs. The major credit for that went to the tight off-spin bowling of Emburey, whose figures read 11-5-16-0. He had also contributed a hard-hitting innings of 28. Emburey had had to wait until he was 25, and Fred Titmus's retirement, before he commanded a regular place in the Middlesex team in 1977. Just a year later, however, he made his Test debut and from then was England's premier off-spin bowler for over a decade, although he missed three years of Test cricket for his rebel tour of South Africa. In his 40s he was recalled for three further Tests (1993-5), and his final figures of 147 wickets at 38.40 hardly do him justice, for his tight control helped others to take wickets. He was also a most useful unorthodox batsman with seven centuries in a first-class career which brought him 12,021 runs and 1,608 wickets.

Emburey's batting style was unusual but effective

visitors down for a Gold Award-winning return of four wickets for 22 runs, while Kent had set Worcestershire a daunting target of 252 which proved beyond even Graeme Hick's reach. It looked like a good contest, and so it proved.

It was no surprise that Christopher Cowdrey should put Middlesex in to bat on a murky morning, or that Clive Radley, appearing in his seventh Cup Final, should hold their innings together in his inimitable style with a score of 54. Middlesex

found it hard going early on, and reached lunch on 89 for four off 35 overs. But Radley found good support from Paul Downton, Emburey and Phil Edmonds to set a target of 199.

That still should have been within Kent's reach. But their bowlers had taken far too long getting through their overs – a tardiness which would later count against their batsmen when the match finished in near-darkness.

Kent's reply started disastrously, with Norman

Above: The rain did not deter the crowd, nor spoil an excellent match. Above right: Miller, closely watched by Ellison, keeps the scoreboard ticking over during his innings of 37

1986 IN CRICKET

Mike Gatting has his nose broken by a **Malcolm Marshall** bouncer before the West Indies fast bowlers bring about a second series 'blackwash'... Two centuries by **Dilip Vengsarkar** give India a 2-0 series win in England. **David Gower** is replaced as captain by Gatting... **Ian Botham** is suspended for two months for admitting smoking marijuana. He returns to take a wicket with his first ball against New Zealand, to equal **Dennis Lillee**'s world record of 355 Test wickets. "Who writes your scripts?"' asks **Graham Gooch**, as Botham proceeds to take another wicket in his next over. He later hits 24 off an over, but NZ win the series 1-0... Botham quits Somerset after they sack **Viv Richard**s and **Joel Garner**... **Geoffrey Boycott** is sacked by Yorkshire.

1986 IN SPORT

Jack Nicklaus becomes the oldest US Masters champion at 46 with a storming last round. **Greg Norman** wins the Open – but he had led all four majors going into last round... **Kenny Dalglish**'s Liverpool do the Double, and Dalglish himself scores the League-clinching goal against Chelsea... Argentina win the World Cup after **Diego Maradona**'s Hand of God goal against England in the quarter-final. **Gary Lineker** scores a hat-trick against Poland... **Lloyd Honeyghan** shocks the world by destroying 'unbeatable' **Don Curry** in Atlantic City... A dramatic burst tyre in last race at Adelaide costs **Nigel Mansell** the Formula One motor racing title.... **Mike Tyson** becomes the youngest heavyweight champion by beating **Trevor Berbick**.

The sun may not have beamed but Mike Gatting did, after one of the closest one-day games ever at Lord's

Cowans and Wayne Daniel snapping up the wickets of Mark Benson, Simon Hinks and Chris Tavaré with just 20 on the scoreboard. Then John Emburey took the stage with 11 overs for 16 runs, calling such an exacting tune that Kent's hopes looked faint indeed.

But Graham Cowdrey launched an exhilarating counter-attack, adding 69 with Eldine Baptiste in a dozen overs and 37 with Richard Ellison in another four. Amazingly, Kent were back in the frame.

With the rain sheeting down in a Stygian gloom, Kent needed 22 off the last 13 balls when Cowdrey was out, caught Radley bowled Hughes. But Richard Ellison had thumped 29 off 17 balls, and was quite capable of getting the runs required.

Not for the first time, Mike Gatting showed his deft command in a tight finish to a B&H Final. For the penultimate over Gatting recalled Edmonds, who bowled Ellison to leave Kent

wanting 14 runs off the last over with two wickets in hand.

For that over, Gatting turned to Simon Hughes – a cool head in a nerve-jangling situation. The man on strike was wicketkeeper Steven Marsh, relishing the spotlight in his first full season since replacing Alan Knott. He bravely pulled a full toss for six, and with three balls to go there were just six more runs required. But Hughes didn't crumble. The next two balls produced just a single between them, which left Graham Dilley needing to slog the last delivery for six. He could manage only a two.

Emburey's immaculate spell of defensive slow bowling, and his pragmatic innings of 28, earned him the Gold Award nomination from David Gower.

Britannic Assurance County Champions: Essex
John Player League Champions: Hampshire
NatWest Bank Trophy Winners: Sussex

FINAL SCOREBOARD 1986

LORD'S • 12TH JULY

– Middlesex –

W N Slack, b Dilley	0
A J T Miller, c Marsh, b C S Cowdrey	37
*M W Gatting, c Marsh, b Ellison	25
R O Butcher, c Marsh, b Ellison	0
C T Radley, run out	54
†P R Downton, lbw, b Ellison	13
J E Emburey, b Baptiste	28
P H Edmonds, not out	15
S P Hughes, not out	4
Extras (lb 8, w 11, nb 4)	23
Total (55 overs, for 7 wkts)	**199**

Did not bat: N G Cowans, W W Daniel

Fall of wickets: 1-6, 2-66, 3-66, 4-85, 5-131, 6-163, 7-183.

Bowling: Dilley 11-2-19-1, Baptiste 11-0-61-1, C S Cowdrey11-0-48-1, Ellison 11-2-27-3, Underwood 11-4-36-0.

– Kent –

won the toss

M R Benson, c Downton, b Cowans	1
S G Hinks, lbw, b Cowans	13
C J Tavaré, c Downton, b Daniel	3
N R Taylor, c Miller, b Edmonds	19
*C S Cowdrey, c Emburey, b Hughes	19
G R Cowdrey, c Radley, b Hughes	58
E A E Baptiste, b Edmonds	20
R M Ellison, b Edmonds	29
†S A Marsh, not out	14
G R Dilley, not out	4
Extras (lb 9, w 8)	17
Total (55 overs, for 8 wkts)	**197**

Did not bat: D L Underwood

Fall of wickets: 1-17, 2-20, 3-20, 4-62, 5-72, 6-141, 7-178, 8-182.

Bowling: Cowans 9-2-18-2, Daniel 11-1-43-1, Gatting 4-0-18-0, Hughes 9-2-35-2, Emburey 11-5-16-0, Edmonds 11-1-58-3.

Umpires: D J Constant & D R Shepherd

Gold Award Winner: J E Emburey
(Adjudicator: D I Gower)

– Middlesex won by 2 runs –

1987

– Northants suffer the cruellest fate –

*If the 1986 B&H Final was close, this was like Russian roulette.
Northants thought they'd made a winning total. But Jim Love knew
that when the scores are equal, some are more equal than others*

It was six years since Northamptonshire's last Lord's final, but the agony and the trauma had not receded. As they went into the 1987 Benson & Hedges Cup Final, the terrible memory kept coming back. In 1981, the NatWest Final between Derbyshire and Northants had finished with the scores level. A tie – but one team had to lose, and that team was Northants. Surely history could not possibly repeat itself...

Yet it did. In yet another dramatic B&H finish, Yorkshire's Jim Love calmly blocked the last ball bowled and Northants trooped off utterly dejected, the two-time losers in a tied Lord's final. Amazingly, there have only ever been two ties at Lord's in a domestic final – and Northants have lost them both. This really was a cruel torture.

> *Northants discovered
> that sometimes
> lightning does
> strike twice ...*

Six years earlier, they had needed to stop Derbyshire drawing level, because Northants had lost three more wickets. Derbyshire made it with the very last ball. This time, Yorkshire were already level. Northants had made 244 for seven. Yorkshire were on 244 for six. And there was nothing Northants could do to stop the Tykes taking the trophy.

Even if Love had perished to the last ball, Yorkshire would still have won. They had scored 110 off their first 30 overs; Northants had got 109. One wicket, one run; so near and yet so far.

The result might have been different if Arnie Sidebottom, scrambling a desperate single to level the scores off the fifth ball of the final over, had not survived a close-range run out. Had Robert Bailey's throw from mid-on hit the

*Right: Ashley Metcalfe
(47) and Martyn Moxon
(45) ensured that
Yorkshire's reply got
off to a good start
with a well-controlled
opening stand of 97*

David Capel batted superbly for Northamptonshire and was unlucky to miss a century by only three runs

Jim Love

g o l d e n   m e m o r i e s

love blocked the final ball of the match – and Yorkshire won with the scores level by virtue of taking one more wicket. His 75 not out brought Love the B&H Gold Award, perhaps the finest moment in a career which did not quite live up to its promise. Born in Leeds on 22 April 1955, Love made his Yorkshire debut at the age of 20, and his free-scoring abilities were recognised by England when he played in three limited-overs internationals against Australia in 1981. He scored 43 in the second of these, but never again received international recognition. Indeed he only twice passed 1,000 runs and only once averaged over 40 in a first-class season. He was at his best in the Benson and Hedges competition, in which he won three Gold Awards in all, and where his career average was a highly respectable 41.22 for 1,113 runs.

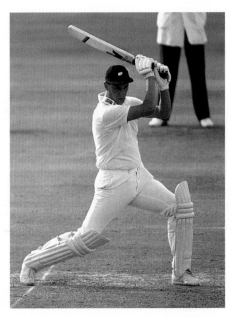

Love hits out during his match-winning innings

stumps, Yorkshire would have needed a run from the last ball. A maiden ball or a wicket would then have given the match to Northants.

But it was not to be. Love carried his bat for 75, and Mike Gatting made him the Gold Award winner.

For Yorkshire, the relief could not have been greater. This was only their second trophy in 18 seasons (they had won the Sunday League in 1983) and as their fans streamed on to the out-field to celebrate, you could hear the echo from London all the way to the Dales.

It was a lovely morning when Phil Carrick and Geoff Cook came out to toss up. For Carrick, that was an event in itself. Whereas Cook had been captain of Northants for six years, Carrick had only been appointed at the beginning of the season. After 17 years with Yorkshire, to walk out at Lord's as captain in a Benson and Hedges Cup Final a week before his 35th birthday was like a dream come true.

Carrick won the toss and put Northampton-shire in to bat, hoping to make the most of any early-morning moisture. Paul Jarvis made a quick breakthrough, having Cook snapped up at short leg. But Wayne Larkins and Bailey were in no mood to spare the horses. And when Larkins mishit Peter Hartley to give a steepling catch to Carrick at cover, Allan Lamb appeared on the scene, wielding his bat with the same attacking philosophy. He and his cavalier partner both perished bravely, Bailey going to a typically spectacular slip catch by Marytn Moxon, and Lamb falling to a tumbling catch by wicketkeeper David Bairstow.

Northants galloped into the 90s at four an over – but for the loss of four good wickets. Carrick put the brakes on with a spell of 11 overs of slow left-arm spin for 30 runs, but David Capel came up trumps as a batsman with 97. His fifth-wicket partnership with Richard Williams of 120 in 28 overs was

Amazingly, there have only ever been two ties at Lord's in a domestic final – and Northants have lost them both. This really was a cruel torture

marked by some hard hitting and smart running between the wickets, and they ensured that Yorkshire would be set a target beyond the reach of any side batting second in a previous domestic final.

Facing a required run rate of 4.45 per over, the exciting Yorkshire opening pair of Moxon and Ashley Metcalfe gave their team a great start in reply. The total was approaching three figures in the 24th over – nicely on target – when Moxon made the fatal mistake of advancing down the pitch to Nick Cook, who beat him in the flight and he was bowled. Metcalfe soon followed, holing out to the other Northants spinner, Williams.

The slow bowlers were getting the upper hand – but they couldn't bowl all day. Capel and Alan Walker were both in expansive mood, giving away far more runs than Northants could afford. So long as Love remained at the crease, his side had to be fancied over the final run-in. A pragmatic, accelerating alliance of 63 with David Bairstow, punishing the loose balls bowled by the medium-pacers, put Yorkshire in the box seat.

Bairstow and Carrick were both run out as Yorkshire desperately threw the bat and chased after every single. When the economical Winston Davis began the last over, Yorkshire needed just five to win, or four to tie. Davis managed to restrict them to three off the first four balls, and if Bailey had hit Sidebottom's stumps on that crucial fifth ball, it all might have been different.

But Northants discovered that sometimes lightning does strike twice … and Yorkshire were able to celebrate their first ever Benson and Hedges Cup.

Britannic Assurance County Champions: Nottinghamshire
Refuge Assurance League Champions: Worcestershire
NatWest Bank Trophy Winners: Nottinghamshire

Jim Love played some timely shots at the end of the Yorkshire innings, before blocking the final ball to seal victory

Above: *Phil Carrick and Jim Love lift aloft the Benson and Hedges cup after a final as close as they come.*
Below: *Hard-hitting Yorkshire opener Ashley Metcalfe strokes the ball away during his innings of 47*

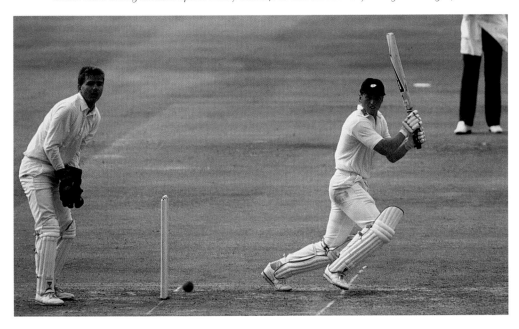

● FINAL SCOREBOARD 1987 ●

LORD'S ● 11TH JULY

– Northamptonshire –

*G Cook, c Blakey, b Jarivs	1
W Larkins, c Carrick, b Hartley	15
R J Bailey, c Moxon, b Fletcher	26
A J Lamb, c Bairstow, b Jarivs	28
D J Capel, b Hartley	97
R G Williams, c Bairstow, b Jarvis	44
D J Wild, b Jarvis	6
W W Davis, not out	10
†D Ripley, not out	6
Extras (b 2, lb 3, w 2, nb 4)	11

Total (*55 overs, for 7 wkts*) **244**

Did not bat: N G B Cook, A Walker

Fall of wickets: 1-3, 2-31, 3-48, 4-92, 5-212, 6-226, 7-232.

Bowling: Jarvis 11-2-43-4, Sidebottom 11-1-40-0, Fletcher 11-1-60-1, Hartley 11-0-66-2, Carrick 11-2-30-0.

– Yorkshire –

won the toss

M D Moxon, b N G B Cook	45
A A Metcalfe, c Davis, b Williams	47
R J Blakey, c Davis, b Williams	1
K Sharp, b Williams	24
J D Love, not out	75
†D L Bairstow, run out	24
*P Carrick, run out	10
A Sidebottom, not out	2
Extras (b 1, lb 4, w 4, nb 7)	16

Total (*55 overs, for 6 wkts*) **244**

Did not bat: P J Hartley, P W Jarvis, S D Fletcher

Fall of wickets: 1-97, 2-101, 3-103, 4-160, 5-223, 6-235.

Bowling: Davis 11-1-37-0, Walker 11-0-62-0, Capel 11-0-66-0, N G B Cook 11-1-42-1, Williams 11-0-32-3.

Umpires: M D Bird & K E Palmer

Gold Award Winner: J D Love
(*Adjudicator: M W Gatting*)

– Yorkshire won –
by losing fewer wickets

1988

– Jefferies swings it Hampshire's way –

Sometimes a Lord's one-day game was decided in the first hour, and this was one such. Was it the conditions or just great cricket? Derbyshire succumbed to the best bowling in any B&H Final

I t don't mean a thing if it ain't got that swing ... and on July 9, 1988, Steve Jefferies certainly did have that swing going just the way he wanted it. The 28-year-old South African left-armer put in a devastating opening burst that reduced Derbyshire to 80 for six at lunch, and their hopes to ashes. Jefferies took the first four wickets to fall in an eight-ball spell which cost him just one run. Game, set and match, barring a miracle which did not occur. Jefferies finished

Right: Devon Malcolm gets the treatment as Robin Smith plays a hook shot during his brief but brilliant innings of 38

Nigel Cowley and Mark Nicholas celebrate victory after Hampshire's first one-day final

with the best bowling figures in the history of the Benson and Hedges Cup Final – five for 13 from 10 overs. And if Chris Smith had held on to a hard slip chance from the first ball of John Morris's innings, Jefferies would have had the second ever B&H Cup Final hat-trick to boot.

There was never any doubt who would pick up the Gold Award from Clive Lloyd.

Jefferies' triumph was all the more sweet considering that he had spent the previous two summers playing League cricket after Lancashire had dropped him as their overseas player. Now

Steve Jefferies

golden memories

after Derbyshire had been put in to bat, Jefferies destroyed their batting with a spell of four wickets for one run in eight balls and final figures of 10-3-13-5, the best ever recorded in a B&H Final. This ensured victory for Hampshire in their first ever Lord's final. Jefferies was a well-built left-arm swing bowler and useful late middle-order batsman from South Africa, who played there for Western Province, for whom he once took all 10 wickets in an innings. He played for three counties in England, starting with Derbyshire in 1982, then three years with Lancashire (1984-6) and two years with Hampshire, (1988-9), as cover for Malcolm Marshall. He achieved better results in England in limited-overs matches than in the first-class games and his 18 wickets in the B&H season of 1988 was a Hampshire record.

If the cap fits... Award winner Steve Jefferies, right

Hampshire had given him another chance in county cricket, and this was his opportunity to repay their faith.

For Hampshire, too, it was a special occasion. Always an attractive, popular team, they were the only county who had never appeared in a Lord's one-day final (Durham later played in seven B&H Cups without reaching the Final). The closest

Then the roar.
The most enormous,
spectacular roar.
And goose pimples.
It has been a long wait
and a lot of trying.
It is a moment I shall
never forget

Hants had previously come to a Benson and Hedges Final was the 1977 semi-final, when Gloucestershire won by seven runs thanks to Mike Procter's famous four-wickets-in-five-balls. They had also lost out in four NatWest semi-finals, including a 1985 nailbiter when they tied with Essex, who had lost fewer wickets.

It was hard to believe that

MARK NICHOLAS

DERBYSHIRE v HAMPSHIRE: THE FINAL, 9TH JULY 1988

THERE WAS A TRADITION OF CAPTAINS WRITING PREVIEWS OF THE B&H FINAL IN THE MATCHDAY PROGRAMME. IN 1989, MARK NICHOLAS WENT ONE BETTER, AND WROTE A REVIEW OF THE PREVIOUS YEAR'S FINAL, WHICH HIS HAMPSHIRE TEAM HAD WON. IT WAS SUCH A SPLENDID PIECE OF WRITING, WE HOPE YOU WILL FORGIVE US FOR REPRODUCING IT HERE...

July 9th, 1988 was a special day for everyone attached to Hampshire CCC. Until that day Hampshire, unbelievably considering the 'star' players on their books since one-day cricket started in 1963, were the only county never to have reached a Lord's final. For the players of 1988 it was a relief to break the duck, a momentous occasion and, not surprisingly, a tense one...

10.35... The dressing room is quiet. Each player has mapped out his perfect day – a hundred, or six wickets, or four awesome catches – but now at the time of reckoning there are doubts – nought, or nought for sixty, or four dropped catches – failure looms all too immediate.

10.55... The ground is virtually full. The umpires are applauded and, from our balcony, they look most assured. In contrast, the players shuffle now, bouncing on their toes, studs clattering, gum revolving from molar to molar. Bowlers extend their arms with awkward rotations, then stretch hamstrings, backs and groins and check haircuts. This must be like the Wembley tunnel. We are so excited we could burst. I say we are lucky to be here so we should enjoy the occasion, smell the air, absorb the fullness of the stands, feel the springy turf on the shaky foot. Orientate yourselves, I urge, quickly, positively, and whatever else, stick together. At 200-1 or 30-5 stick together and we'll be OK. It's noisy now and we leave the security of our dressing room.

10.58... Down the stairs, past gazing, inquisitive eyes. To the Long Room, through the jungle of heavy moustaches and gaudy MCC ties.

To the small white gate and the small gateman, who winked. Then the roar. The most enormous, spectacular roar. And goose pimples. It has been a long wait and a lot of trying. A moment I shall never forget.

10.59... Umpire David Constant is delightful: "Morning, Hampshire. Enjoy the day, 15 other counties didn't make it. Who's bowling at my end? You put on weight, Kippy, or what?" His partner is Nigel Plews, the 6ft 6in former policeman: "Well done, Mark, a lot of people in cricket are glad Hampshire made it." He has made it, too, to the Test panel which, not having played first-class cricket, is an achievement.

11.0... By the start of play, heavy clouds have settled over Lord's and the atmosphere is conducive to swing bowling. We start poorly, however, with a number of wides. The crowd jumps down your throat if you bowl wides, which is fair enough, but hell, it is hard to regain your composure. Then the bowling of Stephen Jefferies becomes part of the history of Lord's finals. He wins the match in half an hour, swinging the ball late, dipping it viciously

"We receive the Cup and Gold Award. The crowd below are delirious. I am so proud..."

to the batsmen's pads. He said afterwards that he had only bowled better once in his life.

(We were pleased to have bowled first. At 9am the pitch had looked firm; the air was clear and the sky blue. We would field first through superstition as much as the notorious batting problems on the morning of Lord's finals. However, these problems are less acute in July at the B&H Final than September and a rumour had circulated that Derbyshire would bat but we didn't believe it. I still don't know if this was true. I probably never shall.)

12.20... Jon Ayling bowls Bernie Maher. I rush

off the pitch, through the Long Room, down the stairs and into the Gents'. My studs crunch on the stone floor and I stand in a cubicle next to the stunned members who can only assume we have come off for rain. We hadn't. I imagine the tension had catalysed such desperation!

1.00pm... Lunch is taken 15 minutes early as the ugly drizzle consumes headquarters. Everyone is buoyant. Seconds earlier Michael Holding had eased our digestion further by hoisting Nigel Cowley high to the Pavilion rails where David Turner safely held the catch.

1.15... Only half the team has gone to see Nancy for lunch. This is unusual. Nancy's lunches are legendary. Most restaurants would shudder in the wake of her lamb chops. Her cooking is delicious – the highlight of Mike Gatting's day. In the dressing room, rolls, milk and cheese are picked at, ice cream is devoured. Peter Sainsbury, who has been with the county for nigh on 40 years in some capacity or other, stalks the dressing room. Now coach, he basks in Jefferies' bowling. He speaks quietly to those that had a quiet morning and reminds us that the match is not yet halfway through.

1.30... Strappings are checked, bandages rewound. More chewing gum, last swigs of orange juice, studs checked and we are bouncing again, eagerly on tip-toe. The drizzle has cleared, the stretching begins, and we're off, back through the prying eyes and sports coats and high-backed Long Room chairs to the arena.

1.40... There is one outstanding moment in the next session of play. John Morris, Derby's precociously talented batsman, is threatening with a major innings. Not only had he survived the morning traumas – he had been dropped at slip first ball, a hat-trick ball – but he had attacked us intelligently. Now risking a second run to long leg, he is run out by a perfect piece of fielding by Nigel Cowley. A clean two-handed pick-up and a fizzing assassin's throw to Bob Parks. Morris was two feet from home. It is the first time that I really believe we will win.

2.30... The dressing room mood is rampant. We need just 118 to win. I urge caution and, for a minute,

Congratulations for Jefferies after taking one of his five wickets in the Derbyshire innings at a cost of just 15 runs

get snappy about it, which is unnecessary. As I pad up I feel I will be in early. Paul and Chris played so faultlessly in the semi-final, and the morning has gone so well, I do not believe things will last.

2.40... Devon Malcolm begins with a fast bouncer to Chris who is alert and ducks convincingly. Kim Barnett attacks with four slips and the first time I look out Paul is caught by the second of them. It was a good outswinger, committing Paul to 'open up', and I pray not to receive another. I am only just ready, having made a late switch to my favourite batting shoes. Watching Derbyshire celebrate pulls the knot in my stomach tighter. I rush out of the dressing room, keen to impose myself on the match. My shoes feel good on the turf and I am suddenly calm. The voice of the audience is muffled, the crowd a sea of background. Malcolm springs from the traps and surges forward menacingly. I see the ball clearly and play it late to cover.

3.35... Robin Smith replaces his brother Chris. Robin is so pumped up I thought he might pop. He askes me how he should approach his innings and thinking of this enormous stage I say: "Show off." Robin smiles and does so. He clubs Holding twice through the covers and clips Mortensen through midwicket. He stands up and strokes Warner off the back foot to the Pavilion, steps and then leans

forward and shovels him past extra cover. In a flash he has made 38 and then just as suddenly he is out, brilliantly caught by Steven Goldsmith at long leg from a mis-hook. (On TV, Richie Benaud was quite breathless about the catch.) I did not, at any stage, think the catch could be taken. It was a dynamic effort and the only way to end Robin's innings.

5.05... We have won the Benson and Hedges Cup. I was at the wicket with David Turner, which is appropriate since David has been with the club through all the previous semi-final agonies. The dressing room is awash with ecstasy.

The first to greet me is Tim Tremlett, who has not played in the match. The day has been full of mixed emotions for him, I'm sure. A natural selection for eight seasons, he has missed the whole B&H campaign through injury. This morning Tim had bowled beautifully in the nets. It was the old bouncy, spitting Tremlett. His eyes implored someone to say: "OK Tim, you're in." But no one had. Now he is showered, groomed and smiling with everyone else, but the agony is still there.

Our chairman, Charles Knott, is delighted as we shake hands; his face shows it. Peter Sainsbury says it is the happiest day of his life. I agree.

5.15... We receive the Cup and Gold Award. The

(Continues overleaf)

MARK NICHOLAS

(From previous page)

crowd below are delirious. I am so proud. There is a deafening roar when Stephen Jefferies is named Gold Award winner.

5.30… Steve and I are whisked away, miles away, for a press conference and interviews. The two of us had sucked on spaghetti the night before and filled our glasses with Chianti. I had awoken 11 hours earlier with a yawn. My head was muggy and thick. The Kent captain calls this a 'woody'. I call it too much Chianti. I had drunk plenty of wine hoping it would cure the likely insomnia – it hadn't, so I ran a bath and made tea with that frightful UHT milk. Jefferies and I had started this fabulous 24 hours with a drink in our hand and here we were, back at it again.

5.45… At last I see Kim Barnett, who shows no jealousy or disappointment and congratulates us. We go to the BBC interview room after dealing with the network radio stations. We agree that swing dictated the match.

6.15… Back to the dressing room, which is by now a free-for-all. Former players, cameras, committee, friends, interviewers, officials, umpires (I think) and Derbyshire players who are generous both in defeat and with our champagne! It was good to see them. The atmosphere in this room is my lingering memory – that 11 o'clock roar and this. It was everyone's day, everyone that has had anything to do with Hampshire cricket was entitled to be in that famous dressing room.

Eventually, I found a bath and soaked there for a full hour, before returning to the now deserted dressing room. Soon I would move on to other frenzied celebrations in London. I took a last look around and reflected, rather morosely, that I had seen just one ball of the whole match from this dressing room – the ball that dismissed Paul Terry. This had been the first time. It could never be the same again.

Hampshire had never made it to Lord's in the era of Richards, Greenidge and Marshall. But now Mark Nicholas's less starry squad was in the Benson and Hedges Cup Final.

It had not been an easy ride. They had had to negotiate a tricky quarter-final against Worcestershire, the team of the year who would finish up as County Champions, Sunday League Champions and NatWest finalists. Hampshire had then had to beat a very strong Essex team at Chelmsford in the semi-final.

But now that they had actually got as far as NW1, they were determined not to go home empty-handed.

It was 10 years since Derbyshire's only previous appearance in a Benson and Hedges Cup Final. In 1978 they had opted to bat and registered a disappointing total of 147 which Kent knocked off with ease. Now they had lost the toss, been put in – and were on their way to an even worse score than in 1978.

As far as the match was concerned, Chris Smith dropping Morris was a bonus. Without Morris's 42, scored off 79 balls, Derbyshire's total would have been slender indeed. Morris resisted Jefferies' swing, only to get himself out in the most embarrassing manner – going for a second run. He was beaten by Nigel Cowley's throw from long leg.

The Derbyshire innings ended on a suitable note of farce. Cardigan Connor began his eighth over with three wides, then bowled Paul Newman and Devon Malcolm with consecutive balls.

With Michael Holding and Malcolm opening the Derbyshire attack, even a target of 118 could have proved difficult. But those two fiery fast bowlers needed not so much an early breakthrough as an early avalanche.

Kim Barnett set extremely attacking fields, and was rewarded with Paul Terry's wicket – caught at second slip by Zambian Paul Roberts off the bowling of Malcolm. But it was not enough.

Mark Nicholas and Chris Smith eased their way in before Chris made way for his brother Robin to play a scintillating cameo innings of 38

off 27 balls, including seven boundaries. It was halted by a remarkable catch by Steven Goldsmith, who had to run over 40 yards to pocket Smith's top-edged hook.

To complete Derbyshire's misery, the match was lost when, with the scores level, Allan Warner bowled a no-ball.

Britannic Assurance County Champions: Worcestershire
Refuge Assurance League Champions: Worcestershire
NatWest Bank Trophy Winners: Middlesex

"The Derbyshire players came to our dressing room. They were generous in defeat and with our champagne…"

◗ FINAL SCOREBOARD 1988 ◗

LORD'S • 9TH JULY

– Derbyshire –

*K J Barnett, b Jefferies	13
P D Bowler, c Nicholas, b Jefferies	4
B Roberts, c Nicholas, b Jefferies	0
J E Morris, run out	42
S C Goldsmith, lbw, b Jefferies	0
†B J M Maher, b Ayling	8
M A Holding, c Turner, b Cowley	7
P G Newman, b Connor	10
A E Warner, b Jefferies	4
O H Mortensen, not out	0
D E Malcolm, b Connor	0
Extras (lb 14, w 12, nb 3)	29
Total (46.3 overs)	**117**

Fall of wickets: 1-27, 2-28, 3-29, 4-32, 5-71, 6-80, 7-101, 8-114, 9-117, 10-117.

Bowling: Connor 7.3-1-27-2, Jefferies 10-3-13-5, Andrew 9-0-25-0, Ayling 9-2-21-1, Cowley 11-2-17-1.

– Hampshire –

won the toss

V P Terry, c Roberts, b Malcolm	2
C L Smith, c Maher, b Mortensen	20
*M C J Nicholas, not out	35
R A Smith, c Goldsmith, b Warner	38
D R Turner, not out	7
Extras (lb 8, w 3, nb 5)	16
Total (31.5 overs, for 3 wkts)	**118**

Did not bat: J R Ayling, S T Jefferies, †R J Parks, N G Cowley, C A Connor, S J W Andrew

Fall of wickets: 1-10, 2-44, 3-90.

Bowling: Holding 11-2-36-0, Malcolm 7-2-25-1, Newman 3-1-11-0, Mortensen 5-1-19-1, Warner 5.5-0-19-1.

Umpires D J Constant & N T Plews

Gold Award Winner: S T Jefferies
(Adjudicator: C H Lloyd)

– Hampshire won by seven wickets –

1989

– Hemmings has a whale of a time –

It was like a shootout in an old black-and-white Western. Two veteran gunmen face to face at 22 paces. John Lever pulled the trigger, but Eddie Hemmings had the last laugh

When all the younger men had had their say through the previous 109.5 overs, it was left to two 40-year-olds born within four days of each other back in 1949 to settle the most tingling and dramatic Lord's final in the history of the Benson and Hedges Cup.

There was Eddie Hemmings with his back to the Nursery End, stout veteran of countless one-day battles around the country on behalf of Warwickshire and Nottinghamshire, indeed around the world on behalf of England, looking for one gap in the field for the boundary he needed if the prize was to decorate the trophy cupboard at Trent Bridge for the first time.

Ranged against him some 50 yards away at the end of his run was John Lever – just the elder of

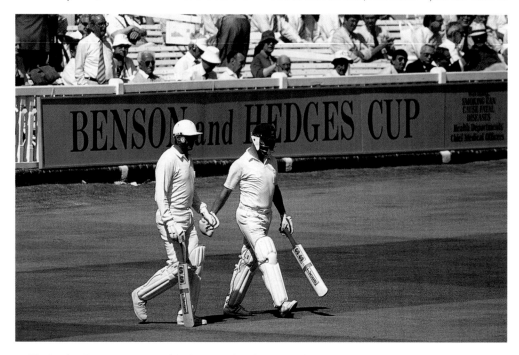

The familiar Essex opening pair of Graham Gooch and Brian Hardie walk out at Lord's after Gooch won the toss

Efficient as ever, Gooch went on to make 48

Coming in at No 3 with the score on four, Alan Lilley batted superbly for 95 not out to set Notts a challenging total

GOLD AWARD WINNER 1989

Tim Robinson

golden memories

Robinson played a captain's innings to help Nottinghamshire to victory. Batting at No 3 he scored 86 from 117 balls when he was needlessly run out. His team just got home, as Eddie Hemmings scored the requisite four off the last ball of the match. Robinson made his debut for Notts in 1978 and established himself in the team after he had left Sheffield University. He progressed steadily until he scored 2,032 runs in the 1984 first-class season to earn selection for the England tour to India. He excelled in his first two Test series, with 444 runs at 63.42 against India and 490 at 61.25 in the following summer against Australia. From seeming the ideal England opener, his technique was exposed by the West Indies pace bowlers in 1986 and he never again recaptured such form in Test cricket. He continued, however, to be a most successful county batsman and captained Notts from 1988 to 1995.

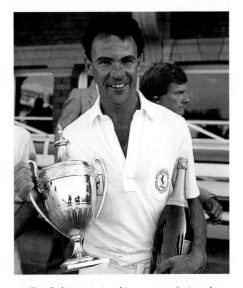

Tim Robinson enjoys his moment of triumph

the two – out to deny him the runs in the way he had denied many others before when limited-over matches had come down to the last ball. Better still, from Essex's point of view, the wicket of Hemmings would have enabled Lever to round off a heroic career with exactly 150 victims in the competition.

Notts had started the over needing nine to win. Now it was down to four, against one of the most reliable bowlers in cricket.

For a moment the 22,000 fascinated watchers were silenced as Graham Gooch, the Essex captain, returned to his position after spending an agonising couple of minutes setting his field, which was heavily biased to the leg side. Then the noise built up as Lever set off on his familiar flowing run, growing in urgency with every stride.

His left-arm delivery was off the line he intended. Not much. Perhaps no more than three or four inches when it reached the waiting Hemmings. But enough for the Nottinghamshire man to seize the chance he wanted. He backed away, making room for himself, and struck the ball unerringly just wide of Brian Hardie at backward point to the welcoming, unprotected boundary rope beyond. Nottinghamshire's joy was com-

1989 IN CRICKET

Allan Border's Aussies regain the Ashes, beating **David Gower**'s team 4-0 in England as **Terry Alderman** takes 41 wickets including 19 lbws. Australian openers **Mark Taylor** and **Geoff Marsh** score 301 in a day. Taylor amasses 839 in the series, while **Steve Waugh** averages 126.5... A tight Benson and Hedges Lord's Final is followed by another last-over finish in the NatWest, as Warwickshire beat Middlesex with two balls to spare.

1989 IN SPORT

Frank Bruno momentarily staggers **Mike Tyson** en route to a fifth round defeat... **Desert Orchid** wins Cheltenham Gold Cup; bookies lose £2million...

95 Liverpool fans are crushed to death before the FA Cup semi-final at Hillsborough... **Stephen Hendry** wins the Benson and Hedges Masters snooker title at 19... FA Cup winners Liverpool lose the League to Arsenal with the last kick of the season by **Michael Thomas** at Anfield... **Peter Scudamore** is the first jump jockey to ride 200 winners in a season... **Nick Faldo** wins the US Masters... **Michael Chang**, 17, wins the French Open — the youngest male Grand Slam event winner ever... **Finlay Calder**'s British Lions triumph 2-1 in Australia when **David Campese** loses the ball on his own line to gift them the third Test... **Adrian Moorhouse** breaks the 100m breaststroke world record.

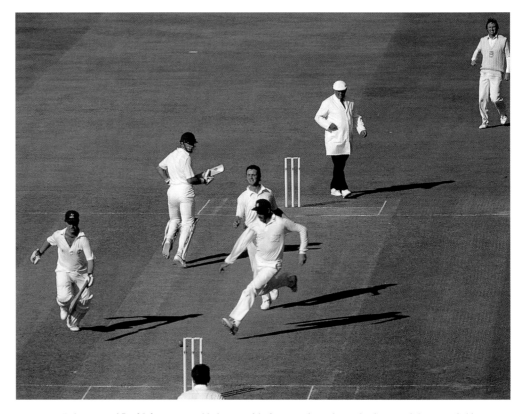

Tim Robinson and Paul Johnson scramble home safely for a quick single, to the dismay of the Essex fielders

plete. Anything less than a four would have presented victory to Essex, to match their feat in 1979 when the Benson and Hedges Cup became the first major honour in their history and launched 10 years of almost non-stop success.

If the scores had finished level, Essex would have won, having heavily outscored Nottinghamshire at the 30-over mark, the next deciding factor.

So Essex, disputing their fourth Benson and Hedges Cup Final in the Eighties, were left to collect their fourth B&H runners-up cheque of the decade. £11,000 made for a handsome payday, but it could never be a substitute for the trophy itself. This was a season when

> *When all the younger men had their say through the previous 109.5 overs, it was left to two 40-year-olds born within four days of each other back in 1949 to settle the most tingling and dramatic Lord's final*

Essex were the Nearly Men: after losing out in the B&H Final, they lost the Sunday League title on the final day, and were pipped to the County Championship by Worcestershire after having 25 points deducted for providing a substandard pitch at Southend. It was a moot point which hurt more: losing a title because of a bad council cricket pitch, or impotently watching Hemmings' shot speed to the boundary on the evening of July 15.

There was little hint some seven hours earlier of the immense drama to come after Essex had decided to bat first and lost Hardie in the third over to Franklyn Stephenson's baffling, almost comical, slower ball. The incoming Alan Lilley

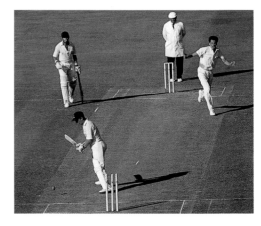

Johnson is bowled by Neil Foster for 54

was the architect of their 243 for seven total with an unbeaten 95 off 144 balls, helped by Graham Gooch and Mark Waugh in stands of 70 and 82 respectively.

The total was short of Gooch's expectations

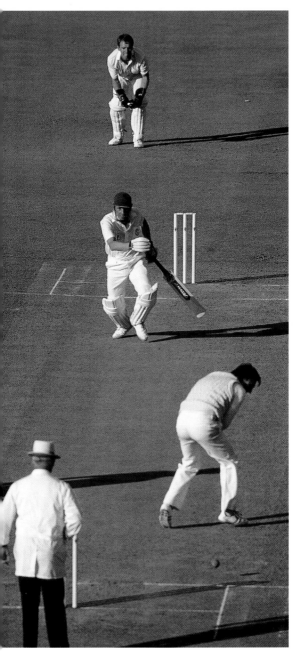

Derek Randall drives straight back past John Lever

Eddie Hemmings and Bruce French finish the job

Then in stepped Nottinghamshire captain Tim Robinson with a masterly 86 off 117 balls to play the role Lilley had done with breezy help from Paul Johnson and Derek Randall, who hustled his way to 49 from 49 balls and thoroughly upset the Essex fielders' concentration.

Randall thumped a mighty six off Gooch over midwicket, then skied a catch to Mark Waugh at long leg, but Essex were looking jittery – as it turned out, with good reason.

Robinson's innings won him the Gold Award for seeing his side to within striking distance of their target before he was run out – an incident which all helped to set up the Hemmings-Lever showdown that had the television watchers as well as those at Lord's sitting on the edge of their seats.

Britannic Assurance County Champions:
Worcestershire
Refuge Assurance League Champions:
Lancashire
NatWest Bank Trophy Winners: Warwickshire

but it still presented Nottinghamshire with the task of equalling the record score by a side batting second and winning the Final. They started disastrously when Lever removed both openers, Chris Broad and Paul Pollard, with only 17 scored.

◊ FINAL SCOREBOARD 1989 ◊

LORD'S • 15TH JULY

– Essex –

won the toss

*G A Gooch, b Afford	48
B R Hardie, b Stephenson	0
A W Lilley, not out	95
M E Waugh, c Robinson, b Evans	41
P J Prichard, lbw b Cooper	1
J P Stephenson, run out	9
D R Pringle, run out	15
†M A Garnham, c Johnson b Evans	0
N A Foster, not out	2
Extras (b 1, lb 26, w 4, nb 1)	32
Total (55 overs, for 7 wkts)	**243**

Did not bat: G Miller, J K Lever

Fall of wickets: 1-4, 2-74, 3-156, 4-162, 5-185, 6-220, 7-235.

Bowling: Stephenson 11-0-61-1, Cooper 11-3-30-1, Evans 11-0-28-2, Afford 11-0-50-1, Hemmings 11-0-47-0.

– Nottinghamshire –

B C Broad, c Garnham, b Lever	6
P Pollard, lbw, b Lever	2
*R T Robinson, run out	86
P Johnson, b Foster	54
D W Randall, c Waugh, b Pringle	49
F D Stephenson, c Gooch, b Miller	0
K P Evans, run out	26
†B N French, not out,	8
E E Hemmings, not out	6
Extras (b 1, lb 3, w 2, nb 1)	7
Total (55 overs, for 7 wkts)	**244**

Did not bat: K E Cooper, J A Afford

Fall of wickets: 1-5, 2-17, 3-149, 4-162, 5-162, 6-221, 7-234.

Bowling: Lever 11-2-43-2, Foster 11-1-40-1, Gooch 11-0-57-0, Pringle 11-1-38-1, Miller 9-0-50-1, Stephenson 2-0-12-0.

Umpires: K E Palmer & D R Shepherd

Gold Award Winner: R T Robinson
(Adjudicator: E R Dexter)

– Nottinghamshire won by three wickets –

1990

– Lancashire are all gold –

David Hughes's team were out to prove that they were the ultimate one-day wonders. Not even Ian Botham could stop them completing the first part of what they hoped would be a unique treble

If there was one man among the throng which packed Lord's on this July Saturday who was not to be envied, it was the Australian manager and former captain Bobby Simpson. To him had been given the job of nominating the player who would receive the Gold Award.

For while Lancashire (brilliant in the field and better all-round on the day) won comfortably enough, there were several performances that had Simpson pondering before he decided that the aggressive 50 scored by Mike Watkinson, together with his tidy bowling figures of two for 37, were sufficient for him to get the nod.

But there were other claimants – two more from Lancashire and just one from a rather lack-lustre Worcestershire side that lost by 69 runs. For the winners, Warren Hegg, the wicketkeeper they call Chucky at Old Trafford, was quite tremendous. He scored 31 runs from just 17 deliveries, with two fours and a six at the end of Lancashire's innings. What he lacked in elegance, he made up

Left: The Worcestershire fielders celebrate the important run-out of Michael Atherton. But at the end of the day the strong Lancashire middle order was still able to set a target too large for Worcestershire to beat

Lord's provided a glorious setting as Gehan Mendis and Graeme Fowler take the field after being put into bat

◊ GOLD AWARD WINNER 1990 ◊

Mike Watkinson

g o l d e n   m e m o r i e s

There were several contenders for the Gold Award from Lancashire's winning team, but Watkinson's all-round contribution of 50 from 79 balls and two early wickets for 37 runs gained the verdict. Watkinson made his Lancashire debut in 1982 and has contributed consistently solid all-round performances ever since, captaining the county from 1994 to 1997. By 1998 he had scored over 10,000 runs in first-class cricket, batting in the middle-order and taken over 700 wickets with his bowling, which initially was mostly at medium-pace, but turning more frequently to off-spin in the second half of his career. He also often opened the innings in one-day games. His talents were belatedly recognised by England as he played in four Tests and one limited-overs international in 1995-6 at the age of 34.

Gold Award winner Mike Watkinson (right) holds the Cup with the Lancashire captain David Hughes

Umpire John Hampshire admires Mike Watkinson carving away a boundary during his innings of 50

A packed Lord's crowd appreciate the sunshine and the cricket

for with his belligerence – and he ensured that his team reached a total (241) that had looked very distant earlier in the afternoon. Then behind the stumps Hegg gave a display that marked him out as one of the keepers England would soon be looking at. It was not just his three catches but the all-round performance that had a touch of real class about it.

Then there was Wasim Akram. Twenty-four a month earlier, left-arm and very fast, he came on as first change. Finding a length and angling the ball across the right-hander's body towards the slips, he tore the heart out of Worcestershire by dismissing Tim Curtis with his second ball, followed by Graeme Hick and Phil Newport.

It was, of course, the Hick dismissal that was so decisive. Two years before in a Lord's final, Hick had been found wanting. Akram knew this and he showed no mercy. The first ball was fearfully fast, a bouncer but a no-ball. Then there was

Phillip DeFreitas made a quick-fire 28 before he charged down the wicket to Stuart Lampitt and was bowled

Wasim Akram was a strong contender for the Gold Award. After hitting 28 runs quickly he tore in to take three wickets at a cost of 30 runs

A vital wicket causes mass jubilation in the Lancashire camp: Warren Hegg catches Graeme Hick off the bowling of Wasim Akram

1989 IN CRICKET
Mike Gatting's rebel tour of South Africa is abandoned due to the release of **Nelson Mandela**... **Graham Gooch**'s England win their first Test against West Indies for 16 years but lose the series 2-1 after **Desmond Haynes** slows down a game to avoid another defeat... **Richard Hadlee** is the first bowler to take 400 Test wickets. He retires and is knighted... India's **Kapil Dev** hits a record four sixes in four balls to save the follow-on at Lord's but **Gooch** outdoes him with 333 and 123 to give England victory.

1989 IN SPORT
Stephen Hendry becomes snooker's youngest world champion at 21... **Mike Tyson** is KO'd by **Buster Douglas** in Tokyo... Farmer's horse **Norton's Coin** at 100-1 shocks **Desert Orchid** to win the Cheltenham Gold Cup... **Monica Seles**, 16, is the youngest winner of a Grand Slam title since 1887... **Bobby Robson**'s England reach the World Cup semi-final in Italy; **Paul Gascoigne** cries when booked... **Steve Backley** breaks the javelin world record... **Ayrton Senna** wins the F1 title when he crashes into rival **Alain Prost** at the final Grand Prix... **Nick Faldo** retains the US Masters and wins the Open by five shots... **Lester Piggott** returns from five years in retirement (and one year in jail) to win the US Breeders' Cup Mile on Royal Academy.

It was already crisis time when he went out to bat. Three down and 41 on the board meant some Botham magic was called for.

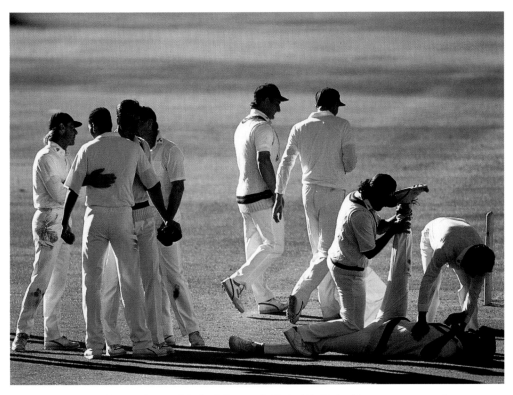

Phillip DeFreitas has just dismissed Richard Illingworth (lbw) while Wasim Akram gets treatment for cramp

LORD'S • 14TH JULY

– Lancashire –

G D Mendis, c Neale, b Botham	19
G Fowler, c Neale, b Newport	11
M A Atherton, run out	40
N H Fairbrother, b Lampitt	11
M Watkinson, c & b Botham	50
Wasim Akram, c Radford, b Newport	28
P A J DeFreitas, b Lampitt	28
I D Austin, run out	17
†W K Hegg, not out	31
*D P Hughes, not out	1
Extras (lb 4, nb 1)	5
Total *(55 overs, for 8 wkts)*	**241**

Did not bat: P J W Allott

Fall of wickets: 1-25, 2-33, 3-47, 4-135, 5-136, 6-191, 7-199, 8-231.

Bowling: Newport 11-1-47-2, Botham 11-0-49-2, Lampitt 11-3-43-2, Radford 8-1-41-0, Illingworth 11-0-41-0, Hick 3-0-16-0.

– Worcestershire –
won the toss

T S Curtis, c Hegg, b Wasim Akram	16
M J Weston, b Watkinson	19
G A Hick, c Hegg, b Wasim Akram	1
D B d'Oliveira, b Watkinson	23
I T Botham, b DeFreitas	38
*P A Neale, c Hegg, b Austin	0
†S J Rhodes, lbw, b Allott	5
N V Radford, not out	26
R K Illingworth, lbw, b DeFreitas	16
P J Newport, b Wasim Akram	3
S R Lampitt, b Austin	4
Extras (lb 9, w 8, nb 4)	21
Total *(54 overs)*	**172**

Fall of wickets: 1-27, 2-38, 3-41, 4-82, 5-87, 6-112, 7-114, 8-154, 9-164, 10-172.

Bowling: Allott 10-1-22-1, DeFreitas 11-2-30-2, Wasim Akram 11-0-30-3, Watkinson 11-0-37-2, Austin 11-1-44-2.

Umpires: J H Hampshire & N T Plews

Gold Award Winner: M Watkinson
(Adjudicator: R B Simpson)

– Lancashire won by 69 runs –

a roar for leg before, but Hick survived. His 12th ball saw him walking back to the pavilion, caught Hegg bowled Akram.

Akram had already backed up his claim for the Gold Award with a sparkling knock that delighted the crowd. Two sixes in an over off the barely fit Neal Radford were massive; one square and the other powered straight into the top of the Pavilion. Watkinson and Michael Atherton had laid the foundations of a big total with a partnership of 88 before they fell in close succession to leave Lancashire still not out of the woods at 136 for five. Akram and DeFreitas then blasted 55 in eight overs to set up Hegg's blaze of glory.

Worcestershire's Gold Award contender was – who else? – Ian Botham. He bowled as well as anyone, taking the wickets of Gehan Mendis and Watkinson. It was already crisis time when he went out to bat. Three down and 41 on the board meant some Botham magic was called for. He did his best, doubling the score with Damian d'O-

liveira, keeping his wicket intact as his partners lost theirs. When Botham was bowled out, trying to pull a straight ball from DeFreitas, to leave the score on 114 for seven, the game was up.

So Worcester went away from their sixth Lord's final beaten for a sixth time and Watkinson marched off with the Benson and Hedges Gold Award.

Later that summer, Lancashire won the NatWest Bank Trophy to become the first team to win both Lord's finals in the same season. And if the weather had not wiped out two of their games in the Sunday League, they probably would have won that as well.

Britannic Assurance County Champions:
Middlesex
Refuge Assurance League Champions:
Derbyshire
NatWest Bank Trophy Winners: Lancashire

1991

– Hick is the saving grace –

Graeme Hick's reputation was on the line. Could he produce the big innings for the big occasion? Lancashire discovered that, yes, he could – and Worcestershire happily avenged their 1990 defeat

Nineteen ninety, the rematch. Lancashire and Worcestershire were old adversaries with scores to settle, and it showed. On a grey, damp day, far from what you expect in July, they circled each other warily.

Lancashire, winners by 69 runs after being put in by Worcestershire 12 months before, now gave their victims first knock and seemed intent on boring them to another defeat. Instead of bowling their overs within three hours and 25 minutes, as stipulated, Lancashire spent a lamentable four hours over their task.

The umpires warned Neil Fairbrother about the slow play four times. This was to cost them a £500 fine and, coupled with the gloom, it meant that the game would go over into Sunday, denying a sell-out crowd the pleasure of seeing the Cup

The Cup, medals and pennants await the winners

won and lost. If it had not been for Graeme Hick, many would have departed on Saturday evening thoroughly disillusioned.

But Hick's battle with himself, as well as with the best attack in the one-day game, was worth the entrance money in its own right.

The Zimbabwean had waited seven years to qualify for England and had begun his Test career being

Right: A view from the new Compton stand at Lord's during the 1991 final between Lancashire and Worcestershire

talked of as a latter-day Bradman. The West Indian quicks had exposed him as mortal, however, and this Final was a watershed. Hick knew that if he failed again, his brief Test career might be over. Too many times before had he fuelled the belief that he couldn't do it when it mattered and here, in the drizzle, came judgement day.

Nor had he long to wait. Tim Curtis played on to the sixth ball of the match which came back at him from Phil DeFreitas and Hick was marching down the Pavilion steps, the score four for one and the wicket no doubt looming like a scaffold. With coach Basil d'Oliveira's words still ringing in

GOLD AWARD WINNER 1991

Graeme Hick

g o l d e n   m e m o r i e s

h ick scored 88 off 126 balls and took three catches at second slip to ensure his selection as the Gold Award winner. A tall, natural games player, Hick has been the most prolific scorer in first-class cricket from his debut in 1983/4 in Zimbabwe and for Worcestershire from 1984. In 1998, at the age of 32, be became the second youngest man ever to score 100 first-class centuries, just 15 days older than Wally Hammond, and his 574 innings to that milestone has been bettered only by Don Bradman and Denis Compton. He is an excellent fielder, a very safe pair of hands in the slips or an outfield with a powerful throw, and a useful off-break bowler. His Test career, long delayed while he took seven years to qualify to play for England, took a while to develop, and he has not managed to cement the place which his talents deserve, although he has had his successes. At county level and often in one-day internationals his power destroys bowling attacks.

Hick hooks Wasim Akram for four during his 88

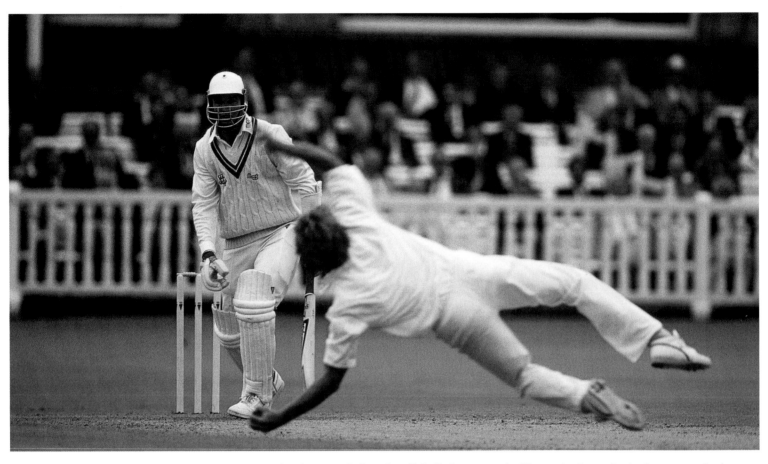

It was going to take something special to remove Graeme Hick and it was Paul Allott who pulled off a fantastic catch off his own bowling to dismiss the master stroke-player

his ears – 'Be positive, that was how you became a good player' -- he square cut his first ball for four. It was the launch pad to two-and-a-half hours' adventurous batting, to a Worcestershire victory at the seventh time of asking in a Lord's final and to the accolade of the Gold Award.

In the appalling conditions he hooked, he pulled and he drove quite magnificently – helped, perhaps, by a curious decision in the Lancashire dressing room. David Hughes, who had captained Lancashire to two one-day titles the previous year, had dropped himself to strengthen the team's batting. His stand-in, Neil Fairbrother, ignored Hick's 1990 nemesis, Wasim Akram, until the 15th over. Had Akram been unleashed earlier, Hick might not have prospered as he did. In the event, he was just 12 short of a richly deserved century when Paul Allott caught him quite stupendously, left-handed and at full stretch, off his own bowling.

Despite Hick's brilliance, Worcestershire were hardly in the driving seat at 166 for four. Another good knock was needed – but Botham, going for a six, was caught on the boundary; Phil Neale sliced to third man; Steve Rhodes and Phil Newport both skied Akram into safe hands; and Worcestershire were 203 for eight as Neal Radford joined Richard Illingworth. They resisted with stiffened sinews, pilfering 33 runs from the last three overs

With seven overs and four balls remaining, and 65 runs to spare, Worcestershire had won their first one-day trophy at Lord's in 28 years in an almost exact reversal of the previous year's result

and carrying their side to 236 and respectability.

Before the umpires were forced to call it a day after 18 overs (in 73 minutes!), Radford unzipped Lancashire's defences. He bowled the big danger, Gehan Mendis, and moved one away from Mike Atherton to give Warren Hegg a catch behind. With the run-out of Fairbrother, the one-day specialist, Lancashire were 32 for three. While Graeme Fowler and Graham Lloyd held firm until the close, they had an uneasy night ahead of them.

Sunday dawned considerably brighter, dry and

Never one to shy away from a challenge, Ian Botham hooks Mike Watkinson and ends up being caught by Graeme Fowler

Lancashire and England opener Graeme Fowler found good form to top score for Lancashire with 54 stylish runs

1991 IN CRICKET

New Zealand's **Martin Crowe** and **Andrew Jones** set a world record Test partnership of 467 against Sri Lanka… **Graham Gooch**'s England are beaten 3-0 in Australia. During a bad-tempered tour, **David Gower** and **John Morris** are fined £1,000 for 'buzzing' the field of play from a hired Tiger Moth… England draw 2-2 with **Viv Richards**' West Indies. **Gooch** carries his bat for 154 out of 252 to win the First Test. **Graeme Hick** makes his Test debut, but after all the hype it's a damp squib… **Ian Botham** and **Dean Jones** join County Cricket new boys Durham… **Gooch** hits 259 in the final Championship match of the season against Middlesex to clinch the title for Essex.

1991 IN SPORT

Kenny Dalglish quits Liverpool at the top of the table, and later becomes Blackburn manager… **Diego Maradona** tests positive for cocaine… **George Foreman** goes the distance with **Evander Holyfield** at 42… **Mark Hughes** scores twice against his old club Barcelona as Manchester United win the Cup Winners' Cup… **Paul Gascoigne**'s free kick against Arsenal takes Spurs to the FA Cup Final, where he injures himself in a mad tackle on Forest's **Gary Charles**… Long-hitting rookie **John Daly** wins the US PGA — his third pro tournament… **Bernhard Langer** misses a six-foot putt which would have retained the Ryder Cup… **Desert Orchid** retires… Australia win the second rugby union World Cup… **Michael Watson** is left in a coma by **Chris Eubank**…. **Mike Powell** beats **Bob Beamon**'s 23-year-old long jump record.

A major blow to Lancashire was the run-out of Pakistan all-rounder Wasim Akram by Richard Illingworth

Victory is sealed and it's a dash for the trophies

Revenge for 1990 as Worcestershire captain Phil Neale celebrates victory over Lancashire with Graeme Hick

sunny. The crowd, let in free, sat in shirt sleeves and it all seemed terribly predictable as Worcestershire took control. Hick snaffled three catches at second slip and once Fowler had gone, Lancashire simply expired.

With seven overs and four balls remaining, and 65 runs to spare, Worcestershire had won their first one-day trophy at Lord's in 28 years in an almost exact reversal of the previous year's result. The scorelines were a mirror image; only the name of the team on the trophy was different.

The public address system failed as Denis Compton named Hick his Gold Award winner but the lights had gone out for Lancashire much earlier.

Britannic Assurance County Champions: Essex
Refuge Assurance League Champions: Nottinghamshire
NatWest Bank Trophy Winners: Hampshire

◊ FINAL SCOREBOARD 1991 ◊

LORD'S • 13TH, 14TH JULY

– Worcestershire –

T S Curtis, b DeFreitas	4
T M Moody, b Allott	12
G A Hick, c & b Allott	88
D B d'Oliveira, c DeFreitas, b Wasim Akram	25
I T Botham, c Fowler, b Watkinson	19
*P A Neale, c Watkinson, b Austin	4
†S J Rhodes, c Allott, b Wasim Akram	13
R K Illingwoth, not out	17
P J Newport, c DeFreitas, b Wasim Akrim	2
N V Radford, not out	25
Extras (lb 8, w 15, nb 4)	27
Total (55 overs, for 8 wkts)	**236**

Did not bat: G R Dilley

Fall of wickets: 1-4, 2-38, 3-97, 4-166, 5-172, 6-175, 7-195, 8-203.

Bowling: DeFreitas 11-1-38-1, Allott 11-3-26-2, Watkinson 11-0-54-1, Wasim Akram 11-1-58-3, Austin 11-0-52-1.

– Lancashire –

won the toss

G D Mendis, b Radford	14
G Fowler, c Hick, b Radford	54
M A Atherton, c Rhodes, b Radford	5
N H Fairbrother, run out	1
G D Lloyd, c Hick, b Botham	10
M Watkinson, c Hick, b Dilley	13
Wasim Akram, run out	14
P A J DeFreitas, c Neale, b Newport	19
†W K Hegg, not out	13
I D Austin, c Illingworth, b Newport	7
P J W Allott, c Neale, b Dilley	10
Extras (lb 5, w 4, nb 2)	11
Total (47.2 overs)	**171**

Fall of wickets: 1-24, 2-31, 3-32, 4-64, 5-92, 6-111, 7-134, 8-140, 9-158, 10-171.

Bowling: Dilley 8.2-2-19-2, Radford 9-1-48-3, Botham 8-1-23-1, Newport 11-1-38-2, Illingworth 11-0-38-0.

Umpires: J W Holder & D W Shepherd

Gold Award Winner: G A Hick
(Adjudicator: D C S Compton)

– Worcestershire won by 65 runs –

1992

– The Judge sentences Kent to defeat –

There are few finer sights than Robin Smith at his aggressive best, and on this day 'The Judge' was not be overruled. With Malcolm Marshall also wreaking havoc, Kent were subjected to a trial by fire

This was a meeting of two teams who had played each other only days before in the NatWest. Kent had been the victors, and must have hoped to repeat the feat at Lord's. But Malcolm Marshall, David Gower, Robin Smith & co were saving their fire for a bigger stage.

The weather forecast was so bad there were fears that the game might even go into a third day, but happily the conditions improved on Sunday morning and Hampshire completed a 41-run victory by early afternoon with 15 balls to spare.

Mark Benson won the toss and asked

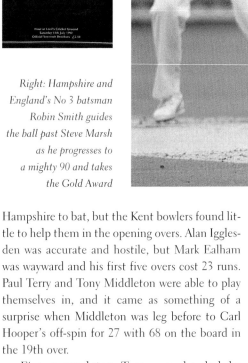

Right: Hampshire and England's No 3 batsman Robin Smith guides the ball past Steve Marsh as he progresses to a mighty 90 and takes the Gold Award

Hampshire to bat, but the Kent bowlers found little to help them in the opening overs. Alan Igglesden was accurate and hostile, but Mark Ealham was wayward and his first five overs cost 23 runs. Paul Terry and Tony Middleton were able to play themselves in, and it came as something of a surprise when Middleton was leg before to Carl Hooper's off-spin for 27 with 68 on the board in the 19th over.

Five overs later, Terry was bowled by Igglesden, but Hampshire had been given an

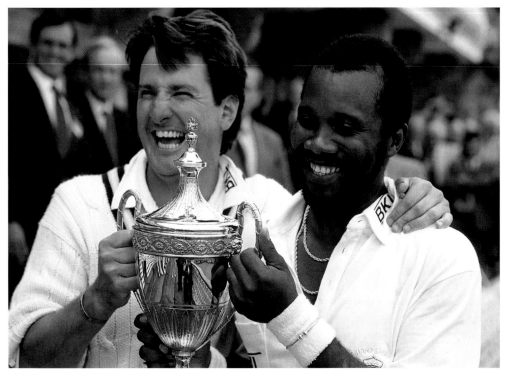

Mark Nicholas and Malcolm Marshall enjoying the media attention after beating Kent.

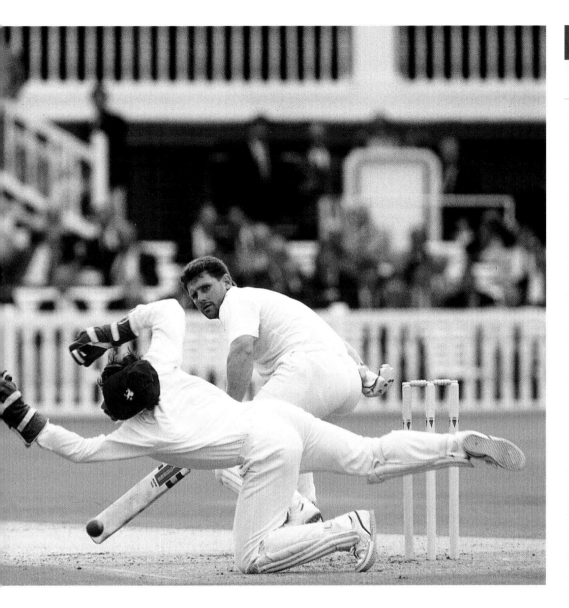

Robin Smith

g o l d e n   m e m o r i e s

Smith's 90 off 108 balls ensured that Hampshire had a comfortable victory in this rain-affected game. Oddly enough this success came in the middle of Smith's least successful season in county cricket for Hampshire. A teenage prodigy and a natural athlete who had excelled at athletics and rugby union as well as cricket, he followed his elder brother, Chris, to Hampshire in 1982, having made his first-class debut for Natal in his native South Africa. 'The Judge' made his Test debut in 1987 and was soon established as an England regular. His Test record of 4,236 runs at an average of 43.67 clearly matches his proven class, but he last played in 1996 after doubts about his ability to cope with top-class spin bowling (notably Shane Warne, Mushtaq Ahmed and Anil Kumble) had increased. He has a superb record in Benson and Hedges matches and took over as Hampshire captain in 1998.

The Gold Award winner was in awesome form

excellent start and Robin Smith was in the sort of bludgeoning form which ensured that they kept their momentum. David Gower, in contrast, was strangely subdued and his 29 took more than an hour, came off 52 balls and did not include a boundary. But 85 runs were added for the third wicket before Gower was leg before to Matthew Fleming and Kent knew that they were going to have to chase a large total.

Mark Nicholas then joined Smith and, having missed Hampshire's NatWest victory the previous year because of injury, he was particularly anxious to do well. He did not let himself or his side down, scoring 25 of a fourth-wicket stand worth 34 and hitting the first six of the day as well as two fours, before becoming Fleming's second victim. But Fleming had proved very expensive, going for 63 runs in eight overs – whereas Richard Davis, who only conceded 18 in five overs, was not asked to bowl again.

When Nicholas was out, Malcolm Marshall strode to the middle, equally anxious to succeed,

An unusually subdued David Gower gave useful support to Robin Smith and took a couple of catches

Carl Hooper finds a gap in the legside field

Hooper joined Benson
and this was obviously
the crucial partnership
if Kent were to have any
chance of reaching the
target. They added 78
together and Hampshire
appeared to be wilting
under the pressure…

as a Lord's Cup-winner's medal was one accolade he had not achieved in his long and distinguished career. He took the tail end of the Hampshire innings by the scruff of the neck, hit a six and two fours while making 29 off only 22 deliveries, and saw Hampshire to a formidable total of 253 for five in their 55 overs.

This meant that if Kent were to win, they would have to make the highest total by a side batting second to win a Benson and Hedges Cup Final – and the conditions were anything but ideal. Only eight balls were bowled, in fact, before the umpires decided that the conditions were unfair, and when drizzle set in to accompany the appalling light, there could be no argument about their decision.

So it was back to Lord's on Sunday morning with the weather happily in a better mood. It was bright and breezy, which was just what the Kent batting needed to be, but was not. Trevor Ward played and missed several times before he eventually got a touch to a magnificent Marshall delivery to give Bobby Parks the first of his two catches. Neil Taylor chased a wide one from Jonathan Ayling. Parks did the necessary once again and Kent were struggling at 43 for two off 20 overs.

Hooper joined Benson and this was obviously the crucial partnership for Kent if they were to have any chance of reaching their target. 78 were added for the third wicket and Hampshire appeared to be wilting under the pressure with far too many runs given away through sloppy fielding.

Just in time, they pulled themselves together. Kevan James bowled Benson – just reward for an economic spell – and then Shaun Udal took the first of his three wickets, bowling Hooper for 28 off his pads.

Fleming started the afternoon with some lusty blows, but he was brilliantly caught by Nicholas at mid-off and then Marshall took over to mop up the tail with the help of another spectacular catch; this one by Gower at slip.

The last five Kent wickets fell for the addition of only 30 runs in four overs and Hampshire

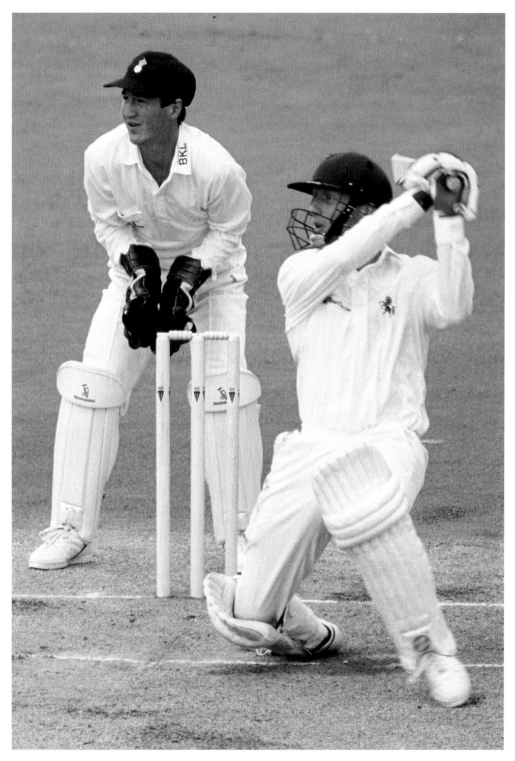

Matthew Fleming, one of the best one-day players in England, attempts to get the scoreboard moving for Kent

Cardigan Connor cannot hide his delight at bowling Mark Ealham, who represented the last real threat

David Gower knows that catches win matches

1992 IN CRICKET

England reach their third World Cup final – and lose their third World Cup Final, as **Imran Khan**'s Pakistan beat **Graham Gooch**'s team by 22 runs in Melbourne...

West Indies beat South Africa in the first Test between the two countries.... Pakistan are accused of ball tampering after the umpires change the ball in a one-day match at Lord's. **Allan Lamb** and **Sarfraz Nawaz** end up battling it out in court...

Keith Fletcher becomes the England team manager.

1992 IN SPORT

Kevin Keegan replaces **Ossie Ardiles** as Newcastle manager and saves them from relegation to Third Division... **Mike Tyson** is jailed for rape... **Will Carling**'s England do their second consecutive Five Nations Grand Slam with a record 118 points... **Eric Cantona** inspires Leeds to the League title, then is transferred to Manchester United... **Andre Agassi** wins Wimbledon at his second attempt... **Martin Offiah** scores twice as Wigan beat Castleford 28-12 to win their fifth successive Challenge Cup... **Graham Taylor**'s England crash out of the European Championships. Captain **Gary Lineker**, stuck on 48 goals (one short of Bobby Charlton's record) is substituted during the Sweden game... At the Barcelona Olympics, **Linford Christie** wins the 100 metres, **Sally Gunnell** wins the 400m hurdles, and **Steve Redgrave** wins his third rowing gold in a row. **Carl Lewis** wins his eighth gold, anchoring the USA 4x100m relay team to a world record, then retires... **Nick Faldo** breaks down in tears as he wins his third Open... **Nigel Mansell** wins the Formula One world title then quits Williams in a contractual dispute and goes to IndyCar.

completed their victory in time for those of us with enough enthusiasm to get to The Oval for most of the Sunday League match.

Malcolm Marshall finished with three for 33 and, together with his 29 not out at the end of the Hampshire innings, was most people's choice for the Gold Award. But Mickey Stewart decided that Robin Smith's 90 was the innings that had won the match for Hampshire, and so 'The Judge' got the verdict.

Britannic Assurance County Champions: Essex
Refuge Assurance League Champions: Middlesex
NatWest Bank Trophy Winners: Northamptonshire

Job well done! Gold Award winner Robin Smith and victorious captain Mark Nicholas

◗ FINAL SCOREBOARD 1992 ◗

LORD'S • 11TH, 12TH JULY

– Hampshire –

V P Terry, b Igglesden	41
T C Middleton, lbw, b Hooper	27
R A Smith, run out	90
D I Gower, lbw, b Fleming	29
*M C J Nicholas, c Ealham, b Fleming	25
M D Marshall, not out	29
K D James, not out	2
Extras (lb 3, w 3, nb 4)	10
Total (*55 overs, for 5 wkts*)	**253**

Did not bat: J R Ayling, †R J Parks, S D Udal, C A Connor

Fall of wickets: 1-68, 2-86, 3-171, 4-205, 5-234.

Bowling: Igglesden 11-1-39-1, Ealham 9-0-46-0, McCague 11-0-43-0, Hooper 11-1-41-1, Davis 5-0-18-0, Fleming 8-0-63-2.

– Kent –
won the toss

T R Ward, c Parks, b Marshall	5
*M R Benson, b James	59
N R Taylor, c Parks, b Ayling	8
C L Hooper, b Udal	28
G R Cowdrey, c Gower, b Marshall	27
M V Fleming, c Nicholas, b Ayling	32
†S A Marsh, b Udal	7
M A Ealham, b Connor	23
M J McCague, b Udal	0
R P Davis, c Gower, b Marshall	1
A P Igglesden, not out	1
Extras (b 1, lb 11, w 5, nb 4)	21
Total (*52.3 overs*)	**212**

Fall of wickets: 1-17, 2-38, 3-116, 4-116, 5-171, 6-182, 7-186, 8-194, 9-204, 10-212.

Bowling: Connor 9.3-2-27-1, Marshall 10-1-33-3, Ayling 11-0-38-2, James 11-1-35-1, Udal 11-0-67-3.

Umpires: J H Hampshire & M J Kitchen

Gold Award Winner: R A Smith
(*Adjudicator: M J Stewart*)

– Hampshire won by 41 runs –

1993
– Every underdog has its day –

When Derbyshire reached the B&H Cup Final and found themselves facing mighty Lancashire, it looked like a bit of a walkover. But Dominic Cork was no respecter of reputations…

I t was the year of the underdog. No one really expected Derbyshire to win the Benson and Hedges Cup Final. Well, let's face it … no one expected them to win anything in 1993. It was going to be a triumph if they survived as one of the 18 County clubs.

Yet, short of money, though they may have been (they were desperately seeking financial help from the Test and County Cricket Board), they were never lacking faith. They went to Lord's

in July believing they were good enough to overturn the odds and Lancashire. As, of course, they did, if only after one of the most dramatic matches that Lord's has staged.

There was huffing and puffing between the two sides even before they reached the Final. Derbyshire's Chris Adams had, two weeks before in a Britannic County Championship match between the two, jestingly asked if he might inspect the ball being bowled – and swung

Neil Fairbrother batted supremely well for his 87 not out, but the Derbyshire target just eluded him and Lancashire

Dominic Cork

g o l d e n   m e m o r i e s

Cork has become best known as a fast-medium swing bowler, but his figures in this final were a modest 1-50 as it was his flamboyant batting that brought him the Gold Award – he hit 92 not out from 124 balls, then his highest county score in any competition. Cork was in his fourth season in first-class cricket, having joined Derbyshire from Minor County Staffordshire, and he had already played for England's one-day team, but it was another two years before he was called up for Tests. Then he made a sensational debut, taking seven for 43 in the second innings against the West Indies at Lord's. In his third Test, at Old Trafford, he took a hat-trick. Some injury problems have held him back, but he was back in the Test team in 1998, when he made a great success of taking over the captaincy of a county troubled by disaffection the previous year.

Dominic Cork was never afraid to celebrate

disconcertingly – by Wasim Akram. Wasim and his Lancashire teammates felt this inferred they were tampering with the ball. Derbyshire later sent the ball to the TCCB for inspection, which was officially the end of the matter. Unofficially, it still rumbled on. Confrontation was inevitable.

Derbyshire batted, and were a modest 32 for two when Adams joined John Morris. Wasim bowled a high full toss – a beamer – at him. Adams was felled, the ground (not to mention the Derbyshire dressing room) was in uproar and the tension was, well … pretty tense. Adams departed swiftly, Wasim bowled less so, the two had a lunch-room confrontation – and Derbyshire consolidated after their poor start.

Dominic Cork was the hero. He had already been suggested as a successor to Botham, but he was only 21 and was still two years away from his first Test cap. He came in after just 16 overs, with Derbyshire rocking at 66 for four, and laid down a

Chris Adams receives treatment after being hit by a controversial 'beamer' from Wasim Akram

1993 IN CRICKET

Graham Gooch's England leave **David Gower** at home for the winter tour of India and Sri Lanka, and lose all four Tests... **Shane Warne**'s magic first ball in Tests in England bamboozles **Mike Gatting**, bowling him behind his pads. With Australia leading 3-0 after four Tests, Gooch quits as captain. England win the final Test of the series and Gooch overtakes Gower to become England's top run-scorer.

1993 IN SPORT

Lennox Lewis beats **Frank Bruno** in the first world heavyweight fight between two Britons this century... Manchester United win their last seven matches to clinch the title, inspired by **Eric Cantona**... The Grand National is declared void after two false starts when starting tapes fail to rise properly... **Jana Novotna** loses the Wimbledon final after leading Steffi Graf 4-1 in the final set... **Nigel Mansell** wins the IndyCar title... **Monica Seles** is stabbed on court in Hamburg by a Graf fan... San Marino score against England after eight seconds of their World Cup qualifier. England fail to qualify and **Graham Taylor** resigns.... England beat the All Blacks 15-9 – "Our greatest win ever," says **Will Carling**... **Sally Gunnell** and **Colin Jackson** break world records at the Stuttgart World Championships.

Wasim Akram was unusually expensive and only collected one wicket, that of Kim Barnett, bowled for 19

quality innings in a pressure situation. With Tim O'Gorman he put on 109 and then his partnership with the effervescent wicketkeeper Karl Krikken added another 77 in the final 11 overs. He was unbeaten on 92 (with seven boundaries) as Derbyshire's 55 overs expired. Bothamesque, indeed. Derbyshire posted a total of 252 for six. Lancashire needed more to win than any team before batting second in a 55-over final.

It was all wonderful stuff (aided in fairness by slightly inept Lancashire bowling and very inept fielding) but tended towards the frenetic. Derbyshire's anxiety one could understand, stemming from a poor start and fanned by the flames licking around their very existence. Lancashire? Perhaps the Wasim beamer had an effect. Perhaps they thought it was going to be all too easy. And despite losing Stephen Titchard at nine in the second over, so it must have seemed for a while. Nick Speak and Michael Atherton carried Lancashire to 80 before Speak was bowled by Ole Mortensen. Then the rain came down…

When play restarted 70 minutes later, at around 7.10pm, Lancashire should have been in command. They required 112 to win off 17 overs with eight wickets in hand. A team of old hands at the one-day game should have seen the underdogs off. Yet it was Derbyshire who kept their nerve, and Derbyshire who went on 80 minutes later to collect the (for them crucial) £30,000 winners' cheque which had their bank manager cheering louder than any other Derbyshire supporter.

Atherton and Fairbrother had taken the score along to 150 for two before Atherton, the sheet anchor, was caught and bowled by Griffith. Graham Lloyd and Wasim Akram both fell to Allan Warner, whose three for 31 was the highlight of the season for this deceptive spin bowler.

Thus, and not for the first time, Lancashire were looking to their captain, Neil Fairbrother. And well though he batted and bustled for his unbeaten 87 off 85 balls, his side went to the penultimate over requiring 21 and the final one still needing 11.

Kim Barnett, with a confidence others might

Derbyshire celebrate as Lancashire opener Stephen Titchard departs for a duck with the score on nine

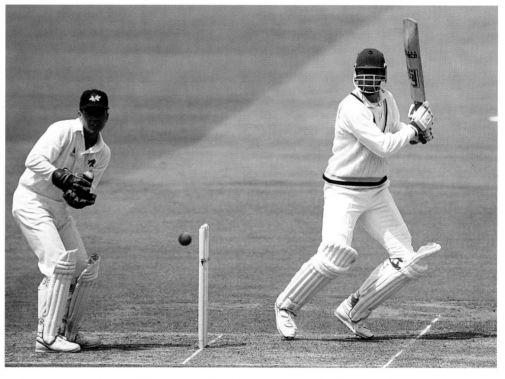

Warren Hegg watches as Gold Award winner Dominic Cork strokes another boundary in his score of 92 not out

MIKE ATHERTON
SURREY V LANCASHIRE: 11TH MAY 1993

FOR TWO SEASONS – 1993 AND 1994 – THE BENSON AND HEDGES CUP WAS PLAYED AS A PURE KNOCKOUT, INSTEAD OF HAVING THE GROUP LEAGUES TO DECIDE THE QUARTER-FINALISTS. IT REQUIRED A PRELIMINARY ROUND WHICH, IN 1993, SAW THE ELIMINATION OF KENT AND GLOUCESTERSHIRE BEFORE THE END OF APRIL. IN MAY, LANCASHIRE TRAVELLED TO THE OVAL FOR A FIRST-ROUND MATCH...

Historically the Benson and Hedges match between Surrey and Lancashire in 1993 may be remembered as the first match in which the third umpire was called upon to adjudicate a run-out. Indeed, presaging many of the problems since its introduction, it was highly ironic that the first time it was needed, the BBC failed to find the correct pictures and Wasim Akram was erroneously given in. Without the third umpire he would surely have gone. Instead he remained and smashed a potentially match-winning 38. Amidst the present debate over widening the use of television replays, it is worth recalling this incident and remembering that, no matter what, there will always be doubtful occasions in cricket. It is part of the game.

It is unlikely, though, that the players involved will recall this match as the first in which technology intervened. Most will remember the remarkable way in which Surrey collapsed from a seemingly invincible 212 for one to 230 all out, six runs short of victory.

The morning was humid and Alec Stewart called correctly and chose rightly to bowl. Early movement pegged Lancashire back and only Wasim Akram and Neil Fairbrother (87) steered us to a total that was seemingly insufficient.

Stewart and Thorpe, during a classy 211 partnership, took Surrey to the brink of victory. Indeed, it was such a foregone conclusion that Henry Blofield and Martin Johnson, who were covering the game, left early. 'Scoop' Johnson, having written it up as a Surrey win, left for dinner in London. 'Blowers', likewise, had a dinner engagement and had sent in his copy and left the result blank for his 'sub' to fill in. He must surely have choked on his caviar and

Graham Thorpe must have thought his century had won the match

Burgundy, when he rang through to check copy that evening. For, as cricket all too often reminds us, nothing is ever certain. Stewart was bowled by Martin, wafting from the crease, and there followed an extraordinary collapse. Lynch was caught down the leg side. Thorpe reached his century before being caught at mid on, and must still have thought his innings had won the match. But then Ward was caught at mid off, Brown lbw, Butcher bowled, Waqar Younis bowled and, when Boiling was run out, we had recorded an improbable victory by six runs.

Most of us, after that victory, felt that Lancashire's name was on the cup. Several bets were taken by Mr W Hill to that effect. It would be nice to record a happy ending, but I'm afraid Derbyshire spiked our guns in the Final.

No matter; Lancashire-Surrey matches are always keenly contested. There are many England players on either side, which always increases the edge, and May 11th 1993 was the sweetest victory of them all.

Lancashire 236 (54.1 overs)
(N H Fairbrother 87; M A Atherton 11;
M P Bicknell 3-27)
Surrey 230 (55 overs) (G P Thorpe 103;
A J Stewart 95; I D Austin 3-40)
Lancashire won by six runs

Above: Phillip DeFreitas appeals unsuccessfully for lbw against Dominic Cork

Fairbrother and DeFreitas after O'Gorman's dismissal.
Below: All smiles at the trophy presentation

have lacked, saved medium-pacer Frank Griffith for the final over. Lancashire hopes rose, as Mike Watkinson recalls:

"Harvey (Neil Fairbrother) had batted magnificently. With him facing their youngster, Frankie Griffith, we thought we had a real chance. Griffith had already conceded over 50 runs. But he produced a superb over and that was it."

Griffith bowled without apparent nerves, perfectly accurately, and even picked up the wicket of Phillip DeFreitas into the bargain. Griffith epitomised the Derbyshire effort: he kept his nerve as they had done; he was committed, as they were the more committed. Lancashire ended up six runs short.

One could feel sorry for Fairbrother, proving again a giant in the one-day game. But Derbyshire could always point to Cork, who can look to this match as the one in which he came of age on the big scene.

Britannic Assurance County Champions: Middlesex
AXA Equity & Law League Champions: Glamorgan
NatWest Trophy Winners: Warwickshire

◗ FINAL SCOREBOARD 1993 ◗

LORD'S • 10TH JULY

— Derbyshire —
won the toss

*K J Barnett, b Wasim Akram	19
P D Bowler, lbw, b DeFreitas	4
J E Morris, c Hegg, b Watkinson	22
C J Adams, b Watkinson	11
T J O'Gorman, c Hegg, b DeFreitas	49
D G Cork, not out	92
F A Griffith, c Hegg, b DeFreitas	0
†K M Krikken, not out	37
Extras (b 1, lb 11, w 1, nb 5)	18
Total *(55 overs, 6 wkts)*	**252**

Did not bat: A E Warner, D E Malcolm, O H Mortensen

Fall of wickets: 1-7, 2-32, 3-61, 4-66, 5-175, 6-175.

Bowling: Austin 11-2-47-0, DeFreitas 11-2-39-3, Wasim Akram 11-0-65-1, Watkinson 11-2-44-2, Barnett 11-0-45-0.

— Lancashire —
won the toss

M A Atherton, c & b Griffith	54
S P Titchard, c Adams, b Warner	0
N J Speak, b Mortensen	42
*N H Fairbrother, not out	87
G D Lloyd, lbw, b Warner	5
Wasim Akram, c & b Warner	12
M Watkinson, b Cork	10
P A J DeFreitas, b Krikken, b Griffith	16
I D Austin, not out	0
Extras (lb 11, w 3, nb 6)	20
Total *(55 overs, for 7 wkts)*	**246**

Did not bat: †W K Hegg, A A Barnett

Fall of wickets: 1-9, 2-80, 3-150, 4-159, 5-184, 6-218, 7-243.

Bowling: Malcolm 11-0-53-0, Warner 11-1-31-3, Cork 11-1-50-1, Mortensen 11-0-41-1, Griffith 11-0-60-2.

Umpires: B J Meyer & D R Shepherd

Gold Award Winner: D G Cork
(Adjudicator: Cricket Writers' Club)

— Derbyshire won by 6 runs —

1994

– Smith makes a name for himself –

The 1994 Final was billed as the battle of the giants – Brian Lara versus Hick and Moody. But the headlines were stolen by a man who was more used to being anonymous. Well, he was called Smith…

Brian Lara is off and running with a quick single, but his innings came to a premature end when he had scored just eight

Right: Paul Smith fires in a delivery during his excellent bowling spell of 11-1-34-3

Everyone knows that 1994 was Brian Lara's annus mirabilis. In April he began rewriting the record books with his innings of 375 against England in Antigua – the highest score in a Test match. Then in June he added the highest first-class score ever to his portfolio with an astounding innings of 501 not out against Durham, the day before being his team's top scorer, with 70, in the B&H semi-final against Surrey. But do you remember what Lara scored just a month later in the Benson and Hedges Final? A crowd of 25,000 gathered to see the man of the moment score … eight runs!

In the event, it made no difference to the

Paul Smith

golden memories

S mith's all-round effort of three wickets for 34 runs and a run-a-ball 42 not out as Warwickshire secured an easy win over Worcestershire earned this talented but insecure cricketer the Gold Award. Smith played for Warwickshire from 1982 to 1996; he had a fine year with the bat, 1,508 first-class runs, in 1986, but was mostly a bits and pieces player, not always sure of his place, in the first-class game. His fast medium bowling proved to be most effective in limited-overs matches; compare for instance his first-class average of 35.72 for 283 wickets to 27.62 for 161 in the Sunday League. He was, though, a useful player to have around, capable of some quick runs or of a burst of pace to get wickets, even if he did not fulfil his promise. His father played first-class cricket for Leicestershire, and his brother David preceded him in the Warwickshire team (1973-85).

Paul Smith after dismissing Graeme Hick for 27

result, because 1994 was also Warwickshire's annus mirabilis. No county had ever won more than two trophies in an English season. In 1994 Warwickshire took an unprecedented three, and were beaten finalists in the one competition they didn't win: the NatWest.

The only really sticky part of their summer was the controversial way they reached the B&H semi-finals – by winning a "bowl-out" against Kent behind closed doors after two days of rain and imperfect pitch coverage prevented any play at Edgbaston.

Lara is credited, quite rightly, with having played a major role in Warwickshire's County Championship success. But a successful team consists of more than one man – and if ever a match proved that adage, it was this Benson and Hedges Cup Final.

The man who would dominate events was from a quite different mould to Lara. Paul Smith had never, as far as we know, broken a record. Five years older than Lara, he will never be a household name. Even the Cup Final programme notes were slightly disparaging. As Smith sat in the dressing room leafing through its glossy pages – where he read that Lara was "the supreme signing who will be the central figure today for sure" – he came upon his own mini-biography: "Born

Above: Cricket, lovely cricket… Opposite: Worcestershire's Australian star Tom Moody drives strongly on the off-side during his innings of 47

Jesmond, 13th April 1964. A talented player… A very positive right-handed batsman… A useful medium pace bowler in the one-day game. However, when he reflects upon his career he may well think that he might not have made enough of his ability down the years."

There were plenty who would argue that it was a fair point, but Smith disagreed. "I'll show him," he grumbled. And, with his captain Dermot Reeve winning the toss and inviting Worcestershire to bat on a damp pitch, he did not have long to wait to start doing so.

After a superb opening spell by Gladstone Small, who shrugged off a hamstring problem by bowling out his 11 overs, and Tim Munton, Smith joined the attack and with the panache and aggression of Ian Botham, hustled Worcestershire towards defeat. Even Graeme Hick and Tom Moody could not escape the chains of the Warwickshire medium pacers, and top scorer Moody became so desperate that he

Paul Smith came up with the match-winning performance and entertained the crowd with some bold shots

Top scorer Dominic Ostler is run out for 55

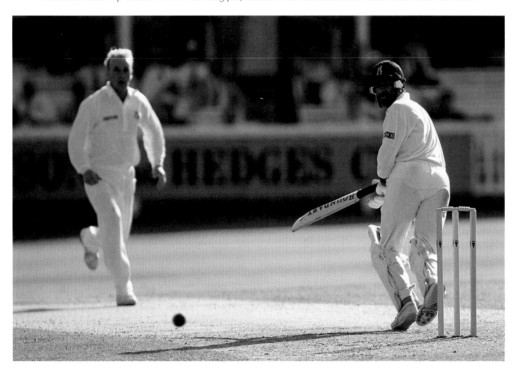

Asif Din guides the ball away down the leg side. He and Smith put on 34 to steady things after a brief flurry of wickets

1994 IN CRICKET

Brian Lara overtakes fellow West Indian **Gary Sobers** to score the highest Test innings ever – 375 against England at St John's... England, needing 194 to beat West Indies in Trinidad, are all out for 46... Lara becomes the first man to score over 500 in an innings, with 501 not out for Warwickshire against Durham at Headingley. It is his seventh century in eight innings... England captain **Michael Atherton** is accused of rubbing dirt into the ball as South Africa celebrate their return to Lord's with a victory by 356 runs.... **Devon Malcolm**, knocked over by a ball from South Africa's **Fanie de Villiers**, says "You guys are history" and takes nine for 57 in 99 balls at The Oval to level the series.

1994 IN SPORT

Tonya Harding is accused of plotting to break rival US skater **Nancy Kerrigan**'s legs... Manchester United do the Double... **Willie Carson** wins the Derby at 51... **Miguel Indurain** wins his fourth Tour de France in a row. Briton **Chris Boardman** briefly wears the yellow jersey... At the USA World Cup, Brazil beat Italy on a penalty shootout. **Maradona** is banned for taking drugs. **Andres Escobar** of Colombia is gunned down after scoring an own goal... **Ayrton Senna** and **Roland Ratzenberger** die in crashes at Imola... **Michael Schumacher** wins the title when he appears to deliberately collide with **Damon Hill** in the final Grand Prix... **George Foreman**, 45, becomes the oldest heavyweight champion.

got himself run out. Paul Smith took three for 34 as the rivals from "next door" were restricted to an inadequate 170 for nine.

On a drier pitch, Warwickshire received such a solid start that if the result wasn't assured before Worcestershire were halfway through their 55 overs, it was when openers Dominic Ostler and Roger Twose put on 91 runs in quite serene style.

There was a small flutter when Lara was caught by Hick off the bowling of Phil Newport, but that was merely the cue for Paul Smith to take centre stage again. He finished the match unbeaten on 42, and collected the Gold Award as clearly the outstanding player of the day while Warwickshire, six-wicket winners, held aloft the first of their record-breaking three trophies of the summer. And the fourth? Ah, that went to Worcestershire.

Britannic Assurance County Champions:
Warwickshire
AXA Equity & Law League Champions:
Warwickshire
NatWest Bank Trophy Winners: Worcestershire

FINAL SCOREBOARD 1994

LORD'S • 9TH JULY

– Worcestershire –

*T S Curtis, c Piper, b Small	13
A C H Seymour, b Munton	3
G A Hick, lbw, b P A Smith	27
T M Moody, run out	47
G R Haynes, c Piper, b N M K Smith	22
D A Leatherdale, c Ostler, b P A Smith	4
†S J Rhodes, lbw, b Twose	0
S R Lampitt, c Penney, b P A Smith	1
R K Illingworth, lbw, b Reeve	18
N V Radford, not out	23
P J Newport, not out	1
Extras (lb 2, w 5, nb 4)	11
Total (55 overs, for 9 wkts)	**170**

Fall of wickets: 1-10, 2-28, 3-55, 4-100, 5-124, 6-124, 7-125, 8-126, 9-168.

Bowling: Small 11-4-26-1, Munton 11-3-29-1, P A Smith 11-1-34-3, Reeve 9-1-38-1, N M K Smith 5-0-16-1, Twose 8-1-25-1.

– Warwickshire –
won the toss

D P Ostler, run out	55
R G Twose, run out	37
B C Lara, c Hick, b Newport	8
P A Smith, not out	42
Asif Din, c Rhodes, b Moody	15
*D A Reeve, not out	9
Extras (lb 1, w 5)	6
Total (44.2 overs, for 4 wkts)	**172**

Did not bat: T L Penney, †K J Piper, N M K Smith, G C Small, T A Munton

Fall of wickets: 1-91, 2-98, 3-103, 4-147.

Bowling: Moody 11-2-31-1, Newport 8-0-29-1, Lampitt 9.2-1-38-0, Ilingworth 6-0-22-0, Radford 8-0-39-0, Hick 2-0-12-0.

Umpires: H D Bird & K E Palmer

TV Replay umpire: B Leadbeater

Gold Award Winner: P A Smith
(Adjudicator: Cricket Writers' Club)

– Warwickshire won by six wickets –

Paul Smith and Dermot Reeve seem well contented with their big day out

1995

– Gold for de Silva is no consolation–

In only one Cup Final did the Gold Award go to a member of the losing side. Kent's Aravinda de Silva scored 112 off 95 balls – but Lancashire lifted the Cup and his magnificent effort was in vain

Every now and then in life you are lucky enough to be able to boast "I was there". And that is how it was for the 25,000-strong packed house at Lord's for the 1995 Benson and Hedges Cup Final. They were all there to see one of the finest one-day innings ever played – a blistering, breath-taking century from Aravinda de Silva.

When he went in, at 37 for two and chasing Lancashire's 274 for seven, Kent already had the look of losers. While he was batting, a Kent victory even seemed possible. Quick of eye and foot, scorning defence and playing with aggression and artistry, the Sri Lankan scored 112 off 95 balls. He hit three sixes and 11 fours and it was little wonder that Graham Lloyd was mobbed by his Lancashire team-

In the first over, Tim Wren bowled the ball that might have turned the match. Ironically, it was de Silva who failed to hold the catch...

mates when he held the catch that sent de Silva back to a Pavilion that roared its appreciation of a quite sensational innings.

It was only the third century in 24 Benson and Hedges Cup Finals (Graham Gooch and Viv Richards were the pace-setters) and it was the only time that the Gold Award went to a member of the losing finalists. Ian Botham had no

Cheer up, Mike – your team won! Atherton celebrates with captain Mike Watkinson

compunction in naming him; indeed, had he not done so he might have started a riot.

Thus Lancashire collected their first trophy since 1990, and did so deservedly. They had started the 1995 season like a rocket, scoring over 300 in three B&H matches against first-class

teams. In the semi-final they had come up against the previous year's losing finalists, Worcester-shire, for whom Graeme Hick and Tom Moody were in majestic form. Hick, who averaged 116 in this year's competition, scored his third B&H century of the summer. Moody added an

Michael Atherton's innings of 93 was the base upon which Lancashire built an unassailable total

Aravinda de Silva

golden memories

d e Silva deputised for Carl Hooper as Kent's overseas player in 1995, and had a hugely successful season. He came into this match in superb form, with double-centuries in his last two Championship innings, although surprisingly no fifties in 19 one-day innings for the county, and he made a wonderful hundred, his 112 coming from just 95 balls. Yet even this was not enough to take Kent to victory, and so he became the first player to win the Gold Award in a B&H Final and be on the losing side. He also bowled eight overs of off-breaks for 36 runs. Hugely popular, de Silva added to this triumph with 1,781 first-class runs for Kent that summer at an average of 59.36. Since his international debut for Sri Lanka in 1983, he has delighted limited-overs and Test crowds with some exhilarating batting, maturing into Sri Lanka's top batsman.

De Silva batting in unfettered Sri Lankan style

unbeaten 75 to set a tough target of 261. Lancashire then struggled to 169 for seven, 96 short of victory with just 11 overs and three wickets left – whereupon Wasim Akram lashed an amazing 64 off 47 balls to secure a highly unlikely last-gasp victory. Lancashire were in the mood...

Kent, on the other hand, had suffered a serious setback in the run-up to the Final. Their prolific opener and captain, Mark Benson, was out of the game with a broken finger. It was a series of five century opening partnerships between Benson and Trevor Ward that had taken Kent into the

Now he's out we can have an aerobics break! It's obvious to everyone that Fulton is lbw to Chapple for 25

Jason Gallian made a useful contribution of 36 runs

1995 IN CRICKET

Dominic Cork takes a hat-trick as England beat the West Indies by six wickets at Old Trafford... England are 344 behind South Africa in Johannesburg with four wickets down and over a day to go, but **Michael Atherton** prevents a South African victory with a magnificent rearguard action, scoring185 not out. On the same tour, teenage spinner **Paul Adams**, playing his third match, takes nine England wickets with a bizarre action as South Africa A beat the tourists.

1995 IN SPORT

Eric Cantona of Manchester United aims a karate kick at an abusive Crystal Palace supporter... **Nelson**

Mandela's South Africa win the rugby union World Cup. **Rob Andrew**'s drop goal in injury time beats Australia but **Jonah Lomu** runs over England in the semi-final... **Gerald McClellan** has emergency surgery on a blood clot on his brain after losing to **Nigel Benn**... **Frank Bruno** wins the WBC world title by beating **Oliver McCall** on points at Wembley... **Jonathan Edwards** shatters the world triple jump record... **Bernard Gallacher**'s Europe regain the Ryder Cup... Blackburn win the title thanks to the SAS — **Alan Shearer** and **Chris Sutton** — with 58 goals... **Lester Piggott** retires... **Naseem Hamed** wins the world featherweight title... **John Daly** wins the Open at St Andrews.

De Silva is finally out, caught by Graham Lloyd off the bowling of Ian Austin, so it's high-fives and cuddles all round

John Crawley showed his range of classy strokes in a memorable innings of 83, and was instrumental in Lancashire setting a target that was out of Kent's reach

semi-finals of the B&H Cup, where they put on 53 together. As Benson modestly put it: "It just so happened that Trevor and I scored a lot of runs. We've been lucky enough to see off the new ball and play on some good wickets. It might be completely different in the Final. Then we might need our other batsmen to pull their weight."

Benson's stand-in as captain, wicketkeeper Steve Marsh, won the toss and asked Mike Watkinson's team to bat. Marsh clearly hoped that the low cloud would help left-arm seamer Tim Wren, who had been extremely successful in the earlier B&H games. "Tim has bowled very well with the new ball," Benson remarked in the Cup Final programme, "and most of his wickets have been top-line batsmen. If it's a cloudy day and we bowl first, Tim will be a dangerous proposition." Benson's words were prophetic. In

ARAVINDA DE SILVA

KENT V LANCASHIRE: THE FINAL, 15TH JULY 1995

ONLY THREE HUNDREDS WERE MADE IN BENSON AND HEDGES CUP FINALS.
ONLY ONE OF THOSE WAS ON THE LOSING SIDE, BUT IT IS AN INNINGS
WHICH STAYS IN THE MEMORY OF ALL WHO SAW IT. IT WAS SCORED BY
KENT'S OVERSEAS PLAYER, THE SRI LANKAN ARAVINDA DE SILVA.

This was a very emotional final for me. I was aware of the history of Kent–Lancashire finals. In Sri Lanka, although there are big games in the domestic competitions and there are the club finals, we don't really have anything quite like this big day out at Lord's.

I enjoyed my season at Kent and all the guys were very supportive and we got on very well, because they were such a nice bunch of lads. We put Lancashire in and Mike Atherton batted very well. He gave maybe a half chance when the ball landed just short of me at fine leg. He made 93, and with John Crawley making 83, they were past 200 before the second wicket fell. I knew then that I was going to have to play a big innings to give Kent a good run at the target.

In the end, we needed 275 and we didn't have a good start. I came in at 37 for two. It was a situation where I thought we had to take charge. Our run rate wasn't all that good and I felt we had to bat positively and that's what I tried to do. There wasn't much of a reception when I came in and I was concentrating my mind on the job in hand. Kent were in trouble.

Aravinda brought up his fifty in 50 balls, with two sixes. He went to his hundred with his tenth four and when he was eventually caught at deep midwicket, he had made 112 from only 95 balls, with 11 fours and three sixes.

I enjoy batting at Lord's, especially in front of a packed house, and I really enjoyed batting on that particular day. When I got out for 112 and went back to the Pavilion with all the members standing and walked through the Long Room, it was a great reception, which I will always cherish.

Standing on the balcony afterwards, when the trophy was presented and I won the Gold Award, I had very mixed emotions. Everything had gone pretty well … except for being on the winning side. That's the most important thing.

Pretty soon after that I was off to Pakistan with Sri Lanka for a Test series which we won and then to Sharjah, where we won the Sharjah Cup. Of course nothing quite compares with what happened eight months later in Lahore, when we won the World Cup and I made a century again, but this was still a very special day.

De Silva hits out during one of the most exciting innings ever seen at Lord's

The winner's cirle: Lancashire enjoy their moment of glory on the Lord's Pavilion balcony

the very first over of the day, Wren bowled the ball that might have turned the Final Kent's way.

Ironically, de Silva was the man who just failed to hold a catch from Mike Atherton. Had he been quicker off the mark as Atherton pulled at Wren, the whole course of the game would have changed. For Atherton, reprieved, then built the foundation for Lancashire's huge score – the second highest in the long history of the Benson and Hedges.

John Crawley, more aggressive, shared a partnership of 121 with Atherton before the England captain gave a catch in the deep when seven runs short of his century. Crawley pressed on, hitting a six off Martin McCague before

> *Every now and then in life you are lucky enough to be able to boast: 'I was there.' And that is how it was for the 25,000-strong packed house at Lord's for the 1995 Benson and Hedges Cup Final*

perishing on 83. De Silva did his best to atone for his dropped catch with the bat, and his was an innings which deserved to win a final. But had it done so it would have been rough justice on a Lancashire team that was never less than vibrantly purposeful and looked as good as any Lancashire side in 50 years.

Kent had their consolation later in the season when they won the Sunday League (and thus prevented Warwickshire from winning a second consecutive Treble).

Britannic Assurance County Champions: Warwickshire
AXA Equity & Law League Champions: Kent
NatWest Bank Trophy Winners: Warwickshire

◊ FINAL SCOREBOARD 1995 ◊

LORD'S • 15TH JULY

– Lancashire –

M A Atherton, c Fulton, b Headley	93
J E R Gallian, b Ealham	36
J P Crawley, c Taylor, b McCague	83
N H Fairbrother, c McCague, b Headley	16
G D Lloyd, run out	12
Wasim Akram, run out	10
*M Watkinson, c McCague, b Fleming	0
I D Austin, not out	5
Extras (lb 2, w 10, nb 7)	19
Total *(55 overs, for 7 wkts)*	**274**

Did not bat: †W K Hegg, G Chapple, G Yates

Fall of wickets: 1-80, 2-201, 3-236, 4-258, 5-259, 6-266, 7-274.

Bowling: Wren 5-0-21-0, Headley 11-0-57-2, McCague 11-0-65-1, Ealham 11-0-33-1, De Silva 8-0-36-0, Fleming 9-0-60-1.

– Kent –

won the toss

D P Fulton, lbw, b Chapple	25
T R Ward, c Hegg, b Chapple	7
N R Taylor, b Yates	14
P A de Silva, c Lloyd, b Austin	112
G R Cowdrey, lbw, b Yates	25
M V Fleming, b Yates	11
M A Ealham, lbw, b Watkinson	3
*†S A Marsh, c Crawley, b Austin	4
M J McCague, not out	11
D W Headley, c Chapple, b Watkinson	5
T N Wren, c Austin, b Watkinson	7
Extras (lb 7, w 2, nb 6)	15
Total *(52.1 overs)*	**239**

Fall of wickets: 1-28, 2-37, 3-81, 4-142, 5-162, 6-180, 7-214, 8-214, 9-219, 10-239.

Bowling: Wasim Akram 10-0-57-0, Chapple 10-1-55-2, Austin 11-4-36-2, Watkinson 10.1-0-42-3, Yates 11-0-42-3.

Umpires: N T Plews & D R Shepherd

T V Replay umpire: J H Hampshire

Gold Award Winner: P A de Silva
(Adjudicator: Cricket Writers' Club)

– Lancashire won by 35 runs –

1996

– Austin reliable takes chequered flag –

*Cup-holders Lancashire were known as the ultimate one-day team –
and there was no more reliable team player than Ian Austin, whose
sterling performance dashed Northants' hopes of a return to glory*

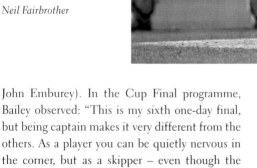

*Left: Gold Award Ian
Austin takes the plaudits
for another wicket.
Right: Austin's main rival
for the Gold Award –
Neil Fairbrother*

*I*f horses played cricket then the Shire would be the equine equivalent of Ian Austin. Not the sleek frame of a Derby winner, but the powerful build of a heavy draught-horse; untiring, unfailingly planting one foot in front of the other hour upon hour, never bothering how heavy the load.

Austin, 30 years old, two inches short of six feet and a solid fifteen stone, is the Lancashire workhorse. A professional's pro, a normally unsung grafter but on this sunlit day at Lord's in July 1996 suddenly a hero as he steered his side to a 31-run victory over Northamptonshire.

Before they even tossed (Mike Watkinson winning it and choosing to bat first), the hearts of the uncommitted were hoping for a victory for the homespun Midlanders – for the new skipper Rob Bailey and the old campaigner 'Ernie' (a.k.a.

John Emburey). In the Cup Final programme, Bailey observed: "This is my sixth one-day final, but being captain makes it very different from the others. As a player you can be quietly nervous in the corner, but as a skipper – even though the butterflies are still going to be there – you need to put on a bit of a front."

Emburey had been brought to Wantage Road as chief coach first, player second. He had already

Ian Austin

golden memories

after he had scored 14 in Lancashire's total of 245 for nine, Austin bowled beautifully in his opening spell of two for seven in seven overs. Later he came back to finish the Northants innings and ended with figures of 9.3-2-21-4. Austin made his Lancashire debut in 1987 and was capped in 1990. A burly, unprepossessing figure, he improved steadily with his pugnacious left-handed batting and right-arm medium-pace bowling to become a vital member of the team. He had by far his best season at first-class level in 1997, with 825 runs and 47 wickets, and in 1998, at the age of 32, was called into the England one-day team, following this with the man of the match award at the NatWest Final. By then, with his guile and unremitting accuracy, he was regarded as the finest bowler of his type in the country.

Ian Austin, a true professional's professional

proved his worth on the pitch, having won the Gold Award in the quarter-final against Kent at the age of 43. Bailey also valued him as a knowledgeable ally in the dressing room. "We get on well," the captain said, "and it's marvellous to be able to talk to someone like him who has seen it all before. He won us the Kent match with good sensible bowling. He came on at a difficult time – as he has done in quite a few limited-overs games

this season – and did the job, keeping the runs down and taking wickets."

But if Northants got the sentimental vote, no-nonsense Lancashire were the team to bet on. This was their sixth Lord's appearance in seven seasons. Not only had they won the trophy 12 months earlier, but they had won 14 B&H games in a row in reaching their second consecutive Final. Their semi-final triumph over their old

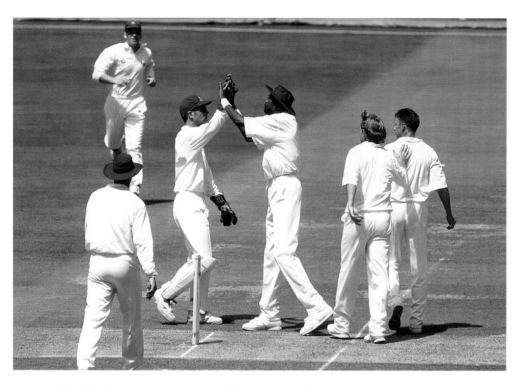

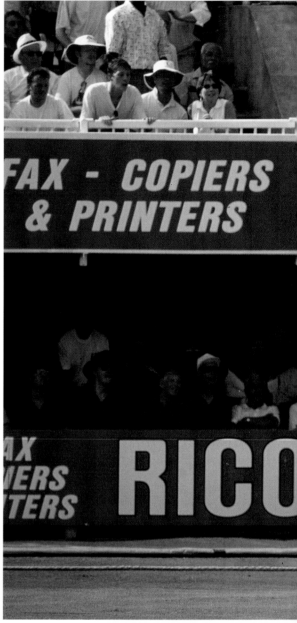

Above: Northamptonshire joy as Jason Gallian is run out. Below: Warren Hegg meets the same fate

rivals Yorkshire was ample testimony to their resolve, their nerve and their bravado in the one-day game. Hailed by Wisden as "one of the greatest matches in the 25-year history of this tournament", it saw Lancashire succeed in a furious run chase, needing 90 runs in the last 10 overs. Miraculously, they made it, winning by just one wicket. They still needed two runs off the last

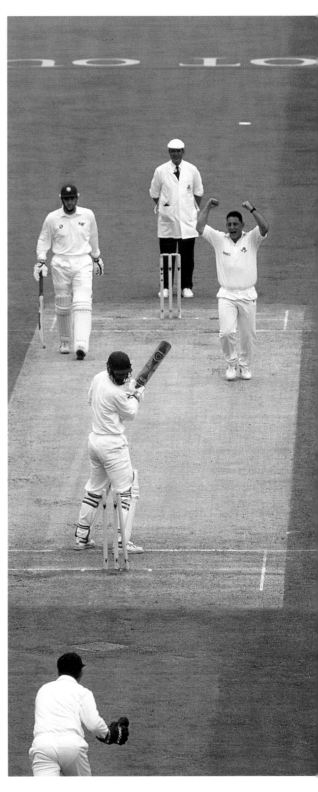

ball of the final over with their last batsman, Peter Martin, facing up to Craig White. Martin hit it square on the off side and just about struggled through for the winning runs. "I felt like I was treading water all the way," he said afterwards.

Northamptonshire were not exactly without big occasion experience, with three September visits to Lord's in seven years to their credit. Nor

Above: John Crawley takes a spectacular catch to dismiss Russell Warren off Mike Watkinson's bowling.
Right: Alan Fordham becomes an early victim of Gold Award winner Ian Austin

1996 IN CRICKET

Hard-hitting Sri Lanka win the World Cup on the subcontinent. Australia and West Indies forfeit games rather than play in Sri Lanka, for fear of violence. Kenya beat West Indies.. A riot causes the India–Sri Lanka semi-final to be abandoned, with Sri Lanka declared winners. **Aravinda de Silva** hits a century in the final against Australia… South African **Shaun Pollock**, in his first game for Warwickshire – a B&H Group match – takes four wickets in four balls… **David Lloyd** becomes England coach… **Ian Botham** and **Allan Lamb** lose a libel action against **Imran Khan**… Zimbabwe's first Test against England ends with the scores level as **Nick Knight** is run out for 96 going for the winning run.

1996 IN SPORT

Steve Redgrave wins his fourth rowing Olympic gold. Carl Lewis wins his fourth long jump gold… **Terry Venables'** England lose to Germany in the Euro 96 semi-final when **Gareth Southgate** misses during a penalty shootout. **Glenn Hoddle** replaces Venables as England boss… Manchester United do the Double, overhauling Newcastle's 12-point lead to win the Premiership… **Greg Norman** loses the US Masters to **Nick Faldo** after going into the final round with six-shot lead… **Frankie Dettori** rides all seven winners in a day at Ascot… **Damon Hill** wins the Formula One world title… **Mike Tyson** takes **Frank Bruno**'s world title. Bruno retires. **Evander Holyfield** beats Tyson.

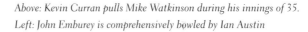

Above: Kevin Curran pulls Mike Watkinson during his innings of 35.
Left: John Emburey is comprehensively bowled by Ian Austin

started early in the year at the World Cup in India, Pakistan and Sri Lanka. David Capel, who had set up Northants' quarter-final victory over Kent with a quickfire 63 batting at No 1, hated being called a pinch hitter; he was due to open the innings again in the Final.

Lancashire's pinch hitter, Mike Watkinson, relished the role. "It has worked well enough so far this season," he said, "and if it comes off in the Final, it might just give us an edge."

Not since Somerset in 1982 had any side managed to retain the trophy. But that Lancashire deserved their victory is beyond dispute. Northants flattered, taking wickets

did they lack men of experience. But Northants' record on the big occasion was not a happy one: they had previously appeared in nine Lord's finals and lost six of them.

In many ways this was a final of great change. Here was the first to be contested over 50 overs, World Cup style; the first allowing only two fielders in the deep for 15 overs; the first with a mid-afternoon lunch.

It was also the year of the 'pinch hitter', the word used to describe the slogging batsman who would open the innings and (in theory, at least) take advantage of the wide open spaces in the deep – a trend that had

just when it seemed Lancashire were settling in for a really big partnership. Mike Atherton was patient without ever setting Lord's alight, John Crawley was magnificent with some fluent drives and Neil Fairbrother was his usual self. Darting the ball here, slicing it there, clipping and chasing for 70 balls which produced 63 runs.

Many a match adjudicator, particularly a batsman by profession, would have given the Gold Award to Fairbrother – but not Graham Gooch. He pondered long and hard, once joking that might stick in a pin! … and came up with the right man.

Austin had chipped in 14 valuable runs when Lancashire's total was looking just a fraction less than secure. He then pinched the wicket of Capel and saw Alan Fordham chop the ball into his

Above: Lancashire do the traditional arms-in-the-air celebration. Below: Mike Watkinson hoists the B&H trophy

stumps while bowling his first seven overs for just seven runs.

Northants were looking for a Fairbrother style knock, as the scorecard showed they needed eight an over from their last 10. They had no one comparable. Austin came back for his final three overs, bowled Emburey, saw Ambrose run out by Glen Chapple and then locked the door on Northants by bowling Tony Penberthy. He put the key in his pocket along with the Gold Award. His four wickets for 21 in 9.3 overs ensured his team retained the gold trophy. The losers knew that, once again, they had not done themselves justice.

Later in the season, Lancashire did the Double – as they had in 1990 – gunning Essex down for just 57 to win the NatWest Trophy.

Britannic Assurance County Champions:
Leicestershire
AXA Equity & Law League Champions: Surrey
NatWest Trophy Winners: Lancashire

FINAL SCOREBOARD 1996

LORD'S • 13TH JULY

– Lancashire –
won the toss

M A Atherton, c Bailey, b Emburey	48
*M Watkinson, c Emburey, b Taylor	7
J E R Gallian, run out	17
J P Crawley, c Warren, b Penberthy	34
N H Fairbrother, b Capel	63
G D Lloyd, b Taylor	26
†W K Hegg, run out	11
I D Austin, c & b Ambrose	14
G Yates, c Penberthy, b Capel	0
G Chapple, not out	6
P J Martin, not out	1
Extras (w 10, nb 8)	18
Total (50 overs, for 9 wkts)	**245**

Fall of wickets: 1-18, 2-52, 3-105, 4-131, 5-180, 6-203, 7-236, 8-236, 9-243.

Bowling: Ambrose 10-2-35-1, Taylor 9-0-55-2, Curran 7-0-48-0, Capel 8-1-37-2, Penberthy 6-0-31-1, Emburey 10-1-39-1.

– Northamptonshire –

D J Capel, c Hegg, b Austin	0
A Fordham, b Austin	4
*R J Bailey, c Hegg, b Chapple	46
R R Montgomerie, c Hegg, b Yates	42
K M Curran, c Crawley, b Chapple	35
†R J Warren, c Crawley, b Watkinson	11
T C Walton, st Hegg, b Watkinson	28
A L Penberthy, b Austin	8
J E Emburey, b Austin	6
C E L Ambrose, run out	10
J P Taylor, not out	0
Extras (lb 10, w 12, nb 2)	24
Total (48.3 overs)	**214**

Fall of wickets: 1-1, 2-10, 3-97, 4-111, 5-132, 6-184, 7-186, 8-194, 9-214, 10-214.

Bowling: Austin 9.3-2-21-4, Martin 9-2-32-0, Chapple 10-1-51-2, Watkinson 10-0-66-2, Yates 10-0-34-1.

Umpires: M J Kitchen & G Sharp
TV Replay umpire: R Julian

Gold Award Winner: I D Austin
(Adjudicator: Cricket Writers' Club)

– Lancashire won by 31 runs –

1997
– A star is confirmed –

Call it destiny. Like Botham rejoining the England team and taking a wicket first ball, like Gower hitting his first Test ball for four. Ben Hollioake's Lord's debut had been sensational. Now he was back…

In May 1997 at Lord's, England completed a whitewash of Australia in the three one-day internationals with a star performance by a young man who had never before stepped inside the historic ground. In July that young man returned with Surrey for his second visit and he graced the occasion no less memorably.

The two finalists had emerged from the same group, with the match between them at The Oval being won by Kent with a six off the last ball. In the quarter-final Kent had to overcome a Warwickshire total of over 300 to win, which they did with a century from Matthew Walker. In the semi-final first Dean Headley and then Zimbabwean leg-spinner Paul Strang ensured that Northamptonshire did not get near a relatively low target.

Surrey's quarter-final had been at Chelmsford, where Martin Bicknell and Chris Lewis had

Left: Surrey captains old and new – Alec Stewart and Adam Hollioake – try to wrest the Benson and Hedges Cup from Gold Award winner Ben Hollioake.
Right: Big Ben chimes in with another four

Ben Hollioake

golden memories

ben Hollioake, batting at No 3, took Surrey to the verge of victory with a superb innings of 98 from 112 balls. Earlier he had bowled six overs for 28 runs. This followed his thrilling 63 at Lord's on his one-day international debut for England two months earler. At 19, the Melbourne-born youngster was hailed as England's new star, and he was later introduced to England's Test team, both he and elder brother Adam making their debut at Trent Bridge. Despite his rich promise, that was perhaps a little premature, for he had still to make a century or take more than four wickets in an innings in first-class cricket. Two first-class centuries came on the England A tour in 1997/8 and one hopes that his uninhibited strokeplay, fast-medium bowling and serene temperament will indeed make him a major star of the future.

The youngest Gold Award winner in B&H history

ALEC STEWART

THE FINAL: KENT V SURREY, 12TH JULY 1997

IN 1996 THE B&H CUP BECAME A 50-OVER COMPETITION, WITH RULES ECHOING THE WORLD CUP. ALL BUT TWO FIELDERS HAD TO BE INSIDE THE 30-YARD CIRCLE FOR THE FIRST 15 OVERS. IN 1997 ALEC STEWART HANDED THE SURREY CAPTAINCY TO ADAM HOLLIOAKE. BUT BOTH HAD TO PLAY SECOND FIDDLE TO A NEW STAR...

We had all learnt from Sri Lanka'a approach in the 1996 World Cup that we really needed to take on the first 15 overs. So we planned to open with Alistair Brown, one of the better stroke-players in county cricket. His task was to make sure that he got it through or over the inner field. I would open with him and try to play my normal way and to pierce the inner field. Ben Hollioake was down to come in at three if we lost a wicket in the first 12 overs. If we hadn't lost a wicket in that time, we would revert to the normal order with Graham Thorpe coming in at three.

We still weren't sure what a par score was for the first 15 overs. It could be anything from 75 to over 100. This was something new and in the earlier matches a perfect example was our group game with Kent, when they beat us, we went too far. We were 108 for one in the 13th over, but soon slipped to 135 for six. We had to accept a cut-off point. But we were learning all the time.

In the Final, Kent had batted first after winning the toss. We had Chris Lewis, who was excellent at bowling in the first 15 overs. He took early wickets or he bowled the ball in the right areas where it's difficult to hit and we didn't get whacked too often in that period when he bowled. The old pattern of one-day cricket, when bowling at the 'death' was the problem, had become almost

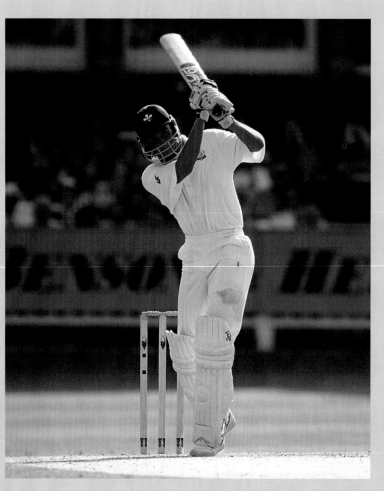

Ben Hollioake outshone even Alec Stewart: "I don't often get outscored by that much..."

reversed. We called it a game of three thirds. The first 15 is almost harder to bowl than the last 10 overs and in the middle it was a normal game of cricket before they had to start knocking it around again at the end.

Kent had made 212 for nine. If we had batted first we would certainly have wanted more. 250 might have been a fair score, even allowing for the pressure of the big occasion. We were fortunate in having quite a few people in our side with international experience who were used to that, so we felt that if we got off to a good start, perhaps 70 in the first 15 overs, the rest should be, if not an easy task, at least more straightforward.

We lost an early wicket when Ali Brown fell to a great catch by Matthew Fleming ... and in came Ben Hollioake to play only his second innings at Lord's – the first having been the one-day international in May, when he had made 63 on his international debut. He showed himself to be a big occasion player and that game against Australia wasn't just a flash in the pan. He just timed the ball straight away. I'm a reasonable stroke-player and can score fairly quickly, but it got to the stage where I was taking one to get him on strike and saying, "There you are, you can hit it for four." We put on 159 together and he made 98 of them. I don't often get outscored by that much.

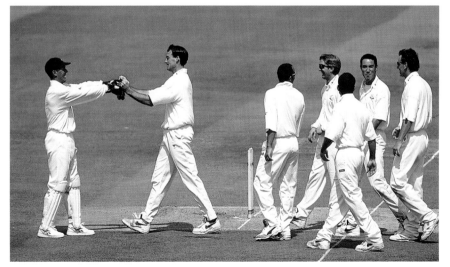

blown away the Essex top order. Then at the Oval the Surrey batsmen had set Leicestershire far too stiff a score.

Kent were at Lord's for their eighth Benson and Hedges Final but, having lost their previous three, it was nine years since they had taken the Cup and this day did not start well for them.

Bicknell and Lewis reduced them to 23 for three in the seventh over. Nigel Llong, first adding 43 with Trevor Ward and then 38 with Mark Ealham, provided some fightback, but they were only just past

Above: Alec Stewart watches a shot by Mark Ealham, Kent's top scorer with 52. Left: Surrey celebrate the fall of a wicket as Kent subside to 212 for nine

1997 IN CRICKET

Following a good tour for **Mike Atherton**'s England in New Zealand early in the year, they have a great start against the unofficial world champions, Australia, with a 3-0 win in the Texaco Trophy and then a convincing win at Egbaston in the first Test. "The Ashes coming home," sing the crowd, but Australia win three of the next four Tests with increasing authority and come to The Oval with the Ashes retained. There England achieve a thrilling win by 19 runs... There is more good news with victory for an England team captained by **Adam Hollioake** in the Sharjah Champions Trophy... The Benson and Hedges Cup's leading player over the years, **Graham Gooch**, retires... The death of the incomparable **Denis Compton** evokes a generation's treasured memories.

1997 IN SPORT

In a world heavyweight rematch, **Mike Tyson** chews champion **Evander Holyfield**'s ear and is disqualified... An IRA bomb threat cancels the Grand National. The race takes place on Monday and 20,000 see **Lord Gyllene** win... **Tiger Woods**, 21, wins the US Masters by a record 12 shots six months after turning professional... Manchester United win the title and **Eric Cantona** retires... Chelsea win the FA Cup Final against Middlesbrough with a goal after 43 seconds by **Roberto Di Matteo**... **Ronnie O'Sullivan** completes the fastest ever maximum break at the snooker world championships, in 5 min 20 sec... **Martina Hingis** is the youngest ever Wimbledon winner. **Tim Henman** and **Greg Rusedski** reach the quarter-finals... The British Lions pull off a historic series victory in South Africa.

Above: Chris Lewis sends Graham Cowdrey back to the pavilion.
Left: Matthew Fleming takes a neat gully catch to dismiss Alistair Brown. But the Kent team's joy was short-lived.
Opposite page: The Surrey lads reflect on a nice day out in north London

100 in the 30th over when Llong fell to Saqlain Mushtaq for 42. Strang and the captain, Steve Marsh, laid about them for 23 and 24 not out respectively and Ealham took his score to 52 to give the total something of a challenge about it at 212 for nine.

It looked better when the hard-hitting Alistair Brown was caught at cover point off McCague in the first over, but that was the last time it did. Nineteen-year-old Ben Hollioake now came in to join Alec Stewart.

He started with the freedom of one who is not overawed by the occasion, though he was nearly caught and run out off the same ball early on. Over the next 33 overs, the pair added 159 runs. Hollioake's contribution to that was 98, hit from 113 balls. The only thing that was missing was his

hundred, but when he was caught at mid-on off Ealham he returned to rapturous reception. A star had surely been born.

It was left to the old firm of Stewart with 75 not out and Thorpe, 17 not out, to complete what was now the formality of a Surrey win by eight wickets, with five overs to spare. Steve Marsh, captaining a B&H losing team for the third time, admitted sadly that Kent "simply did not compete".

To have given the Gold Award to anyone but Ben Hollioake would have caused a riot.

Britannic Assurance County Champions:
Glamorgan
AXA Life League Champions: Warwickshire
NatWest Trophy Winners: Essex

◗ FINAL SCOREBOARD 1997 ◗

LORD'S • 12TH JULY

– Kent –
won the toss

M V Fleming, lbw, b Lewis	7
M J Walker, b Bicknall	6
T R Ward, lbw, b A J Hollioake	15
A P Wells, lbw, b Bicknell	5
N J Llong, c Butcher, b Saqlain Mushtaq	42
M·A Ealham, c Brown, b Lewis	52
G R Cowdrey, b Lewis	8
P A Strang, b Salisbury	23
†*S A Marsh, not out	24
M J McCague, c Thorpe, b Saqlain Mushtaq	0
D W Headley, not out	3
Extras (b 1, lb 7, w 17, nb 2)	27
Total (50 overs, for 9 wkts)	212

Fall of wickets: 1-15, 2-15, 3-23, 4-68, 5-106, 6-135, 7-170, 8-194, 9-198.

Bowling: Bicknell 8-0-33-2, Lewis 10-3-39-3, A J Hollioake 7-0-31-1, B C Hollioake 6-0-28-0, Saqlain Mushtaq 9-1-33-2, Salisbury 10-0-40-1.

– Surrey –

A D Brown, c Fleming, b McCague	2
†A J Stewart, not out	75
B C Hollioake, c Strang, b Ealham	98
G P Thorpe, not out	17
Extras (lb 11, w 6, nb 6)	23
Total (45 overs, for 2 wkts)	215

Did not bat: *A J Hollioake, M A Butcher, C C Lewis, J D Ratcliffe, M P Bicknell, I D K Salisbury, Saqlain Mushtaq

Fall of wickets: 1-2, 2-161.

Bowling: McCague 8-0-45-1, Headley 10-0-53-0, Fleming 7-1-29-0, Ealham 6-0-31-1, Strang 10-1-31-0, Llong 4-0-15-0.

Umpires: G Sharp & D R Shepherd
TV Replay umpire: J H Holder

Gold Award Winner: B C Hollioake
(Adjudicator: Cricket Writers' Club)

– Surrey won by eight wickets –

THE BENSON AND HEDGES CUP YEARS

1998

— The final act of a 27-year drama —

The 27th Final and the strangest result of them all. Leicestershire desperately wanted to regain the Cup they used to see as their own but Paul Prichard's heroics set the seal on Essex's favourite competition

Essex celebrate their second Benson and Hedges Cup win, 19 years after the first. Opposite: Paul Prichard at the crease

Essex had already played at Lord's in the 1998 campaign – in the quarter-finals, when young Stephen Peters played a mature innings to boost their total and Ashley Cowan's five wickets brought an eight-run victory over Middlesex on the second day. Their semi-final victims had been the previously unbeaten Yorkshire side, with Nasser Hussain's batting retrieving an early collapse.

The early-season form of Leicestershire's Darren Maddy had already earned him a one-day international call-up for England and he took the Gold Award in both the quarter-final annihilation of Kent, when he made 93 not out, and in the 20-run semi-final win over Surrey for his 120 not out.

The weather forecast for the weekend of the last Benson and Hedges Cup Final was dire, and

The last Benson and Hedges Cup Final merited a great day. In a poor summer, though, there was no remission for this occasion. But there was some romance about it. Leicestershire, the first winners, were here. And so was Paul Prichard. As a schoolboy, the Essex captain had shared the delight of seeing Keith Fletcher hold up his county's first ever trophy – that same classic gold Cup – in 1979. Now he had fought back from injury with this game as his incentive.

Paul Prichard

golden memories

e ssex captain Prichard had a troubled 1998 season, missing most of his team's matches through injury. He was there, however, for the B&H Final at Lord's in July and, opening the innings, batted commandingly for a fine 92 from 113 balls. That was 16 more than the whole Leicestershire team managed the following day, after rain had ended play early on the Saturday. In his first innings of the year in the Cup, Prichard's batting reminded spectators that he had been thought close to international honours earlier in his career, and indeed he went on an England A tour in 1992/3. Born in Billericay, he made his debut for his native county at the age of 17 and has now scored some 15,000 runs in first-class cricket, his consistent scoring making him one of the most solid and attractive of county cricketers. He succeeded Graham Gooch as Essex captain in 1995.

Prichard's innings was his finest moment for Essex

Left: Nasser Hussain plays a reverse sweep during his innings of 88. Below: Lord's in the rain – not a sight that anyone wanted to see during the very last Benson and Hedges Cup match

1998 IN CRICKET

Mike Atherton resigns as England captain at the end of a series in the West Indies which is lost 3-1. Earlier, the Jamaica Test had been abandoned because of a dangerous pitch... **Alec Stewart** takes over from Atherton and leads an England comeback to take the Test series against South Africa 2-1, thanks to an amazing rescue act at Old Trafford...

Muttiah Muralitharan spins Sri Lanka to victory at The Oval, after they have also taken the Emirates Triangular Tournament... Benson and Hedges are not the only cricket sponsors to bid farewell. Texaco, Britannic and AXA also bow out as domestic cricket in England faces several changes for 1999.

1998 IN SPORT

Mark O'Meara, who recently is best known as **Tiger Woods'** mentor, wins the US Masters and the Open, where English amateur Justin Rose, 18, finishes fourth by chipping in for a birdie at the last hole... France beat favourites Brazil 3-0 in the World Cup Final. England go out on penalties to Argentina, having held on for a 2-2 draw after **David Beckham** was sent off... **Mark McGwire** of the St Louis Cardinals breaks **Roger Maris**'s 37-year-old record of 61 home runs. A week later **Sammy Sosa** of the Chicago Cubs ties him on 62... British athletes win a best ever nine golds in the European Championships. **Iwan Thomas** also wins the 400m at the World Cup and Commonwealth Championships.

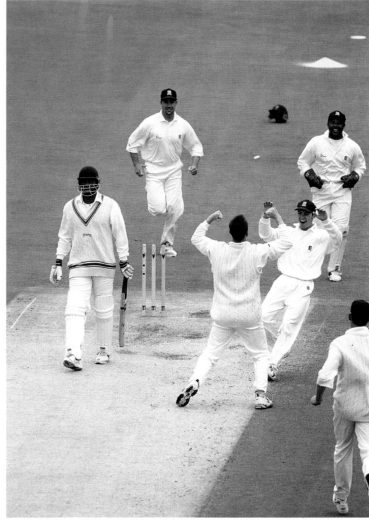

Phil Simmons finds that even a fancy Leicestershire fox haircut can't help him as Mark Ilott clips his off bail and sends him back to the Pavilion for just two runs

looked likely to help swing bowling. Chris Lewis, playing in a Benson and Hedges Final for the second year in a row – but for a different county – put Essex in. Alan Mullally's left-arm swing looked all but unplayable, but he made no early breakthrough. In the circumstances, Essex were not able to take full toll of the first 15 overs with the field in, though they had got to 40 in the 10th when Stuart Law was caught at midwicket for six.

Nasser Hussain, who had led Essex through all the earlier stages of the competition in the absence of the injured Prichard, now joined his captain in a stand of 134 for the second wicket, which occupied the next 25 overs. Gradually the realisation dawned that Essex were liable, despite the unfavourable conditions, to post a fair total.

Prichard, who had only been able to play a couple of matches all season before this while he recovered from a stress fracture of his left leg, was approaching his century when he cut Dominic Williamson to backward point and perished for 92. But the significance of his heroic innings was not lost on an appreciative crowd.

Hussain and Ronnie Irani added an increas-ingly rapid 60, Hussain making 88 and Irani 32 before Mullally returned to take three wickets towards the end of the innings.

Essex had made a surprisingly hefty total of 268 for seven. But even as the players walked off, rain was starting to fall. It intensified during the interval, and it was acknowledged that Leicester-shire would not be able to bat until the next day.

Sunday dawned to a deluge of rain and, despite the comprehensive covering at Lord's, it looked unlikely that any play would be possible. A cut-off time for a start was being agreed and plans were

PAUL PRICHARD

THE LAST FINAL: ESSEX V LEICESTERSHIRE, 11TH/12TH JULY 1998

THE ESSEX CAPTAIN HAD MISSED THE WHOLE OF HIS TEAM'S BENSON AND HEDGES CUP CAMPAIGN WHILE RECOVERING FROM A STRESS FRACTURE OF HIS LEFT LEG. BUT HE MANAGED TO RECOVER JUST IN TIME TO LEAD FROM THE FRONT IN THE FINAL.

It had been the sort of injury where I really didn't know how fit I would be, but I was driven by a determination to play in this Final. I had managed to play a couple of games and I was fairly sore, but I was able to get through with some pain-killers.

I lost the toss and Chris Lewis put us in. The weekend weather forecast was awful, but, as Stuart Law and I went out to bat, with the ground packed, it was completely irrelevant. You just concentrate on every ball and every over and don't look at the clouds building up. It may be said that Leicester's bowlers didn't make the best of the conditions, but we played and missed a bit early on and Alan Mullally bowled exceptionally well in his first spell.

Stuart was caught at midwicket for six in the 10th over, but Nasser Hussain came in and he played really positively. Over the next 25 overs, we added 134 together.

I'd got to 92 when I cut Dominic Williamson to backward point and Phil Simmons took the catch. At the time, not getting the hundred didn't seem so important – but maybe, looking back in future years, I'll kick myself.

By the end of our innings, the clouds had filled in and during the interval it started to rain properly. It soon became clear that there would be no more play that day. There was a bit of anxiety in our dressing room, because we felt that our 268 was a very good score on that pitch and we certainly didn't want the game to come down to a bowl-out on Sunday. We just kept hoping that it would stop raining.

But on Sunday morning it seemed to be pouring even harder and we had meetings with the officials to go through what would happen if we did have to have a bowl-out. They were going to peel back the covers just enough to bowl on the pitch, whatever the conditions. The rules are rather like a football penalty shoot-out. Five bowlers each bowl two balls at a set of stumps and the most hits wins, going into sudden death if they're equal after those 10 balls each.

When it looked as if this might happen and it had eased from a downpour to a steady drizzle, a few of us went over to the artificial nets at the Nursery End and some of the boys bowled at the stumps. No one got anywhere near them, so we went back fairly quickly. Thank goodness it didn't come down to that – because just in time for a full 50-over innings, the covers were peeled off and we started just before half past three.

Paul Prichard gets the lowdown as he throws the ball to wicketkeeper Paul Nixon

Keith Fletcher, Geoff Arnold and I had stressed to all the bowlers in these conditions to bowl straight, aiming to hit the top of the off stump and not to give the batsmen any width, and if it played the way it did on Saturday we should make it difficult for them. And the bowlers did exactly that. In fact Mark Ilott's delivery to bowl Phil Simmons was a perfect example. It hit the top of the off stump. By that time they were 10 for three in the seventh over.

The wickets kept on falling. In the 17th over they were 36 for seven and in the 28th it was all over. All out for 76.

There I was on the Pavilion balcony at Lord's. The last winning captain to hold up the gold Benson and Hedges Cup. There was obviously elation in winning the Cup and it was a special one for us as well, because it had been Essex's first trophy – in 1979. I remember as a small boy watching Keith Fletcher lift it up and we hadn't won it since.

But there was also a tinge of sadness, because it had always been a great competition. I had enjoyed playing in it and watching it as a boy. Now I had won the last Gold Award, too. I had had to take risks to get fit, but as I held up the Cup I knew that it had certainly been worth the fight.

being laid for resolving the outcome with a bowl-out at undefended stumps. But the rain stopped in the nick of time and a start was made just before half past three.

Batting was clearly not going to be easy. Leicestershire had reached only six in as many overs against Mark Ilott and Cowan, when Cowan had Iain Sutcliffe and Ben Smith both caught at slip. Ilott's accuracy was rewarded in his next two overs

Plans were being laid for a bowl-out at undefended stumps, but the rain stopped in the nick of time...

with the wickets of Simmons and Wells and it was 17 for four in the ninth over.

The top order demolition was completed before the end of the 15th over with another wicket for each of them – the dangerous Maddy and Aftab Habib, for five apiece. It was 31 for six.

The game was as good as over, though it was Stuart Law and Irani who completed the job. Leicestershire were all out for 76 in 27 overs and four balls. Essex had won by a massive 192 runs and Paul Prichard not only held aloft the Benson and Hedges Cup for the last time, but took the last Gold Award.

Britannic Assurance County Champions: Leicestershire
AXA League Champions: Lancashire
NatWest Trophy Winners: Lancashire

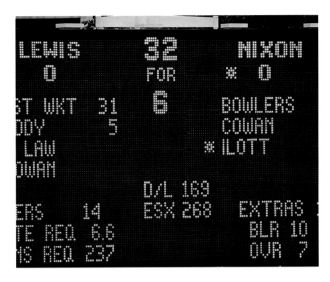

Above: Leicestershire in big trouble. Below: Paul Prichard wonders if he and his Essex chums can keep the Benson and Hedges Cup

FINAL SCOREBOARD 1998

Lord's • 11th, 12th July

– Essex –

*P J Prichard, c Simmons, b Williamson	92
S G Law, c Mullally, b Wells	6
N Hussain, c Smith, b Lewis	88
R C Irani, c Maddy, b Mullally	32
D R C Law, c Lewis, b Williamson	1
A P Grayson, not out	9
†R J Rollins, c Brimson, b Mullally	0
S D Peters, b Mullally	9
A P Cowan, not out	3
Extras (b 2, lb 8, w 18 nb 4)	28
Total (7 wickets, 50 overs)	**268**

Did not bat: M C Ilott, P M Such

Fall of wickets: 1-40, 2-174, 3-234, 4-244, 5-245, 6-250, 7-265.

Bowling: Mullally 10-1-36-3, Lewis 9-0-59-1, Wells 10-0-34-1, Simmons 9-0-67-0, Brimson 2-0-13-0, Williamson 10-0-49-2.

– Leicestershire –

won the toss

D L Maddy, c S Law b Cowan	5
I J Sutcliffe, c S Law, b Cowan	1
B F Smith, c S Law, b Cowan	0
P V Simons, b Ilott	2
V J Wells, lbw, b Ilott	1
Aftab Habib, lbw, b Ilott	5
†P A Nixon, not out	21
*C C Lewis, c Peters, b Irani	0
D Williamson, c Hussain, b S Law	11
A D Mullally, lbw, b Irani	1
M T Brimson, b S Law	0
Extras (lb 8, w 17 nb 4)	29
Total (27.4 overs)	**76**

Fall of wickets: 1-6, 2-6, 3-10, 4-17, 5-31, 6-31, 7-36, 8-67, 9-73, 10-76.

Bowling: Ilott 8-2-10-3, Cowan 10-2-24-3, Irani 6-2-21-2, S Law 3.4-0-13-2.

Umpires: R Julian & M J Kitchen
TV Replay umpire: J C Balderstone

Gold Award Winner: P J Prichard
(*Adjudicator: Cricket Writers' Club*)

– Essex won by 192 runs –

Graham Gooch

– The supreme B&H Cup performer –

He scored the first century in a Benson and Hedges Cup Final. Played the highest innings. Made the most runs. Won the most Gold Awards. Even took the most catches. So who wrote his script?

If there is one player whose name is written indelibly on the Benson and Hedges Cup, it is Graham Gooch. You look at his record, and it is almost the record of the Cup itself.

The most prolific scorer: Graham Gooch. The highest individual innings: Graham Gooch. The first century scored in a Final: Graham Gooch. Most frequent Gold Award winner: Graham Gooch. The most catches by a fielder: Graham Gooch. The most runs in a season: Graham Gooch. The most appearances in the 27-year competition … you guessed it.

For the opposing bowlers, the sight of Gooch shuffling out with that massive bat in his hand must have become a recurring nightmare. Most supporters of Essex could not get enough of their

The 1989 B&H Final, in which Gooch scored 48. Opposite: 130 not out in a B&H match versus Leicestershire in 1994

county talisman, but even at Chelmsford you might hear the odd grumble that "he just never gets out".

In his early days, Gooch loved to start as he meant to go on, clubbing the ball straight back past the bowler in cavalier fashion, enjoying every minute. Later, to the dismay of opening bowlers everywhere, he became more circumspect. A one-day innings would be built, methodically, starting with an iron defence.

While his longtime opening partner Brian Hardie would snick and skitter, Gooch would stand there swaying gently, massive bat dangling lightly above the ground, eyes hooded, walrus moustache bristling like some contemporary of W G Grace, laying a firm dead bat on anything that spelt danger but latching on to every wayward delivery to unleash a thunderous cut, pull or drive.

One of the keys to Gooch's amazing B&H record was his longevity. He began playing for Essex in 1974, two years after the launch of the Benson and Hedges Cup, and retired in 1997, one year before cricket supporters bid a sad farewell to the Cup itself. In 24 years of B&H appearances he maintained an average of over 50 – 52.28 to be precise – which is quite extraordinary for the frenetic pace of one-day cricket, where wickets are

Gooch batting in the Benson & Hedges Cup in 1985. He made 57 in the Final, but finished on the losing side

often sacrificed to a run chase.

His aggregate of 5,176 runs is more than 2,000 ahead of the next highest (Mike Gatting) in the history of the competition. His other B&H records include highest score (198 not out), most centuries (15), most catches (68), most runs in a season (591 in 1979) and most matches (115) – and his 22 Gold Awards is twice that of his closest rivals. In addition to his batting and fielding feats, Gooch took 69 wickets (at an average of 31.81) in B&H matches.

Gooch went on to many triumphs, but Essex supporters will always treasure his innings of 120 in the Benson and Hedges Cup Final at Lord's on July 21, 1979. This was the first century to be made in eight Benson and Hedges Finals. Essex scored 290 for six in their 55 overs, and Surrey fell well short, as they replied with 255.

That innings won Gooch the Gold Award (an easy decision for another Essex man, Trevor Bailey), but most importantly it secured Essex's first trophy since the county club was formed in 1876. Possibly no other B&H result had such lasting significance for the county involved, because it marked the beginning of a great era for Essex under the guidance of Keith Fletcher and Gooch.

Gooch played for Essex in four more B&H finals but, perhaps surprisingly, they lost all of them, all in close contests, even though Gooch played well on each occasion:
1980: Gooch 60 – Essex 203-8 in response to Northants' 209 (Gooch 1-24 in 11 overs).
1983: Gooch 46 – Essex 192 in response to Middlesex's 196 (Gooch 1-21 in 11 overs).
1985: Gooch 57 – Essex 213-8, a total Leicester passed in 52 overs (Gooch 2-40 in 10 overs).
1989: Gooch 48 – Essex 243-7, a total passed by Notts off the last ball, when Eddie Hemmings needed to hit John Lever for four, and did so (Gooch 0-57 in 11 overs).

In 1982 at Hove in a B&H zonal match, Gooch bludgeoned his way to 198 not out – the highest ever individual score in a one-day match in England. He hit five sixes and 22 fours and put on 268 in an unbroken third-wicket partnership with his captain, Keith Fletcher, as Essex amassed

327 – to which Sussex could reply with only 213.

The supreme professional cricketer of the past quarter-century, Gooch was a stalwart of an England team that included such talents as David Gower and Ian Botham. But he outlasted them through dedication and fitness, playing at his best throughout his 30s.

Born in Leytonstone, Essex, on 23 July, 1953, he was encouraged to play cricket by his father, Alf. He joined top Essex club side Ilford while at school, then progressed to play for the Essex Second XI for the first time in 1969 and to make his first-class debut in 1973.

In 1972 he went with the England Young Cricketers side to the West Indies, not only as a batsman but also as reserve wicket-keeper. Any ambitions in that regard were, however, soon abandoned, as he switched to bowling medium pace as his second string. That bowling would prove useful for both Essex and England, although many will best recall his gift for mimicry, most particularly a marvellous rendition of Bob Willis's run-up and action which he revealed when the occasion permitted.

Gooch's ability was evident to all, and he was introduced to Test cricket very early, against the Australians in 1975. This came after a command-ing innings for the MCC against the tourists, but he came up against an attack that included Lillee and Thomson at their ferocious best. Batting at No 5, he collected a 'pair' on his debut at Edgbaston and was discarded after scoring six and 31 in his second Test at Lord's.

In retrospect that selection was too soon, and indeed he averaged less than 30 in both his first two full seasons in first-class cricket in 1974 and 1975. He progressed steadily, however, and the breakthrough came in 1978 when he took over the job of opening the innings for his county, fared well and was reintroduced, as opener, into the Test side. Three fifties that summer ensured his selection for the Ashes tour to Australia, where he played in all six Tests, although with only modest success until he hit a swashbuckling 74 in the final Test.

A familiar sight to bowlers: Gooch drives Roger Knight during his landmark innings of 120 in the 1979 B&H Final

1980: In his second Benson and Hedges Cup Final, Gooch scores 60 against Northamptonshire but ends up on the losing side

From then he was a regular in the England team, although he did not make his first Test hundred until his 36th innings – 123 against the West Indies at Lord's in 1980. Having established his place, however, he accepted an invitation to captain a rebel tour to South Africa in 1982, and as a result had to accept a three-year ban from Test cricket.

These were years of plenty in the county game, for after a previous best season's average of 47.90 in 1980, he scored 2,559 first-class runs at 67.34 in 1984 and 2,208 runs at 71.22 in 1985. On his return to the international team, he scored two centuries in the one-day matches against Australia, followed by 487 runs at 54.11 in the six Tests of 1985.

He succeeded Keith Fletcher as captain of Essex in 1986, but stepped down after two years in which he suffered a decline in batting form. He took on the job again from 1989 to 1994, and by then was into the full flowering of his batting talents. A powerful player, particularly strong off his back foot, he was a destroyer of ordinary bowling and a magnificent player at Test level.

With his heavy bat held aloft as he prepared to face the bowling, Gooch, who looked bigger than he actually was – a powerful upper body on comparatively thin legs – presented an awesome sight to toiling bowlers everywhere when he was in his pomp. His driving could be of tremendous power and he was also a fierce square-cutter.

In 1988, that disastrous Ashes summer for England, he became the fourth man to captain the Test team in one season – but his appointment as captain for the ensuing tour to India precipitated the cancellation of that tour, for the Indian government refused to sanction visas to Gooch and others for their links with South Africa.

Initially thought by some to have an inappropriate demeanour for the job, he returned to the England captaincy in 1990 and led the team by

A 1994 B&H match against Leicestershire at Chelmsford

Gooch runs out Tim Curtis of Worcestershire in the 1991 Benson and Hedges Cup semi-final at Chelmsford

the personal example of his magnificent batting and his disciplined approach to the job. Gooch reached his peak as England batsman and captain with scores of 333 and 123 (a record aggregate for a single Test match) against India at Lord's in 1990. No doubt as a result of these stirring deeds, he was awarded the OBE in 1991.

In 1990 he also became the first player to score 1,000 Test runs in an English summer (306 v New Zealand, 752 at 125.33 v India) and only the fifth player ever to average over 100 in an English first-class season. His 2,746 runs at 101.70 was the highest since 1961. Such high form continued with a first-class average over 50 each year from 1991 to 1996, including twice over 70.

He resigned the captaincy after England lost four of the first five Tests of the Ashes series in 1993, with an overall Test record of 10 wins in his 34 matches as captain. He did, however, continue to bat marvellously well in that series, with 673 runs at 56.08 in the six Tests.

In perhaps one tour too many, he announced his retirement from Test cricket during the 1994/5 series against Australia and retired from first-class cricket in 1997. He has moved seamlessly into coaching and management and was appointed an England selector in 1996.

He became England's highest-ever scorer both in Test cricket (8,900 runs at 42.58) and in limited-overs internationals (4,290 at 36.98), and in all scored 44,841 runs in first-class cricket at 49.11, with 128 centuries.

He is also easily the most prolific scorer in all the one-day competitions: 8,573 (average 34.99) in the Sunday League, including the record score of 176 in 1983; 2,547 (average 48.98) in the Gillette Cup/NatWest Trophy; and of course 5,176 (average 52.28) in the Benson & Hedges Cup.

With Essex he won six County Championships (1979, 1983, 1984, 1986, 1991, 1992) as well as the Sunday League in 1984 and 1985. But it is the Benson & Hedges Cup of 1979 – and Gooch's brilliant century at Lord's – that will live longest in the memory of Essex supporters and of all who loved cricket's big day out.

– B&H statistics –

Every fact you ever wanted to know about the Benson and Hedges Cup – and a lot of other things it probably never occurred to you to ask… It's all here, down to the last decimal point

The competition began in 1972 and consisted of 55 overs. The 17 first-class counties took part, augmented by Minor County teams (designated North and South) and Cambridge University.

In 1973 Cambridge University were replaced by Oxford University and in 1974 Cambridge again alternated with them.

In 1975 the two university teams amalgamated to be Oxford & Cambridge Universities.

In 1976 the minor counties were rearranged to be East & West and this format continued until 1979, when they reverted to North & South.

In 1980 Scotland joined the competition, which reduced the minor counties to one team.

In 1987 Oxford & Cambridge Universities was strengthened by the inclusion of players from other universities – Durham, Exeter, Loughborough and Swansea. The title of the team was Combined Universities and this continued until 1996, when it was changed to British Universities.

In 1992 Durham became the 18th first-class county.

In 1993 the competition changed from the four-group system to be a straight knock-out.

In 1994 Ireland joined the competition and the knock-out format was continued.

In 1995 the group system was re-introduced but the overs were reduced to 50 per side, in line with international limited-overs matches.

Ben Hollioake enters the Pavilion after scoring 98 in the 1997 Benson and Hedges Cup Final at Lord's

— Team Performances —

HIGHEST TOTALS

67 Totals of 300 have been recorded

+ denotes batted first

+388-7	55	Essex v Scotland at Chelmsford	30.4.92
+382-6	50	Leicestershire v Minor Counties CA at Leicester	8.5.98
+371-6	50	Leicestershire v Scotland at Leicester	28.4.97
+396-8	50	Warwickshire v Minor Counties CA at Jesmond	28.4.96
+366-4	55	Derbyshire v Combined Universities at Oxford	25.4.91
+359-6	50	Essex v Ireland at Chelmsford	4.5.98
+353-7	55	Lancashire v Nottinghamshire at Old Trafford	9.5.95
+350-3	55	Essex v Oxford & Cambridge Universities at Chelmsford	19.5.79
+349-7	50	Somerset v Ireland at Taunton	2.5.97
+338-6	50	Kent v Somerset at Maidstone	28.4.96
+333-4	55	Essex v Oxford & Cambridge Universities at Chelmsford	18.5.85
+333-6	50	Surrey v Hampshire at The Oval	28.4.96
+331-5	55	Surrey v Hampshire at The Oval	1.5.90
+331-5	50	Essex v British Universities at Chelmsford	30.4.96
+330-4	55	Lancashire v Sussex at Old Trafford	7.5.91

HIGHEST TOTAL BY A NON-COUNTY TEAM

+312-8	50	British Universities v Glamorgan at Cambridge	28.4.96

HIGHEST TOTAL BATTING FIRST AND LOSING

+312-5	55	Leicestershire v Lancashire at Old Trafford	25.4.95
+312-8	50	British Universities v Glamorgan at Cambridge	28.4.96

HIGHEST TOTAL BY THE SIDE BATTING SECOND AND WINNING

318-5	54.3	Lancashire v Leicestershire at Old Trafford	25.4.95

HIGHEST TOTAL BY THE SIDE BATTING SECOND AND LOSING

303-7	55	Derbyshire v Somerset at Taunton	1.5.90

LOWEST TOTALS

73 Totals of under 100 have been recorded

+ denotes batted first

50	27.2	Hampshire v Yorkshire at Headingley	4.5.91
+52	26.5	Minor Counties CA v Lancashire at Lakenham	5.5.98
56	26.2	Leicestershire v Minor Counties CA at Wellington	27.5.82
59	34	Oxford & Cambridge Universities v Glamorgan at Cambridge	14.5.83
+61	26	Sussex v Middlesex at Hove	13.5.78
+61	25.3	Essex v Lancashire at Chelmsford	21.4.92
62	26.5	Gloucestershire v Hampshire at Bristol	3.5.75
63	37.4	Minor Counties (East) v Sussex at Eastbourne	29.4.78
63	30.3	Hampshire v Surrey at Southampton	5.5.97
+66	40.2	Minor Counties (East) v Northamptonshire at Horton	7.5.77
+67	34.1	Minor Counties (North) v Nottinghamshire at Newark	17/19.5.75
+67	45.5	Minor Counties (North) v Kent at Lincoln	28.4.79
68	36.5	Glamorgan v Lancashire at Old Trafford	13.6.73
+68	32	Oxford & Cambridge Universities v Somerset at Taunton	20.5.78
70	32.4	Gloucestershire v Hampshire at Moreton-in-Marsh	6.5.72
70	47.4	Minor Counties (North) v Derbyshire at Derby	11/13.5.74
+70	35.5	Minor Counties CA v Lancashire at Leek	23.4.95
73	37.4	Kent v Middlesex at Canterbury	12.5.79
+73	29.1	Middlesex v Essex at Lord's	16.5.85
+74	32.4.	Nottinghamshire v Leicestershire at Leicester	13.5.87
+75	38.2	Minor Counties (West) v Warwickshire at Edgbaston	29.4.78
+76	32.1	Minor Counties CA v Glamorgan at Swansea	11.5.85
76	27.4	Leicestershire v Essex at Lord's	12.7.98

1986: Graham Cowdrey is bowled by John Inchmore

1996: Lancashire celebrate beating Northamptonshire in the Final

HIGHEST AGGREGATES

Runs	Wkts			
631	15	Kent v Somerset	Maidstone	28.4.96
630	10	Lancashire v Leicestershire	Old Trafford	25.4.95
629	14	Lancashire v Notinghamshire	Old Trafford	9.5.95
628	15	Lancashire v Warwickshire	Old Trafford	14.5.96
626	10	Combined Universities v Glamorgan	Cambridge	28.4.96
615	11	Surrey v Gloucestershire	Oval	30.4.96
613	10	Somerset v Derbyshire	Taunton	1.5.90
610	8	Sussex v Kent	Hove	16/17.5.95
610	14	Kent v Warwickshire	Canterbury	27.5.97
609	18	Surrey v Sussex	Oval	12.5.97
607	10	Surrey v Hampshire	Oval	28.4.96

LOWEST AGGREGATES

Runs	Wkts			
105	13	Minor Counties CA v Lancashire	Lakenham	5.5.98
122	12	Sussex v Middlesex	Hove	13.5.78
126	12	Essex v Lancashire	Chelmsford	21.4.92
134	10	Minor Counties (East) v Northamptonshire	Horton	7.5.77
135	13	Nottinghamshire v Minor Counties (North)	Newark	17/19.5.75
135	11	Minor Counties (North) v Kent	Lincoln	28.4.79
140	10	Somerset v Oxford & Cambridge Universities	Taunton	20.5.78
147	16	Middlesex v Essex	Lord's	16.5.85
150	12	Leicestershire v Nottinghamshire	Leicester	12/13.5.87

HIGHS AND LOWS BY COUNTY

	Totals 300+		Totals -100		Hundreds		5 Wkts/innings	
	For	Agst	For	Agst	For	Agst	For	Agst
Derbyshire	3	2	1	2	20	11	8	9
Durham	-	-	-	-	4	8	1	-
Essex	8	-	1	5	32	7	9	5
Glamorgan	3	2	5	6	16	15	6	4
Gloucestershire	3	3	2	3	15	16	8	6
Hampshire	3	3	3	5	21	14	5	7
Kent	5	4	1	4	21	13	9	8
Lancashire	6	4	3	6	17	14	12	8
Leicestershire	5	3	4	3	20	9	11	8
Middlesex	2	2	2	6	15	9	10	8
Northamptonshire	2	2	1	3	18	17	9	7
Nottinghamshire	-	1	3	2	14	17	10	5
Somerset	7	3	1	5	16	19	5	6
Surrey	7	3	1	7	15	17	6	7
Sussex	3	5	4	4	13	14	8	4
Warwickshire	5	5	1	3	16	14	11	6
Worcestershire	2	-	3	3	18	9	10	9
Yorkshire	2	-	1	4	13	8	10	7
Minor Counties CA	-	3	5	1	3	17	1	8
Universities	1	9	8	1	5	25	5	12
Scotland	-	8	3	-	-	21	-	7
Ireland	-	4	2	-	-	5	-	3
Cambridge University	-	-	2	-	-	2	-	-
Oxford University	-	-	-	-	-	1	-	1
Minor Counties N	-	-	4	-	-	3	-	4
Minor Counties S	-	1	6	-	-	4	-	1
Minor Counties E	-	-	4	-	2	5	-	3
Minor Counties W	-	-	2	-	-	-	-	1
	67	67	73	73	314	314	154	154

Alan Ealham steers Kent to victory in the low-scoring 1978 Final

TEN-WICKET WINS

There have been 19 ten-wicket wins
(in county order)

Derbyshire	beat Scotland at Titwood	14.5.80	Sc 116 (50.2)	D 121-0 (27.2)
Essex	beat Middlesex at Harlow	2.6.73	M 133 (54.3)	E 136-0 (33.5)
	beat Glamorgan at Chelmsford	11.5.89	Gm 98 (44.3)	M 99-0 (23.2)
Glamorgan	beat Minor Counties CA at Swansea	17.5.80	MC 175-9 (55)	Gm 176-0 (42.5)
Hampshire	beat Glamorgan at Southampton	3.5.88	Gm 157-9 (55)	H 158-0 (47)
Kent	beat Minor Counties (South) at Canterbury	26.4.75	MC 117-9 (55)	K 118-0 (36.5)
	beat Ireland at Comber	9.5.95	I 146 (54)	K 149-0 (32.1)
Lancashire	beat Scotland at Old Trafford	8.5.82	Sc 154 (54)	La 156-0 (49.2)
Leicestershire	beat Minor Counties (West) at Leicester	1.5.76	MC 139-8 (55)	Le 140-0 (36.2)
	beat Gloucestershire at Cheltenham	21.4.92	Gs 110 (47.5)	Le 111-0 (34.5)
Middlesex	beat Sussex at Hove	5.5.92	Sx 141 (48.5)	M 145-0 (44.3)
Northamptonshire	beat Minor Counties (East) at Horton	8.5.77	MC 66 (40.2)	Nh 68-0 (23)
Somerset	beat Oxford & Cambridge Universities at Taunton	20.5.78	Un 68 (32)	Sm 72-0 (13.1)
Warwickshire	beat Minor Counties (West) at Coventry	7.5.77	MC 139-8 (55)	Wa 141-0 (37.3)
Worcestershire $	beat Somerset at Worcester	23/24.5.79	Sm 1-0 dec (1)	Wo 2-0 (1.4)
	beat Scotland at Worcester	23.4.95	Sc 118 (53.1)	Wo 119-0 (27.1)
Yorkshire	beat Minor Counties (North) at Jesmond	12.5.79	MC 85 (42.5)	Y 86-0 (30.5)
	beat Warwickshire at Edgbaston	2-4.5.87	Wa 208-8 (55)	Y 211-0 (50)
	beat Scotland at Glasgow	2.5.95	Sc 129 (51.1)	Y 130-0 (22.3)

$ Somerset were disqualified from the competition at a special meeting of the TCCB on 1.6.79. The action of the Somerset captain was seen as being against the spirit of the competition. Somerset's place in the quarter-finals was taken by Derbyshire and the rules of the competition were amended the following year, expressly forbidding declarations.

1998: Essex get the wicket of Darren Maddy and they're on the way to victory

Right: Adam Hollioake and his Surrey teammates celebrate beating Kent in the 1997 Benson and Hedges Cup Final

WINNING BY A LARGE MARGIN OF RUNS

Runs		
272	Essex beat Scotland at Chelmsford	1.5.92
256	Leicestershire beat Minor Counties CA at Leicester	8.5.98
233	Somerset beat Ireland at Eglinton	16.5.95
221	Somerset beat Ireland at Taunton	2.5.97
217	Glamorgan beat Combined Universities at Cardiff	25.4.95
214	Essex beat Oxford & Cambridge Universities at Chelmsford	19.5.79
206	Derbyshire beat Combined Universities at Oxford	25.4.91
192	Essex beat Leicestershire at Lord's (Final)	12.7.98
189	Yorkshire beat Hampshire at Headingley	4.5.91
186	Sussex beat Cambridge University at Hove	18.5.74
184	Leicestershire beat Warwickshire at Coventry	13.5.72
184	Yorkshire beat Minor Counties CA at Headingley	12.5.97

NARROW MARGINS OF VICTORY

23 matches were won by one wicket

WINS BY 1 RUN

There have been 10 wins by 1 run

Warwickshire beat Derbyshire at Derby	17.5.77
Glamorgan beat Oxford & Cambridge Universities at Oxford	15.5.78
Glamorgan beat Gloucestershire at Bristol	10.5.80
Middlesex beat Somerset at Taunton	17.5.80
Kent beat Hampshire at Canterbury	21.5.80
Yorkshire beat Leicestershire at Leicester	11.5.85
Middlesex beat Surrey at The Oval	10.5.88
Worcestershire beat Middlesex at Lord's	26.4.89
Glamorgan beat Nottinghamshire at Cardiff	4.5.91
Warwickshire beat Surrey at The Oval	7.5.91

NARROW MARGINS OF VICTORY

35 matches have been won on the last ball

TIED MATCHES

Lancashire beat Worcestershire by a faster scoring rate at 30 overs at Worcester 13.5.86.
Middlesex beat Sussex by a faster scoring rate at 30 overs at Hove 8.5.90.

DECISION ON THE TOSS OF A COIN

The result of a match was decided only once in this way. Middlesex beat Gloucestershire in the quarter-final at Bristol 3.6.83.

As a result of this, a new way of deciding the outcome in a match where no play was possible -- from the quarter-final stage onwards -- was brought in. Five bowlers from the teams selected were to bowl two balls each at a set of unguarded stumps, with the team hitting them the most times being the winner.

DECISION BY BOWLING AT STUMPS

Derbyshire beat Somerset in the quarter-final at Chelmsford 30.4.92.
Warwickshire beat Kent in the quarter-final at Edgbaston 25.5.94.

1996 semi-final, Lancashire v Yorkshire: Celebrations as Byas catches Atherton

1998: The last Benson and Hedges Cup Final, won by Essex

WINS BY UNIVERSITY TEAMS

Oxford University beat Northamptonshire by two wickets at Northampton	12.5.73
Oxford & Cambridge Universities beat Worcestershire by 66 runs at Cambridge	3.5.75
Oxford & Cambridge Universities beat Northamptonshire by three wickets at Oxford	21.5.75
Oxford & Cambridge Universities beat Yorkshire by seven wickets at Barnsley	22.5.75
Oxford & Cambridge Universities beat Gloucestershire by 27 runs at Bristol	15.5.84
Combined Universities beat Surrey by 9 runs at Cambridge	25/26.4.89
Combined Universities beat Worcestershire by five wickets at Worcester	11.5.89
Combined Universities beat Yorkshire by two wickets at Headingley	8/9.5.90
British Universities beat Sussex by 19 runs at Cambridge	30.4.97
British Universities beat Gloucestershire by 7 runs at Bristol	6.5.98

WINS BY MINOR COUNTIES CRICKET ASSOCIATION

MCCA beat Gloucestershire by 3 runs at Chippenham	22.5.80
MCCA beat Hampshire by 3 runs at Southampton	13.5.81
MCCA beat Leicestershire by 131 runs at Wellington	27.5.82
MCCA beat Glamorgan by seven wickets at Christchurch, Oxford	14/15.5.87
MCCA beat Sussex by 19 runs at Marlow	30.4/1.5.92
MCCA beat Leicestershire by 26 runs at Leicester	2.5.95

WINS BY SCOTLAND

Scotland beat Lancashire by 3 runs at Perth	10/11.5.86
Scotland beat Northamptonshire by 2 runs at Northampton	10.5.90

WINS BY IRELAND

Ireland beat Middlesex by 46 runs at Dublin	28/29.4.97

BENSON AND HEDGES CUP
RESULTS BY COUNTY

	Home				Away				Total			
	P	W	L	NR	P	W	L	NR	P	W	L	NR
Derbyshire	62	32	23	7	59	31	27	1	121	63	50	8
Durham	13	6	6	1	13	5	7	1	26	11	13	2
Essex	69	46	22	1	67	38	26	3	136	84	43	4
Glamorgan	58	25	31	2	56	25	28	3	114	50	59	5
Gloucestershire	57	30	24	3	59	26	32	1	116	56	56	4
Hampshire	61	28	30	3	64	34	28	2	125	62	58	5
Kent	69	46	22	1	76	47	26	3	145	93	48	4
Lancashire	65	44	17	4	75	46	26	3	140	90	43	7
Leicestershire	65	43	21	1	66	30	30	6	131	73	51	7
Middlesex	65	34	26	5	64	33	28	3	129	67	54	8
Northamptonshire	57	25	29	3	66	33	28	5	123	58	57	8
Nottinghamshire	62	43	15	4	63	28	32	3	125	71	47	7
Somerset	60	36	23	1	67	33	32	2	127	69	55	3
Surrey	65	41	22	2	67	36	29	2	132	77	51	4
Sussex	56	30	26	-	59	25	32	2	115	55	58	2
Warwickshire	59	33	24	2	70	39	26	5	129	72	50	7
Worcestershire	66	34	30	2	65	34	29	2	131	68	59	4
Yorkshire	62	35	24	3	62	33	25	4	124	68	49	7
Minor Counties	36	4	29	3	39	2	36	1	75	6	65	4
British Universities	22	2	20	-	25	3	21	1	47	5	41	1
Scotland	35	1	31	3	35	1	33	1	70	2	64	4
Ireland	8	1	5	2	9	-	9	-	17	1	14	2
Minor Counties(North)	10	-	10	-	10	-	10	-	20	-	20	-
Minor Counties(South)	10	-	9	1	10	-	10	-	20	-	19	1
Minor Counties(East)	6	-	6	-	6	-	6	-	12	-	12	-
Minor Counties(West)	6	-	6	-	6	-	6	-	12	-	12	-
Cambridge University	4	-	4	-	4	-	4	-	8	-	8	-
Oxford University	2	-	2	-	2	1	1	-	4	1	3	-
Oxford/Cambridge Universities	24	2	21	1	24	2	21	1	48	4	42	2

Finals are counted as away matches for all teams except Middlesex (1975, 1983, 1986)

The 1981 quarter-final between Kent and Warwickshire, which was moved to The Oval, is counted as an away match for both teams.

Every run is vital: Neal Radford saves four for Worcestershire against Surrey in 1987

Graham Gooch in action during his 120 against Surrey in the 1979 Final

COUNTIES' RECORDS

The successes of each first-class county in the competition are as follows:

Derbyshire	Winners	1993
	Finalists (2)	1978, 1988
	Semi-finalists	1979
	Quarter-finalists (5)	1982, 1985, 1986, 1992, 1994
Durham	Quarter-finalists	1998
Essex	Winners (2)	1979, 1998
	Finalists (4)	1980, 1983, 1985, 1989
	Semi-finalists (2)	1988, 1991
	Quarter-finalists (8)	1973, 1975, 1976, 1984, 1986, 1990, 1994, 1997
Glamorgan	Semi-finalists	1988
	Quarter-finalists (7)	1972, 1973, 1977, 1978, 1979, 1990, 1996
Gloucestershire	Winners	1977
	Semi-finalists	1972
	Quarter-finalists (5)	1983, 1987, 1989, 1995, 1996
Hampshire	Winners (2)	1988, 1992
	Semi-finalists (3)	1975, 1977, 1994
	Quarter-finalists (7)	1973, 1974, 1983, 1985, 1987, 1991, 1993
Kent	Winners (3)	1973, 1976, 1978
	Finalists (5)	1977, 1986, 1992, 1995, 1997
	Semi-finalists (5)	1981, 1983, 1985, 1987, 1989
	Quarter-finalists (6)	1974, 1982, 1991, 1994, 1996, 1998
Lancashire	Winners (4)	1984, 1990, 1995, 1996
	Finalists (2)	1991, 1993
	Semi-finalists (4)	1973, 1974, 1982, 1983
	Quarter-finalists (7)	1972, 1975, 1976, 1980, 1989, 1992, 1998
Leicestershire	Winners (3)	1972, 1975, 1985
	Finalists (2)	1974, 1998
	Semi-finalists (3)	1981, 1993, 1997
	Quarter-finalists (3)	1973, 1976, 1982
Middlesex	Winners (2)	1983, 1986
	Finalists	1975
	Semi-finalists (3)	1980, 1985, 1998
	Quarter-finalists (9)	1972, 1977, 1978, 1979, 1982, 1988, 1990, 1992, 1995
Northamptonshire	Winners	1980
	Finalists (2)	1987, 1996
	Semi-finalists (3)	1977, 1993, 1997
	Quarter-finalists (5)	1983, 1985, 1986, 1989, 1991

Nottinghamshire	Winners	1989
	Finalists	1982
	Semi-finalists (3)	1984, 1986, 1990
	Quarter-finalists (8)	1973, 1976, 1978, 1980, 1981, 1988, 1994, 1995
Somerset	Winners (2)	1981, 1982
	Semi-finalists (6)	1974, 1978, 1989, 1990, 1992, 1995
	Quarter-finalists (5)	1975, 1984, 1987, 1993, 1997
Surrey	Winners (2)	1974, 1997
	Finalists (2)	1979, 1981
	Semi-finalists (5)	1976, 1987, 1992, 1994, 1998
	Quarter-finalists (4)	1980, 1984, 1990, 1996
Sussex	Semi-finalists	1982
	Quarter-finalists (8)	1972, 1977, 1978, 1980, 1981, 1984, 1986, 1993
Warwickshire	Winners	1994
	Finalists	1984
	Semi-finalists (5)	1972, 1975, 1976, 1978, 1996
	Quarter-finalists (7)	1977, 1979, 1981, 1983, 1988, 1991, 1997
Worcestershire	Winners	1991
	Finalists (4)	1973, 1976, 1990, 1994
	Semi-finalists (3)	1980, 1986, 1995
	Quarter-finalists (7)	1974, 1979, 1985, 1987, 1988, 1992, 1993
Yorkshire	Winners	1987
	Finalists	1972
	Semi-finalists (5)	1979, 1984, 1991, 1996, 1998
	Quarter-finalists (5)	1974, 1975, 1981, 1995, 1997

Tim Robinson leads the Nottinghamshire
players out of the Lord's Pavilion in 1989

HIGHS AND LOWS

+ denotes batted first

Derbyshire

Highest Total For:	+366-4 (55 overs)	v Combined Universities at Oxford	24.4.91
Highest Total Against:	+310-3 (55 overs)	Somerset at Taunton	1.5.90
Lowest Total For:	+98 (44 overs)	v Worcestershire at Derby	25.5.94
Lowest Total Against:	70 (47.4 overs)	Minor Counties (North) at Derby	13.5.74
Highest Score For:	142 D M Jones	v Minor Counties CA at Derby	14.5.96
Highest Score Against:	127* G A Hick	Worcestershire at Worcester	9.5.95
Best Bowling For:	6-33 E J Barlow	v Gloucestershire at Bristol	6-9.5.78
Best Bowling Against:	6-26 S R Lampitt	Worcestershire at Derby	25.5.94

Durham

Highest Total For:	+287-5 (50 overs)	v Leicestershire at Leicester	14.5.96
Highest Total Against:	289-6 (49.4 overs)	Leicestershire at Leicester	14.5.96
Lowest Total For:	162 (40.4 overs)	v Derbyshire at Chesterfield	26.4.96
Lowest Total Against:	+150-8 (50 overs)	Scotland at Forfar	2.5.97
Highest Score For:	145 J E Morris	v Leicestershire at Leicester	14.5.96
Highest Score Against:	121* M A Atherton	Lancashire at Old Trafford	28/29.4.96
Best Bowling For:	6-30 S J E Brown	v Northamptonshire at Chester-le-Street	30.4.97
Best Bowling Against:	4-26 M Frost	Glamorgan at Durham University	21.4.92
	4-26 D G Cork	Derbyshire at Jesmond	5.5.92
	4-26 D J Millns	Leicestershire at Stockton	23.4.95

Essex

Highest Total For:	+338-7 (55 overs)	v Scotland at Chelmsford	30.4.92
Highest Total Against:	295 (54.2 overs)	Warwickshire at Edgbaston	25.4.91
Lowest Totals For:	+61 (25.3 overs)	v Lancashire at Chelmsford	21.4.92
Lowest Totals Against:	+73 (29.1 overs)	Middlesex at Lord's	16.5.85
Highest Score For:	198* G A Gooch	v Sussex at Hove	25.5.82
Highest Score Against:	115* G R J Roope	Surrey at Chelmsford	19/21.5.93
Best Bowling For:	5-13 J K Lever	v Middlesex at Lord's	16.5.85
Best Bowling Against:	5-16 P A J DeFreitas	Lancashire at Chelmsford	21.4.92

Glamorgan

Highest Total For:	+318-3 (55 overs)	v Combined Universities at Cardiff	25.4.95
Highest Total Against:	+312-8 (50 overs)	British Universities at Cambridge	28.4.96
Lowest Total For:	68 (36.5 overs)	v Lancashire at Old Trafford	13.6.73
Lowest Totals Against:	59 (34 overs)	Combined Universities at Cambridge	14.5.83
Highest Score For:	151* M P Maynard	v Middlesex at Lord's	7.5.96
Highest Score Against:	155* R A Smith	Hampshire at Southampton	9.5.89
Best Bowling For:	6-20 S D Thomas	v Combined Universities at Cardiff	25.4.95
Best Bowling Against:	5-30 E A E Baptiste	Kent at Cardiff	4.5.85

Gloucestershire

Highest Total For:	+308-3 (50 overs)	v Ireland at Dublin	7.5.96
Highest Total Against:	+311-4 (55 overs)	Hampshire at Bristol	27.4.74
Lowest Total For:	62 (26.5 overs)	v Hampshire at Bristol	3.5.75
Lowest Totals Against:	83 (38 overs)	Combined Universities at Bristol	23.4.91
Highest Score For:	154* M J Procter	v Somerset at Taunton	3.6.72
Highest Score Against:	138* I T Botham	Worcestershire at Bristol	24.4.90
Best Bowling For:	6-13 M J Procter	v Hampshire at Southampton	26.6.77
Best Bowling Against:	6-33 E J Barlow	Derbyshire at Bristol	6.5.78

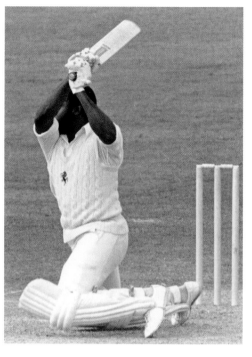

John Shepherd batting for Kent in the 1977 Final

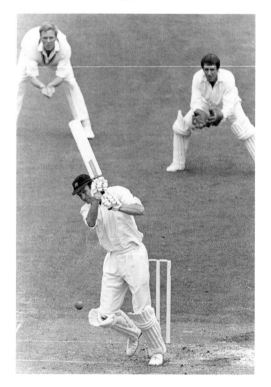

Mike Smith scores 83 for Middlesex in the 1975 Final

Hampshire

Highest Total For:	+321-1 (55 overs)	v Minor Counties (South) at Amersham	28.4.73
Highest Total Against:	+333-6 (50 overs)	Surrey at The Oval	28.4.96
Lowest Total For:	50 (27.2 overs)	v Yorkshire at Headingley	4.5.91
Lowest Total Against:	62 (26.5 overs)	Gloucestershire at Bristol	3.5.75
Highest Score For:	173* C G Greenidge	v Minor Counties (South) at Amersham	28.4.73
Highest Score Against:	160 A J Stewart	Surrey at The Oval	28.4.96
Best Bowling For:	6-25 S J Renshaw	v Surrey at Southampton	5.5.97
Best Bowling Against:	7-22 J R Thomson	Middlesex at Lord's	9.5.81

Kent

Highest Total For:	+338-4 (50 overs)	v Somerset at Maidstone	28.4.96
Highest Score Against:	+308-5 (55 overs)	Worcestershire at Worcester	29.5.91
Lowest Total For:	73 (37.4 overs)	v Middlesex at Canterbury	12.5.79
Lowest Total Against:	+67 (45.5 overs)	Minor Counties (North) at Lincoln	28.4.79
Highest Score For:	143 C J Tavaré	v Somerset at Taunton	14.5.85
Highest Score Against:	137* B C Rose	Somerset at Canterbury	10.5.80
Best Bowling For:	6-41 T N Wren	v Somerset at Canterbury	2.5.95
Best Bowling Against:	5-23 S T Clarke	Surrey at The Oval	15.5.80

Lancashire

Highest Total For:	+353-7 (55 overs)	v Nottinghamshire at Old Trafford	9.5.95
Highest Total Against:	+ 314-5 (55 overs)	Worcestershire at Old Trafford	12.6.80
Lowest Total For:	+82 (47.2 overs)	v Yorkshire at Bradford	29.4-1.5.72
Lowest Total Against:	+52 (26.5 overs)	Minor Counties CA at Lakenham	5.5.98
Highest Score For:	136 G Fowler	v Sussex at Old Trafford	7.5.91
Highest Score Against:	158 W J Cronje	Leicestershire at Old Trafford	25.4.95
Best Bowling For:	6-10 C E H Croft	v Scotland at Old Trafford	8.5.82
Best Bowling Against:	6-29 J D Inchmore	Worcestershire at Old Trafford	17.5.84

Leicestershire

Highest Total For:	+382-6 (50 overs)	v Minor Counties CA at Leicester	8.5.98
Highest Total Against:	+325-5 (55 overs)	Middlesex at Leicester	2.5.92
Lowest Total For:	56 (26.2 overs)	v Minor Counties CA at Wellington	27.5.82
Lowest Total Against:	+74 (32.4 overs)	Nottinghamshire at Leicester	13.5.87
Highest Score For:	158* B F Davison	v Warwickshire at Coventry	13.5.72
Highest Score Against:	145 J E Morris	Durham at Leicester	14.5.96
Best Bowling For:	6-25 V J Wells	v Minor Counties CA at Leicester	8.5.98
Best Bowling Against:	6-21 S M Pollock	Warwickshire at Edgbaston	26.4.96

Middlesex

Highest Total For:	+325-5 (55 overs)	v Leicestershire at Leicester	2.5.92
Highest Total Against:	+322-4 (50 overs)	Somerset at Lord's	26.4.96
Lowest Total For:	+73 (29.1 overs)	v Essex at Lord's	16.5.85
Lowest Total Against:	+61 (26 overs)	Somerset at Hove	13.5.78
Highest Score For:	143* M W Gatting	v Sussex at Hove	14/15.5.85
Highest Score Against:	151* M P Maynard	Glamorgan at Lord's	7.5.96
Best Bowling For:	7-12 W W Daniel	v Minor Counties (East) at Ipswich	22.4.78
Best Bowling Against:	5-13 J K Lever	Essex at Lord's	16.5.85

Northamptonshire

Highest Total For:	+304-6 (55 overs)	v Scotland at Northampton	16.5.95
Highest Total Against:	+303-7 (55 overs)	Middlesex at Northampton	21.5.77
Lowest Total For:	85 (40.3 overs)	v Sussex at Northampton	6-9.5.78
Lowest Total Against:	+66 (40.2 overs)	Minor Counties (East) at Horton	7.5.77
Highest Score For:	134 R J Bailey	v Gloucestershire at Northampton	12.5.87
Highest Score Against:	129 G D Barlow	Middlesex at Northampton	21.5.77
Best Bowling For:	5-14 F A Rose	v Minor Counties CA at Luton	29.4.98
Best Bowling Against:	6-22 C E B Rice	Nottinghamshire at Northampton	9.5.81

A classic hook shot from Gordon Greenidge

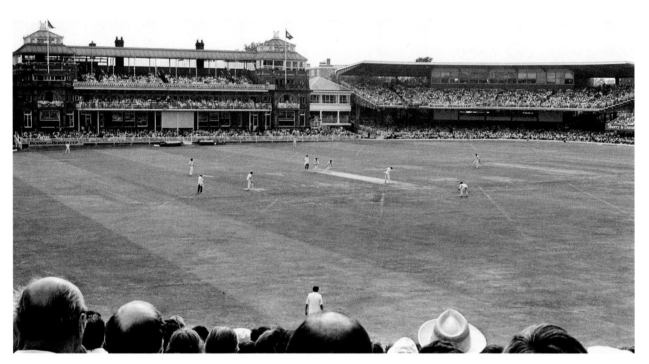

The 1976 Benson and Hedges Cup Final saw Kent beat Worcestershire by 43 runs at Lord's

Below: Geoff Arnold celebrates after Surrey beat Leicestershire in the 1974 Cup Final

Nottinghamshire

Highest Total For:	+296-6 (55 overs)	v Kent at Trent Bridge	14.6.89
Highest Total Against:	+353-7 (55 overs)	Lancashire at Old Trafford	9.5.95
Lowest Total For:	+74 (32.4 overs)	v Leicestershire at Leicester	13.5.87
Lowest Total Against:	+67 (34.1 overs)	Minor Counties (North) at Newark	17.5.75
Highest Score For:	130* C E B Rice	v Scotland at Glasgow	25.5.82
Highest Score Against;	134 J E R Gallian	Lancashire at Old Trafford	9.5.95
Best Bowling For:	6-22 M K Bore	v Leicestershire at Leicester	17.5.80
	6-22 C E B Rice	v Northamptonshire at Northampton	9.5.81
Best Bowling Against:	5-26 W K M Benjamin	Leicestershire at Leicester	12.5.87

Somerset

Highest Total For:	+349-7 (50 overs)	v Ireland at Taunton	2.5.97
Highest Total Against:	+338-6 (50 overs)	Kent at Maidstone	28.4.96
Lowest Total For:	+98 (39.3 overs)	v Middlesex at Lord's	15.5.82
Lowest Total Against:	+68 (32 overs)	Combined Universities at Taunton	20.5.78
Highest Score For:	177 S J Cook	v Sussex at Hove	12.5.90
Highest Score Against:	167* A J Stewart	Surrey at The Oval	26.4.94
Best Bowling For:	7-24 Mushtaq Ahmed	v Ireland at Taunton	2.5.97
Best Bowling Against:	6-41 T N Wren	Kent at Canterbury	2.5.95

Surrey

Highest Total For:	+333-6 (50 overs)	v Hampshire at The Oval	28.4.96
Highest Total Against:	+318-8 (55 overs)	Kent at Canterbury	25.4.95
Lowest Total For:	89 (35.3 overs)	v Nottinghamshire at Trent Bridge	7.6.84
Lowest Total Against:	63 (30.3 overs)	Hampshire at Southampton	5.5.97
Highest Score For:	167* A J Stewart	v Somerset at The Oval	26.4.94
Highest Score Against:	137* R J Cunliffe	Gloucestershire at The Oval	30.4.96
Best Bowling For:	5-15 S G Kenlock	v Ireland at The Oval	23.4.95
Best Bowling Against:	6-25 S J Renshaw	Hampshire at Southampton	5.5.97

Sussex

Highest Total For:	+305.6 (55 overs)	v Kent at Hove	27.5.82
Highest Total Against:	+330-4 (55 overs)	Lancashire at Old Trafford	7.5.91
Lowest Total For:	+61 (26 overs)	v Middlesex at Hove	13.5.78
Lowest Total Against;	63 (37.4 overs)	Minor Counties (East) at Eastbourne	29.4.78
Highest Score For:	118 C W J Athey	v Kent at Hove	16.5.95
Highest Score Against:	198* G A Gooch	Essex at Hove	25.5.82
Best Bowling For:	5-8 Imran Khan	v Northamptonshire at Northampton	8.5.78
Best Bowling Against:	6-17 W W Daniel	Middlesex at Hove	13.5.78

Warwickshire

Highest Total For:	+369-8 (50 overs)	v Minor Counties CA at Jesmond	28.4.96
Highest Total Against:	+327-4 (55 overs)	Leicestershire at Coventry	13.5.72
Lowest Total For:	+96 (39.5 overs)	v Leicestershire at Leicester	28.6.72
Lowest Total Against:	+75 (38.2 overs)	Minor Counties (West) at Edgbaston	29.4.78
Highest Score For:	137* T A Lloyd	v Lancashire at Edgbaston	11.5.85
Highest Score Against:	158* B F Davison	Leicestershire at Coventry	13.5.72
Best Bowling For:	7-32 R G D Willis	v Yorkshire at Edgbaston	19.5.81
Best Bowling Against:	5-22 P J Newport	Worcestershire at Edgbaston	16.5.87

Worcestershire

Highest Total For:	+314-5 (55 overs)	v Lancashire at Old Trafford	12.6.80
Highest Total Against:	292-4 (49.1 overs)	Yorkshire at Worcester	28.4.96
Lowest Total For:	81 (34.4. overs)	v Leicestershire at Worcester	7.5.83
Lowest Total Against:	+88 (48.5 overs)	Yorkshire at Headingley	30.5.95
Highest Score For:	143* G M Turner	v Warwickshire at Edgbaston	23.6.76
Highest Score Against:	142 G Boycott	Yorkshire at Worcester	17.5.80
Best Bowling For:	6-8 N Gifford	v Minor Counties (South) at High Wycombe	12.5.79
Best Bowling Against:	6-35 L B Taylor	Leicestershire at Worcester	15.5.82

Yorkshire

Highest Total For:	+317-5 (55 overs)	v Scotland at Headingley	15.5.86
Highest Total Against:	+289-3 (50 overs)	Worcestershire at Worcester	28.4.96
Lowest Total For:	+88 (48.5 overs)	v Worcestershire at Headingley	30.5.95
Lowest Total Against:	50 (27.2 overs)	Hampshire at Headingley	4.5.91
Highest Score For:	142 G Boycott	v Worcestershire at Worcester	17.5.80
Highest Score Against:	127 A R Butcher	Glamorgan at Cardiff	7.5.91
Best Bowling For:	6-27 A G Nicholson	v Minor Counties (North) at Middlesbrough	20.5.72
Best Bowling Against:	7-32 R G D Willis	Warwickshire at Edgbaston	19.5.81

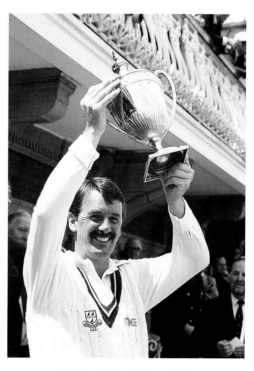

Phil Neale lifts the Cup in 1991

Graham Thorpe dives back to safety during his innings of 103 for Surrey against Lancashire at The Oval in 1993

Norman Gifford, best known for his bowling, was also a handy batsman, as shown here during his innings of 33 in the 1973 Benson and Hedges Cup Final

Minor Counties Cricket Association

Highest Total For:	+273-2 (55 overs)	v Sussex at Marlow	1.5.90
Highest Total Against:	+382-6 (50 overs)	Leicestershire a Leicester	8.5.98
Lowest Total For:	+52 (26.5 overs)	v Lancashire at Lakenham	5.5.98
Lowest Total Against:	56 (26.2 overs)	Leicestershire at Wellington	27.5.82
Highest Score For:	121 M J Roberts	v Sussex at Marlow	1.5.90
Highest Score Against:	151 D L Maddy	Leicestershire at Leicester	8.5.98
Best Bowling For:	6-43 D Nicholls	v Worcestershire at Wellington	22.5.82
Best Bowling Against:	6-25 V J Wells	Leicestershire at Leicester	8.5.98

British Universities (including Combined Universities)

Highest Total For:	+312-8 (50 overs)	v Glamorgan at Cambridge	28.4.96
Highest Total Against:	+366-4 (55 overs)	Derbyshire at Oxford	25.4.91
Lowest Total For:	59 (34 overs)	v Glamorgan at Cambridge	14.5.83
Lowest Total Against:	92 (49.3 overs)	Worcestershire at Cambridge	3.5.75
Highest Score For:	147 G A Khan	v Glamorgan at Cambridge	28.4.96
Highest Score Against:	154* C L Smith	Hampshire at Southampton	12.5.90
Best Bowling For:	6-36 R H Macdonald	v Gloucestershire at Bristol	23.4.91
Best Bowling Against:	6-20 D V Lawrence	Gloucestershire at Bristol	23.4.91
	6-20 S D Thomas	Glamorgan at Cardiff	24.4.95

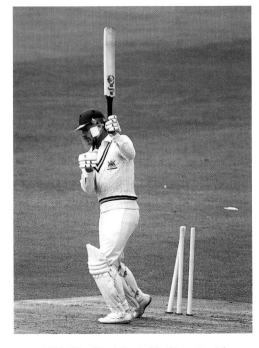

1986: Clive Rice is bowled by Wayne Daniel

Scotland

Highest Total For:	+231-8 (55 overs)	v Northamptonshire at Northampton	10.5.90
Highest Total Against:	+388-7 (55 overs)	Essex at Chelmsford	30.4.92
Lowest Total For:	82 (39.2 overs)	v Northamptonshire at Glasgow	15.5.82
Lowest Total Against: $	153-9 (55 overs)	Lancashire at Perth	11.5.86
Highest Score For:	96 B M W Patterson	v Northamptonshire at Forfar	21.4.92
Highest Score Against:	130* C E B Rice	Nottinghamshire at Glasgow	25.5.82
Best Bowling For:	4-16 C L Parfitt	v Nottinghamshire at Glasgow	8/9.5.85
Best Bowling Against:	6-10 C E H Croft	Lancashire at Old Trafford	8.5.82

$ Scotland did not dismiss any side in fewer than 55 overs

Ireland

Highest Total For:	+281-4 (50 overs)	v Middlesex at Dublin	28.4.97
Highest Total Against:	+359-6 (50 overs)	Essex at Chelmsford	4.5.98
Lowest Total For:	+80 (32 overs)	v Surrey at The Oval	23.4.95
Lowest Total Against: $$	235 (46.4 overs)	Middlesex at Dublin	28.4.97
Highest Score For:	94* W J Cronje	v Middlesex at Dublin	28.4.97
Highest Score Against:	124* J P Stephenson	Hampshire at Southampton	26.4.96
Best Bowling For:	3-38 W J Cronje	v Middlesex at Dublin	28/29.4.97
Best Bowling Against:	7-24 Mushtaq Ahmed	Somerset at Taunton	2.5.97

$$ Middlesex are the only side to be dismissed by Ireland in the competition

Cambridge University

Highest Total For:	+179-9 (55 overs)	v Warwickshire at Edgbaston	29.4.72
Highest Total Against:	+280-5 (55 overs)	Sussex at Hove	1.6.74
Lowest Total For:	94 (31.4 overs)	v Surrey at The Oval	18.5.74
	94 (49.2 overs)	v Sussex at Hove	1.6.74
Lowest Total Against:	*Cambridge University never dismissed a side in the competition*		
Highest Score For:	46 D R Owen-Thomas	v Warwickshire at Edgbaston	29.4.72
Highest Score Against:	114* P J Graves	Sussex at Hove	1.6.74
Best Bowling For:	4-29 J Spencer	v Worcestershire at Cambridge	6.5.72
Best Bowling Against:	4-27 R A Woolmer	Kent at Cambridge	27.4.74

Somerset's Peter Roebuck loses his stumps in the match against Combined Universities at Taunton in 1989

Oxford University

Highest Total For:	175-8 (54.2 overs)	v Northamptonshire at Northampton	12.5.73
Highest Total Against:	+274-8 (55 overs)	Worcestershire at Worcester	19.5.73
Lowest Total For:	112 (46.2 overs)	v Worcestershire at Worcester	19.5.73
Lowest Total Against:	+172 (53.3 overs)	Northamptonshire at Northampton	12.5.73
Highest Score For:	82 A K C Jones	v Northamptonshire at Northampton	12.5.73
Highest Score Against:	132 R G A Headley	Worcestershire at Worcester	19.5.73
Best Bowling For:	3-31 C B Hamblin	v Worcestershire at Worcester	19.5.73
Best Bowling Against:	5-32 N M McVicker	Warwickshire at Oxford	8.5.73

Minor Counties (North)

Highest Score For:	+205-5 (55 overs)	v Nottinghamshire at Trent Bridge	19.5.79
Highest Total Against:	+275-5 (55 overs)	Lancashire at Old Trafford	28.4.73
Lowest Total For:	+67 (34.1 overs)	v Nottinghamshire at Newark	17-19.5.75
	+67 (45.5 overs)	v Kent at Lincoln	28.4.79
Lowest Total Against:	+186 (54.1 overs)	Derbyshire at Derby	11/13.5.74
Highest Score For:	83 D Bailey	v Nottinghamshire at Trent Bridge	19.5.79
Highest Score Against:	113 D Lloyd	Lancashire at Old Trafford	28.4.73
Best Bowling For:	4-45 P Bradley	v Derbyshire at Derby	11.5.74
Best Bowling Against:	6-27 A G Nicholson	Yorkshire at Scunthorpe	20.5.72

Minor Counties (South)

Highest Total For:	193 (52.1 overs)	v Hampshire at Amersham	28.4.73
Highest Total Against:	+321-1 (55 overs)	Hampshire at Amersham	28.4.73
Lowest Total Against:	83 (50 overs)	v Essex at Bedford	10.5.75
Lowest Total Against:	+123 (53.2 overs)	Glamorgan at Amersham	4.5.74
Highest Score For:	78 H B Hollington	v Gloucestershire at Bristol	20.5.72
Highest Score Against:	173* C G Greenidge	Hampshire at Amersham	28.4.73
Best Bowling For:	4-35 B G Collins	v Gloucestershire at Bristol	18.5.74
Best Bowling Against:	6-8 N Gifford	Worcestershire at High Wycombe	12.5.79

Minor Counties (East)

Highest Total For:	+213-6 (55 overs)	Nottinghamshire at Trent Bridge	24.4.76
Highest Total Against:	+294-4 (55 overs)	Essex at Norwich	8.5.76
Lowest Total For:	63 (37.4 overs)	v Sussex at Eastboune	29.4.78
Lowest Total Against:	*No side was dismissed by Minor Counties (East)*		
Highest Score For:	109* N A Riddell	v Northamptonshire at Longton, Stoke	22.5.76
Highest Score Against:	131 Mushtaq Mohammed	Northamptonshire at Longton, Stoke	22.5.76
Best Bowling For:	4-15 N T O'Brien	v Leicestershire at Chesham	9.5.78
Best Bowling Against:	7-12 W W Daniel	Middlesex at Ipswich	22.4.78

Minor Counties (West)

Highest Total For:	+173-4 (55 overs)	v Derbyshire at Derby	13.5.78
Highest Total Against:	+209-5 (55 overs)	Lancashire at Watford	20.5.78
Lowest Total For:	+75 (38.2 overs)	v Warwickshire at Edgbaston	29.4.78
Lowest Total Against:	*No side was dismissed by Minor Counties (West)*		
Highest Score For:	62 W M Osman	v Derbyshire at Derby	13.5.78
Highest Score Against:	88 E J Barlow	Derbyshire at Watford	23/24.4.77
Best Bowling For:	3-19 W Merry	v Derbyshire at Derby	13.5.78
Best Bowling Against:	5-23 D P Hughes	Lancashire at Watford	20.5.78

Bob Willis put in many fine performances for Warwickshire in the Benson and Hedges Cup

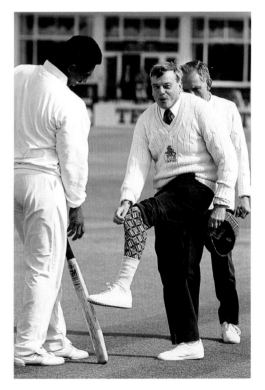

Leicestershire v Ireland at Grace Road in 1994: Dickie Bird shows Phil Simmons how to keep warm in April

PETER BAXTER
THE DRAW FOR THE QUARTER-FINALS AND SEMI-FINALS

IN HIS CAPACITY AS A PRODUCER AND ON-AIR COMMENTATOR FOR BBC RADIO SPORT, PETER BAXTER OBSERVED EVERY DRAW FOR THE LATER STAGES OF THE BENSON AND HEDGES CUP

I have been asked often about the draws for the quarter-finals and semi-finals, because, you see, I was always there. County members have asked, journalists have asked, players have asked and even county chairmen have asked: "It is rigged, isn't it?"

"Nothing to do with me, I just broadcast it – but I think they'd make a better fist of it if it was."

The quarter-final draw in this competition was always the one to send a shiver down an administrative spine. At some stage it was decided that it would be sensible to keep the two qualifiers from each group apart, and to guarantee the group winners a home tie. This meant two red velvet bags, each holding four numbered ping-pong balls.

We would do these draws in the BBC Radio commentary box at the top of the Pavilion at Lord's. Donald Carr presided as the then Secretary of the Test and County Cricket Board. He took the first time it went wrong remarkably well. We were live on Radio 2 and the draw seemed to be going well, until he suddenly pointed out that two teams from the same group had been drawn together. Back went the balls into the bags, while, as I tried to gloss over the hiatus for listeners, I heard Terry Wogan from the studio: "Plough on, me boys. Keep going till you get the draw you want!"

We sorted it out at the second attempt and resolved to give the balls coloured tags to represent the groups, so that a similar mistake could be avoided. Thus it was some years before it went wrong again. Alan Smith was now chief executive

With Willis and Botham and all Sky's equipment, surely nothing could go wrong?

of the Board and he had a new assistant secretary, Tim Lamb, experiencing this performance for the first time. This time it all went wrong not once, but twice. The gentlemen in the box were sweating with embarrassment and the studio proved to have rather less of a sense of humour about such things than had Mr Wogan of days gone by.

With the building of the state-of-the-art offices of the ECB we were able in 1997 to do the draw in relaxed mode in the office of the new cricket operations manager. As it happened, it was John Carr – Donald's son. But in 1998, Sky TV decided to broadcast it live. New sets were built. All the panoply of a television outside broadcast was wheeled into the ECB's conference room, together with star guests. My little self-operated box of tricks was relegated to a distant corner where I couldn't see what was going on. With all that technology everything must be fine.

Well, not exactly everything. We had agreed a time, the TV and me, and at that time I started my prepared half-minute lead-in to the draw. As I went on, I gradually became aware that the television presenter, Charles Colville, had not started his spiel. Ten minutes later, when I had described the set, run through most of the history of the Benson and Hedges Cup and resorted to poking fun at the waxwork appearance of the assembled ECB hierachy, the Radio Five Live studio took pity on me and put on another item. It turned out that, in this space age, the TV van had run out of diesel for its generator.

– Individual Performances –

HIGHEST CAREER TOTALS IN THE BENSON AND HEDGES CUP

	M	I	N/O	HS	Runs	Av	100s	50s
G A Gooch	114	114	15	198*	5176	52.28	15	30
M W Gatting	95	90	18	143*	2921	40.56	3	18
C J Tavaré	94	93	8	143	2761	32.48	2	16
K J Barnett	85	76	5	115	2749	38.71	4	19
W Larkins	87	83	4	132	2718	34.40	7	11
G A Hick	62	61	12	127*	2717	55.44	7	18
D W Randall	98	95	13	103*	2663	32.47	2	17
A J Lamb	73	67	11	126*	2636	47.07	5	17
R J Bailey	69	66	10	134	2626	46.89	4	19
A J Stewart	65	65	10	167*	2598	47.23	4	18
N H Fairbrother	74	71	21	116*	2580	51.60	1	21
R T Robinson	78	75	9	120	2567	38.89	3	18
C W J Athey	84	79	11	118	2551	37.51	1	20
M R Benson	65	64	7	119	2450	42.98	4	17
A I Kallicharran	68	64	7	122*	2392	41.96	4	17
C G Greenidge	62	62	2	173*	2274	37.90	5	14
R A Smith	57	54	8	155*	2186	47.52	5	9
D R Turner	80	77	12	123*	2179	33.52	1	13
T E Jesty	75	71	11	105	2150	35.83	1	15

MOST WICKETS IN A CAREER IN THE BENSON AND HEDGES CUP

	Overs	M	Runs	W	Av	BB	4wI	RPO
J K Lever	904.1	173	2789	149	18.71	5-13	8	3.08
I T Botham	829.4	148	2815	132	21.32	5-41	6	3.39
S Turner	771.2	130	2232	107	20.85	4-19	3	2.89
D L Underwood	832.4	170	2435	107	22.75	5-35	5	2.92
J N Shepherd	649	86	2116	102	20.74	4-25	2	3.26
R D Jackman	561	95	1981	101	19.61	4-24	5	3.53
D R Pringle	685.5	87	2402	101	23.78	5-35	3	3.50

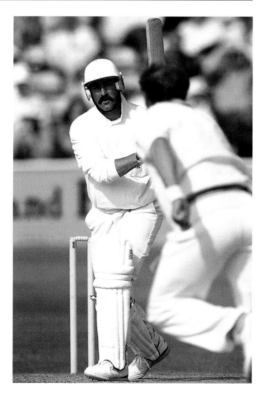

Graham Gooch scored more runs in Benson and Hedges matches than anyone else. He is seen here during his innings of 130 for Essex against Leicestershire at Chelmsford in 1994

Far right: Gooch's county colleague John Lever of Essex was the leading wicket-taker in Benson and Hedges matches

LEADING WICKETKEEPERS

Dis	Ct	St	
122	117	5	D L Bairstow (Yorkshire)
100	90	10	S J Rhodes (Worcestershire)
88	79	9	A P E Knott (Kent)
86	81	5	W K Hegg (Lancashire)
83	80	3	G W Humpage (Warwickshire)
83	77	6	S A Marsh (Kent)
80	68	12	B N French (Nottinghamshire)
77	65	12	R W Taylor (Derbyshire)
75	63	12	R C Russell (Gloucestershire)
72	62	10	P R Downton (Kent/Middlesex)
70	64	6	D J S Taylor (Somerset)

Alan Ealham fielding in the 1977 Final

LEADING FIELDSMEN

68	G A Gooch (Essex)
55	C J Tavaré (Oxford & Cambridge U/Kent/Somerset)
53	I T Botham (Somerset/Worcestershire/Durham)
45	D W Randall (Nottinghamshire)
44	J E Emburey (Middlesex/Northamptonshire)
37	D M Smith (Surrey/Worcestershire/Sussex)
37	G A Hick (Worcestershire)
35	G Miller (Derbyshire/Essex/Minor Counties CA)

HIGHEST INDIVIDUAL SCORES

314 hundreds were scored

198*	G A Gooch	Essex v Sussex at Hove	25.5.82
177	S J Cook	Somerset v Sussex at Hove	12.5.80
173*	C G Greenidge	Hampshire v Minor Counties (South) at Amersham	28.4.73
167*	A J Stewart	Surrey v Somerset at The Oval	26.4.94
160	A J Stewart	Surrey v Hampshire at The Oval	28.4.96
158*	B F Davison	Leicestershire v Warwickshire at Coventry	13.5.72
158	W J Cronje	Leicestershire v Lancashire at Old Trafford	25.4.95
155*	R A Smith	Hampshire v Glamorgan at Southampton	9.5.89
155	M D Crowe	Somerset v Hampshire at Southampton	12.5.97
154*	M J Procter	Gloucestershire v Somerset at Taunton	3.6.72
154*	C L Smith	Hampshire v Combined Universities at Southampton	12.5.90
151*	M P Maynard	Glamorgan v Middlesex at Lord's	7.5.96
151	D L Maddy	Leicestershire v Minor Counties CA at Leicester	8.5.98

RECORD PARTNERSHIPS

1st	252	V P Terry & C L Smith	Hampshire	Oxford & Cambridge U.	Southampton	12.5.90
2nd	285*	C G Greenidge & D R Turner	Hampshire	Minor Counties (S)	Amersham	28.4.73
3rd	269*	P M Roebuck & M D Crowe	Somerset	Hampshire	Southampton	12.5.87
4th	184*	D Lloyd & B W Reidy	Lancashire	Derbyshire	Chesterfield	17.5.80
5th	160	A J Lamb & D J Capel	Northamptonshire	Leicestershire	Northampton	13.5.86
6th	167*	M G Bevan & R J Blakey	Yorkshire	Lancashire	Old Trafford	11/12.6.96
7th	149*	J D Love & C M Old	Yorkshire	Scotland	Bradford	21.5.81
8th	109	R E East & N Smith	Essex	Northamptonshire	Chelmsford	16.5.77
9th	83	P G Newman & M A Holding	Derbyshire	Nottinghamshire	Trent Bridge	16.5.85
10th	80*	D L Bairstow & M Johnson	Yorkshire	Derbyshire	Derby	11.5.81

BEST BOWLING

There were 154 returns of five wickets in an innings.
Six or seven wickets were registered on 26 occasions.

7-12	W W Daniel	Middlesex v Minor Counties (East) at Ipswich	22.4.78
7-22	J R Thomson	Middlesex v Hampshire at Lord's	9.5.81
7-24	Mushtaq Ahmed	Somerset v Ireland at Taunton	2.5.97
7-32	R G D Willis	Warwickshire v Yorkshire at Edgbaston	19.5.81
6-8	N Gifford	Worcestershire v Minor Counties (South) at High Wycombe	12.5.79
6-10	C E H Croft	Lancashire v Scotland at Old Trafford	8.5.82
6-13	M J Procter	Gloucestershire v Hampshire at Southampton	22.6.77
6-17	W W Daniel	Middlesex v Sussex at Hove	13.5.78
6-20	D V Lawrence	Gloucestershire v Combined Universities at Bristol	23.4.91
6-20	S D Thomas	Glamorgan v British Universities at Cardiff	25.4.95
6-21	S M Pollock	Warwickshire v Leicestershire at Edgbaston	26.4.96
6-22	M K Bore	Nottinghamshire v Leicestershire at Leicester	17.5.80
6-22	C E B Rice	Nottinghamshire v Northamptonshire at Northampton	9.5.81
6-25	S J Renshaw	Hampshire v Surrey at Southampton	5.5.97
6-25	V J Wells	Leicestershire v Minor Counties CA at Leicester	8.5.98

Allan Donald congratulates Shaun Pollock after his 6 for 21 for
Warwickshire against Leicestershire at Edgbaston in 1996

HAT-TRICKS

There were 11 hat-tricks in Benson and Hedges matches

G D McKenzie	Leicestershire v Worcestershire at Worcester	3.6.72
K Higgs	Leicestershire v Surrey at Lord's (Final)	20.7.74
A A Jones	Middlesex v Essex at Lord's	10.5.77
M J Procter	Gloucestershire v Hampshire at Southampton (Semi-final)	22.6.77
W Larkins	Northamptonshire v Oxford & Cambridge Universities at Northampton	10.5.80
E A Moseley	Glamorgan v Kent at Cardiff	20.5.81
G C Small	Warwickshire v Leicestershire at Leicester	12.5.84
N A Mallender	Somerset v Combined Universities at Taunton	9.5.87
W K M Benjamin $$	Leicestershire v Nottinghamshire at Leicester	12.5.87
A R C Fraser	Middlesex v Sussex at Lord's	3.5.88
S M Pollock $	Warwickshire v Leicestershire at Edgbaston	26.4.96

$ Took four wickets in four balls – it was his debut match for Warwickshire
$$ Took four wickets in six balls

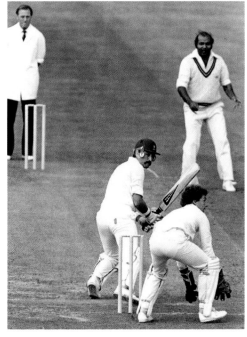

1979: Graham Gooch cuts Intikhab Alam

MOST RUNS IN A SEASON

629	D L Maddy (Leicestershire)	1988

MOST WICKETS IN A SEASON

19	J K Lever (Essex)	1979
19	C E H Croft (Lancashire)	1982

GOLD AWARD WINNERS

1,204 Gold Awards were distributed.
Kent won the most Gold Awards: 90
Most Gold Awards in a season: D L Maddy 5 in 1998

LEADING GOLD AWARD WINNERS

22	G A Gooch (Essex)
11	K J Barnett (Derbyshire)
	M W Gatting (Middlesex)
	G A Hick (Worcestershire)
	T E Jesty (Hampshire/Surrey/Lancashire)
	B Wood (Lancashire/Derbyshire)
10	J C Balderstone (Leicestershire)
	I T Botham (Somerset/Worcestershire/Durham)

Benson and Hedges matches often captured the public's imagination, ensuring large and lively crowds

BENSON AND HEDGES GOLD AWARD WINNERS

90 Awards

Kent in 145 matches

N R Taylor (8), C S Cowdrey (7), M V Fleming (7), M A Ealham (5), R M Ellison (5), R A Woolmer (5), Asif Iqbal (4), M R Benson (4), A G E Ealham (4), C J Tavaré (4), G W Johnson (3), B D Julien (2), D W Headley (2), B W Luckhurst (2), J N Shepherd (2), J B D Thompson (2), D L Underwood (2), M J Walker (2), T R Ward (2), H L Alleyne, E A E Baptiste, G S Clinton, G R Cowdrey, M C Cowdrey, R P Davis, M H Denness, P A De Silva, G R Dilley, J N Graham, R W Hills, S G Hinks, C L Hooper, K B S Jarvis, A P E Knott, N J Llong, A P Wells, T N Wren.

84 Awards

Essex in 136 matches

G A Gooch (22), K W R Fletcher (8), K S McEwan (6), P J Prichard (4), D R Pringle (4), S Turner (4), R E East (3), N A Foster (3), M C Ilott (2), K D Boyce (2), B E A Edmeades (2), B R Hardie (2), R C Irani (2), J K Lever (2), K R Pont (2), J P Stephenson (2), T D Topley (2), M E Waugh (2), N Hussain (2), D D J Robinson (2), A R Border, A P Cowan, R N S Hobbs, S G Law, A W Lilley, Salim Malik.

77 Awards

Lancashire in 140 matches

B Wood (10), N H Fairbrother (9), P A J DeFreitas (4), B E Reidy (4), Wasim Akram (4), G Fowler (3), H Pilling (3), M Watkinson (3), M A Atherton (3), J Abrahams (2), P J W Allott (2), F C Hayes (2), D Lloyd (2), G D Lloyd (2), G D Mendis (2), S J O'Shaughnessy (2), J Simmons (2), I D Austin (2), M R Chadwick, G Chapple, J P Crawley, C E H Croft, A Flintoff, J E R Gallian, W K Hegg, D P Hughes, S T Jefferies, T E Jesty, A Kennedy, P Lever, C H Lloyd, K L Snellgrove, N J Speak, J Sullivan.

72 Awards

Leicestershire in 131 matches

J C Balderstone (10), D L Maddy (7), B F Davison (6), N E Briers (5), J F Steele (5), P Willey (5), B Duddleston (4), R W Tolchard (4), R Illingworth (3), W K M Benjamin (2), G J Parsons (2), J J Whitaker (2), P V Simmons (2), J P Agnew, T J Boon, P B Clift, W J Cronje, J M Dakin, G J F Ferris, M A Garnham, D I Gower, K Higgs, N M McVicker, D J Millns, L Potter, P E Robinson, I J Sutcliffe, V J Wells.

69 Awards

Yorkshire in 124 matches

G Boycott (9), D L Bairstow (7), M D Moxon (7), A A Metcalfe (5), C W J Athey (3), M G Bevan (3), J D Love (3), C M Old (3), A Sidebottom (3), R J Blakey (2), J H Hampshire (2), P J Hartley (2), R A Hutton (2), C E W Silverwood (2), D S Lehmann (2), D Byas, P Carrick, G M Hamilton, S N Hartley, C Johnson, A McGrath, A G Nicholson, S Oldham, P E Robinson, R D Stemp, G B Stevenson, M P Vaughan, C White, D Wilson.

67 Awards

Derbyshire in 121 matches

K J Barnett (11), E J Barlow (4), A J Borrington (4) G Miller (4), C J Adams (4), P D Bowler (3), D G Cork (3), M Hendrick (3), J G Wright (3), R G A Headley (2), A Hill (2), M A Holding (2), J E Morris (2), B Roberts (2), F E Rumsey (2), H Cartwright, V P Clarke, D J Cullinan, R J Finney, W P Fowler, S C Goldsmith, J H Hampshire, D M Jones, P N Kirsten, A P Kuiper, D E Malcolm, P J Sharpe, R W Taylor, T A Tweats, A Ward, B Wood.

67 Awards

Nottinghamshire in 125 matches

C E B Rice (9), R J Hadlee (7), R T Robinson (7), D W Randall (6), P Johnson (3), J A Afford (2), B C Broad (2), K E Cooper (2), K P Evans (2), M J Harris (2), M J Smedley (2), G St A Sobers (2), F D Stephenson (2), W Taylor (2), G F Archer (2), R T Bates, J D Birch, M K Bore, C L Cairns, B N French, J E R Gallian, N A Gie, B Hassan, E E Hemmings, N Nanan, R A Pick, K Saxelby, B Stead, M N S Taylor, P A Todd.

67 Awards

Worcestershire in 131 matches

G A Hick (11), T M Moody (7), G M Turner (5), S R Lampitt (4), J A Ormrod (4), I T Botham (3), R G A Headley (3), E J O Hemsley (3), J D Inchmore (3), T S Curtis (2), B L d'Oliveira (2), D M d'Oliveira (2), N Gifford (2), S J Rhodes (2), P A Neale (2), P J Newport (2), D N Patel (2), Younis Ahmed (2), G R Haynes, Imran Khan, N V Radford, D M Smith, G G Watson, M J Weston.

67 Awards

Surrey in 132 matches

J H Edrich (9), A R Butcher (5), A J Stewart (5), M A Lynch (4), G R J Roope (4), D J Bicknell (3), M P Bicknell (3), S T Clarke (3), G S Clinton (3), T E Jesty (3), M A Feltham (2), R D V Knight (2), P I Pocock (2), D M Smith (2), B C Hollioake (2), A D Brown (2), J E Benjamin, M A Butcher, A J Hollioake, G P Howarth, Intkhab Alam, R D Jackman, S G Kenlock, I R Payne, I D K Salisbury, L E Skinner, D M Ward, G P Thorpe, Younis Ahmed.

65 Awards

Somerset in 127 matches

I T Botham (6), I V A Richards (6), T W Cartwright (4), G D Rose (4), V J Marks (4), M D Crowe (3), P W Denning (3), C J Tavaré (3), S J Cook (2), J Garner (2), A N Hayhurst (2), A N Jones (2), M N Lathwell (2), Mushtaq Ahmed (2), N F M Popplewell (2), P M Roebuck (2), B C Rose (2), J D Batty, P D Bowler, M Burns, D B Close, R C Cooper, M R Davis, S C Ecclestone, K F Jennings, A A Jones, M J Kitchen, J M Parks, D J S Taylor, R J Turner, S R Waugh.

63 Awards

Hampshire in 125 matches

C G Greenidge (9), T E Jesty (7), C L Smith (5), R A Smith (5), V P Terry (4), D R Turner (4), B A Richards (3), S J W Andrew (2), R S Herman (2), S T Jefferies (2), T C Middleton (2), J P Stephenson (2), T M Tremlett (2), R M C Gilliat, D I Gower, M L Hayden, M D Marshall, M C J Nicholas, R J Parks, J M Rice, A M E Roberts, P J Sainsbury, G R Stephenson, J P Stephenson, S D Udal, P R Whitaker, J R Wood.

60 Awards

Middlesex in 129 matches

M W Gatting (11), J E Emburey (6), J M Brearley (4), C T Radley (4), P H Edmonds (3), D L Haynes (3), M R Ramprakash (3), P N Weekes (3), K R Brown (3), G D Barlow (2), R O Butcher (2), W W Daniel (2), A A Jones (2), N G Cowans, N G Featherstone, A G J Fraser, H A Gomes, D W Headley, P H Parfitt, A Roseberry, M W W Selvey, W N Slack, M J Smith, V A P Van der Bijl, N F Williams.

59 Awards

Warwickshire in 129 matches

D L Amiss (5), R B Kanhai (5), R G D Willis (5), A I Kallicharran (4), P A Smith (3), G W Humpage (2), J A Jameson (2), N V Knight (2), T A Lloyd (2), B M McMillan (2), A J Moles (2), D L Murray (2), D A Reeve (2), S J Rouse (2), G C Small (2), N M K Smith (2), R N Abberley, Asif Din, D J Brown, D R Brown, A F Giles, D L Hemp, B C Lara, T A Munton, C M Old, D P Ostler, S P Perryman, A R K Pierson, S M Pollock, K D Smith, J Whitehouse.

56 Awards
Gloucestershire in 116 matches
A W Stovold (9), M J Procter (6), Sadiq Mohammad (4), C W J Athey (2),
P Bainbridge (2), A S Brown (2), R J Cunliffe (2), K M Curran (2), G D Hodgson (2),
R D V Knight (2), D V Lawrence (2), P W Romaines (2), R C Russell (2),
J R Srinath (2), A Symonds (2), A J Wright (2), M W Alleyne, J H Childs, M J Church,
J S Foat, J Lewis, M A Lynch, I R Payne, D R Shepherd, A M Smith, S Young,
Zaheer Abbas.

55 Awards
Northamptonshire in 123 matches
A J Lamb (9), R J Bailey (9), W Larkins (5), R G Williams (4), G Cook (3),
A Fordham (3), D J Capel (2), J C J Dye (2), N A Felton (2), J G Thomas (2),
P Willey (2), R M H Cottam, J E Emburey, T M Lamb, M B Loye, D Ripley, F A Rose,
Sarfraz Nawaz, J N Snape, J P Taylor, T C Walton, P J Watts, D J Wild.

54 Awards
Sussex in 115 matches
Imran Khan (6), P W G Parker (5), J R T Barclay (3), I J Gould (3), G D Mendis (3),
J Spencer (3), C M Wells (3), P J Graves (2), G S Le Roux (2), C P Phillipson (2)
R M Prideaux (2), D M Smith (2), J A Snow (2), M P Speight (2), K C Wessels (2),
C W J Athey, M G Bevan, M A Buss, I A Greig, J W Hall, P W Jarvis, A N Jones,
R D V Knight, N J Lenham, I D K Sailsbury, F D Stephenson, N R Taylor.

51 Awards
Glamorgan in 114 matches
M P Maynard (7), R C Ontong (5), J A Hopkins (4), H Morris (3), M A Nash (3),
A Dale (2), S P James (2), Javed Miandad (2), M J Llewellyn (2), G Richards (2),
S R Barwick, A R Butcher, R D B Croft, W W Davis, G P Ellis, M Frost, D L Hemp,
A Jones, A A Jones, E W Jones, M J Khan, A R Lewis, E A Moseley, R J Shastri,
J W Solanky, P D Swart, S D Thomas, S L Watkin, D L Williams.

18 Awards
Minor Counties in 75 matches
P A Todd (2), K A Arnold, D Bailey, B L Cairns, I Cockbain, R D Dalton, S Davis,
R Evans, N A Folland, R E Hayward, R Herbert, D Nicholls, N T O'Brien, S G Plumb,
L Potter, M J Roberts, M J Saggers.

13 Awards
Durham in 26 matches
W Larkins (3), P Bainbridge, I T Botham, S J E Brown, P D Collingwood, J M Dakin,
M J Foster, A R Fothergill, J J B Lewis, J I Longley, M Saxelby.

12 Awards
Oxford and Cambridge Universities in 48 matches
A J T Miller (2), C J Tavaré (2), P J Hayes, A J Hignell, Imran Khan, J M Knight, A
Odendaal, G Pathmanathan, N Russom, C D M Tooley.

12 Awards
British Universities in 47 matches
M J Chilton (2), W J House (2), J Boiling, M A Crawley, N Hussain,
R S C Martin-Jenkins, A Singh, J N Snape, C M Tolley, W van der Merwe.

10 Awards
Scotland in 70 matches
I L Philip (4), R G Swan (2), Asif Butt, O Henry, D Lockhart, M J Smith.

6 Awards
Ireland in 17 matches
W J Cronje, J D Curry, N G Doak, A G Dunlop, D A Lewis, M P Rea.

4 Awards
Minor Counties (North) in 20 matches
D Bailey, A J Burridge, R M O Cooke, J A Sutton.

3 Awards
Minor Counties (East) in 12 matches
M Maslin, N T O'Brien, N A Riddell.

1 Award
Oxford University in 4 matches – R J Lee
Minor Counties (West) in 12 matches – M D Nurton
Minor Counties (South) in 20 matches – H B Hollington

Cambridge University played 8 matches but did not win any Gold Awards

Ian Botham won six Gold Awards for Somerset

— Benson & Hedges Cup Finals —

The Benson and Hedges Cup was won 15 times by the side batting first, and 12 times by the side batting second.

TOTALS OF 250 AND OVER IN THE FINAL

+	*batted first*				
+	290-6	55 overs	Essex	v Surrey	1979
+	274-7	55 overs	Lancashire	v Kent	1995
+	268-7	50 overs	Essex	v Leicestershire	1998
	255	51.4 overs	Surrey	v Essex	1979
+	253-5	55 overs	Hampshire	v Kent	1992
+	252-6	55 overs	Derbyshire	v Lancashire	1993

TOTALS OF UNDER 150 IN THE FINAL

	76	27.4 overs	Leicestershire	v Essex	1998
+	117	46.3 overs	Derbyshire	v Hampshire	1988
+	130	50.1 overs	Nottinghamshire	v Somerset	1982
+	136-9	55 overs	Yorkshire	v Leicestershire	1972
+	139	50.4 overs	Warwickshire	v Lancashire	1984
	143	54 overs	Leicestershire	v Surrey	1974
+	146	52.4 overs	Middlesex	v Leicestershire	1975
+	147	54.4 overs	Derbyshire	v Kent	1978

HIGHEST TOTAL FOR A SIDE BATTING FIRST AND LOSING

244-7	55 overs	Northamptonshire v Yorkshire	1987

LOWEST TOTAL FOR A SIDE BATTING FIRST AND WINNING

170	54.1 overs	Surrey	v Leicestershire	1974

HUNDREDS IN A FINAL

120	G A Gooch	Essex	v Surrey	1979
132*	I V A Richards	Somerset	v Surrey	1981
112	P A de Silva	Kent	v Lancashire	1995

FIVE WICKETS IN A FINAL

5-14	J Garner	Somerset	v Surrey	1981
5-13	S T Jefferies	Hampshire	v Derbyshire	1988

HAT-TRICK IN A FINAL

K Higgs	Leicestershire	v Surrey	1974

Dean Headley of Kent bowls to Surrey's Alec Stewart during the 1997 B&H Final